The
INN
ON LAKE
SUPERIOR

Know Your Ships 2008

Guide to Boats & Boatwatching
Great Lakes & St. Lawrence Seaway

Marine Publishing Co. Inc.
P.O. Box 68, Sault Ste. Marie, MI 49783
(734) 668-4734

ISBN: 978-1-891849-11-4

Founder
Tom Manse, 1915-1994

Editor & Publisher
Roger LeLievre

Front: *Calumet* passes Port Huron in 2007. *(Roger LeLievre)*

This: *Paul R. Tregurtha* departs Duluth. *(Sam Lapinski)*

Back: *Montrealais* in the Welland Canal. *(Chris Winters)*

Researchers: Mac Mackay, Matt Miner, Gerry Ouderkirk, Wade P. Streeter, Franz VonRiedel, John Vournakis, George Wharton and Chris Winters

Crew: Kathryn Lengell, Nancy Kuharevicz, Audrey LeLievre, Neil Schultheiss, William Soleau

kysbook@concentric.net

KnowYourShips.com

CONTENTS '08

***Reserve* anchored off Detroit's Renaissance Center in 2007.** *(Wade P. Streeter)*

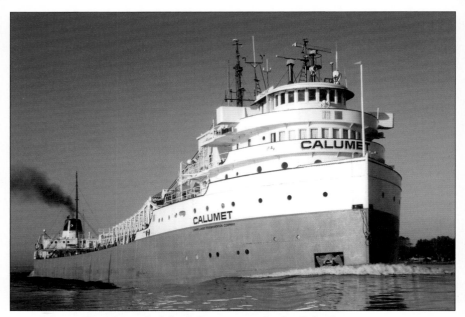

***Calumet* downbound under full power on the St. Clair River.** *(John Meyland)*

GOODBYE TO THE CALUMET

Vessel of the Year

An impressive, 77-year sailing career came to an end late in 2007, when the familiar motor vessel *Calumet* was sold for scrap.

The *Calumet*, built in 1929 by the Great Lakes Engineering Works, River Rouge (Detroit), Mich., was launched as the *Myron C. Taylor* for the Pittsburgh Steamship Co. Constructed as a traditional-styled straight decker, the *Myron C. Taylor* was one of three new vessels joining the Pittsburgh fleet that year, the other two being the *William G. Clyde* (now *Maumee*) and *Horace Johnson* (scrapped 1984).

Stack view. *(Neil Schultheiss)*

Upon entering service, the *Myron C. Taylor* was named the fleet's flagship, an honor retained until 1938, when the designation was passed to the *William A. Irvin* (now a museum at Duluth). The vessel was built with an extra deck directly below the wheelhouse to accommodate company management and corporate guests.

The boat served the Pittsburgh fleet until spring 1956. Due to an increase in limestone demand, she was transferred to the Bradley Transportation Co. fleet, managed by the Pittsburgh fleet. In 1956, the *Taylor* was converted to a self-unloader, and over the winter of 1967/68 her steam engine was replaced with a new Nordberg diesel. By 1967, when the Bradley and Pittsburgh fleets merged (as the USS Great Lakes Fleet), the *Taylor* was one of the fleet's smallest carriers. However the *Taylor*'s smaller size permitted access to many of the smaller Great Lakes ports.

(Continued on Page 7)

***Myron C. Taylor* before conversion.** *(Tom Manse Collection)*

As the *Taylor* appeared after conversion to a self-unloader. *(George Haynes)*

The *Taylor* laid up for the final time in Great Lakes Fleet colors Nov. 11, 2000 in Sarnia, Ont. In late March 2001, the *Taylor* and her fleet mate, *Calcite II*, were sold to Grand River Navigation Co., Cleveland, Ohio, an affiliate of Lower Lakes Towing Ltd., Port Dover, Ont. On April 21, 2001, the vessel was christened *Calumet* in honor of the Calumet River, which empties into Lake Michigan at Chicago. Also christened was the *Calcite II*, which became the *Maumee*. A third former fleet mate, the *George A. Sloan*, was reflagged Canadian and christened *Mississagi* as part of the ceremony.

The *Calumet*'s activities for her new owners continued to be concentrated in the limestone, stone, aggregates, coal, sand and salt trades, primarily on the lower lakes, servicing many of the customers she had previously serviced before her sale.

On Nov. 15, 2007, the *Calumet* struck a concrete wall along the Old River in Cleveland after unloading at Ontario Stone. The incident only hastened the ending of the *Calumet*'s career, as it was expected that the veteran laker would be scrapped at the end of the 2007 season. The *Calumet* headed for Port Colborne under her own power, ultimately tying up at International Marine Salvage's dismantling dock, ending the active life of another proud laker. – ***George Wharton***

At the dock in Sarnia. *(Marc Dease)*

***Calumet* heads off into the sunset.** *(Chris Winters)*

Tug *Radium Yellowknife* tows the long-idled *Aquarama* into Port Colborne on the first leg of her trip overseas for scrapping, July 15, 2007. *(Brad Jolliffe)*

PASSAGES

Changes in the shipping scene since our last edition

Fleets & Vessels

Lower Lakes Towing Ltd. continues its expansion, acquiring three former Oglebay Norton Co. vessels, *David Z*, *Earl W.* and *Wolverine*, from the Wisconsin & Michigan Steamship Co. The *Wolverine* is now under Canadian registry as *Robert S. Pierson*, while the others sail under the U.S. flag for the firm's Grand River Navigation Co. division as *Manitowoc* and *Calumet* (replacing another vessel of that name that is being scrapped). *Voyageur Independent* and *Voyageur Pioneer* are now under the Lower Lakes flag as well, with the new names *Ojibway* and *Kaministiquia*, and the company has also contracted for the use of *Maritime Trader*.

The *Edward L. Ryerson* wandered far from her familiar Great Lakes stomping grounds in 2007, making three trips out the St. Lawrence Seaway to Quebec with ore and returning with cargoes of magnesium slag. In between, the *Ryerson* maintained the taconite run from Superior, Wis., to Lorain, Ohio, that she started in 2006. Look for the *Ryerson* to run taconite to Hamilton in 2008.

While laying up for the winter at Superior, Wis., in early January 2008, the 1,000-footer *Walter J. McCarthy Jr.* hit an underwater obstruction and punctured her hull, flooding the engine room. Repairs delayed her return to service this season.

The long-inactive passenger vessel *Aquarama*, which last ran in 1962, and the former Upper Lakes Group steamer *Canadian Mariner* were towed overseas for scrap during 2007, both winding up far from home in Aliaga, Turkey.

The former Inland Steel steamer *L.E. Block* was cut up at International Marine Salvage in 2007. *(Roger LeLievre)*

LAST LOOK AT THE S.S. RESERVE

The 1953-built, steam turbine-powered *Reserve* was cut down to a barge in late 2007 and renamed *James L. Kuber*. She's shown upbound on the St. Marys River on one of her final trips as an operating steamboat. *(Roger LeLievre)*

The *Reserve*'s stern has been removed and a notch fitted for a tug in this late 2007 view. *(Dick Lund)*

***Canadian Mariner* at Port Colborne.** *(Jim Hoffman)*

***Voyageur Pioneer* has new owners.** *(John C. Knecht)*

***Algobay,* laid up since 2002, will get a major refit this year and return to service in 2009. She's shown at St. Catharines in 1999.** *(Roger LeLievre)*

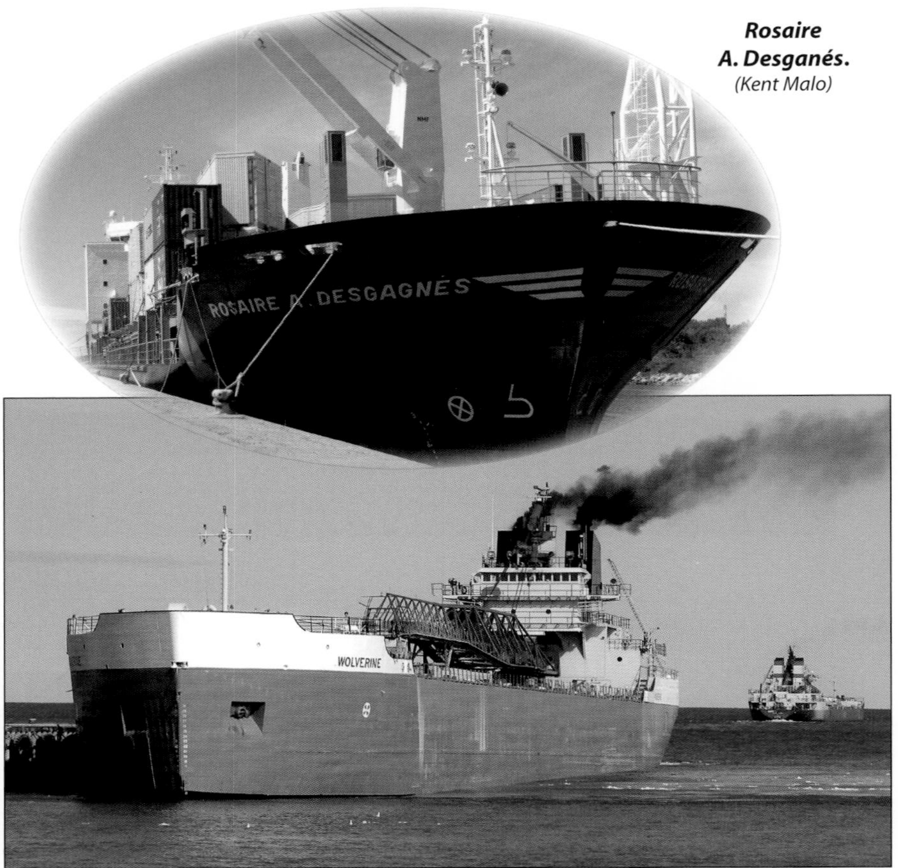

Rosaire A. Desganés. *(Kent Malo)*

***Wolverine* arrives at Stoneport as fleet mate *David Z.* departs.** *(Ben McClain)*

Two new tankers built in Turkey for Great Lakes and Seaway trades enter service this year for Algoma Central Marine's tanker division as *Algocanada* and *Algonova*. Algoma Central Marine's *Algoville* resumed operation last season with a new engine, and the fleet has announced that the *Algobay*, idled since 2002, will get a new forebody and return to service in 2009. The *Algoport* will also receive a new forebody by 2010.

Transport Desgagnés lost one vessel and added another in 2007. *Cecilia Desgagnés* was sold to a Panamanian company for saltwater use. However, the fleet purchased the *Rosaire A. Desgagnés*, built in China in 2007.

Lay-up Log

John Sherwin, which hasn't sailed under its own power since 1981, remains in use as a grain storage hull at South Chicago. The cement carrier *J.A.W. Iglehart* continued its role as a storage hull at Superior, Wis., in 2007, taking over for the *J.B. Ford*, which is laid up at Superior. *C.T.C. #1* still stores cement at South Chicago., while the *S.T. Crapo* at Green Bay, *E.M. Ford* at Saginaw and *Paul H. Townsend* at Muskegon are also used for cement storage. Other vessels remain in limbo at various Great Lakes ports, including *Windoc* (Port Colborne), the car ferry *Viking* (Marinette) and the former Lake Michigan ferry *Spartan* (Ludington).

Shipwrecks

Almost exactly 100 years after she sank on Lake Superior, wreck hunters from the Great Lakes Shipwreck Historical Society located the final resting place of the steamer *Cyprus*, lost on Oct. 11, 1907. The vessel was just on its second trip; it rests in 400 feet of water.

The *Carl D. Bradley* was the first vessel to lock through the new MacArthur Lock at Sault Ste. Marie on July 11, 1943. Note the well-wishers on the lock wall.

BRADLEY LOST 50 YEARS AGO

***Bradley* under the Ambassador Bridge.**

Nov. 18, 2008, marks the 50th anniversary of the sinking of the *Carl D. Bradley* on Lake Michigan. The limestone carrier was upbound for Rogers City and winter layup when she encountered 65 mph winds and 20-foot waves.

The ship was about 12 miles southwest of Gull Island when, around 5:30 p.m., the hull began breaking in two. Although First Mate Elmer Fleming was able to broadcast a mayday call before his vessel headed for the bottom, launching a massive lake search, only two of the 35-man of the crew were saved, including Fleming.

In August 2007, divers removed the *Bradley*'s bell and returned it to Rogers City, Mich., the ship's home port, where it was restored and unveiled in a ceremony the weekend of the 49th anniversary of the tragedy.

J.W. WESTCOTT II

GREAT LAKES GLOSSARY

AAA CLASS – Vessel design popular on the Great Lakes in the early 1950s. *Arthur M. Anderson* is one example.

AFT – Toward the back, or stern, of a ship.

AHEAD – Forward.

AMIDSHIPS – The middle point of a vessel, referring to either length or width.

ARTICULATED TUG/BARGE (ATB) – Tug-barge combination. The two vessels are mechanically linked in one axis but with the tug free to move, or articulate, on another axis. *Jacklyn M/Integrity* is one example.

BACKHAUL – The practice of carrying a revenue-producing cargo (rather than ballast) on a return trip from hauling a primary cargo.

BARGE – Vessel with no engine, either pushed or pulled by a tug.

BEAM – The width of a vessel measured at the widest point.

BILGE – Lowest part of a hold or compartment, generally where the rounded side of a ship curves from the keel to the vertical sides.

BOW – Front of a vessel.

BOW THRUSTER – Propeller mounted transversely in a vessel's bow under the water line to assist in moving sideways. A stern thruster may also be installed.

BRIDGE – The platform above the main deck from which a ship is steered/navigated. Also: PILOTHOUSE or WHEELHOUSE.

BULKHEAD – Wall or partition that separates rooms, holds or tanks within a ship's hull.

BULWARK – The part of the ship that extends fore and aft above the main deck to form a rail.

DATUM – Level of water in a given area, determined by an average over time.

DEADWEIGHT TONNAGE – The actual carrying capacity of a vessel, equal to the difference between the light displacement tonnage and the heavy displacement tonnage, expressed in long tons (2,240 pounds or 1,016.1 kilograms).

DISPLACEMENT TONNAGE – The actual weight of the vessel and everything aboard her, measured in long tons. The displacement is equal to the weight of the water displaced by the vessel. Displacement tonnage may be qualified as light, indicating the weight of the vessel without cargo, fuel and stores, or heavy, indicating the weight of the vessel loaded with cargo, fuel and stores.

DRAFT – The depth of water a ship needs to float. Also, the distance from keel to water line.

FIT OUT – The process of preparing a vessel for service after a period of inactivity.

FIVE-YEAR INSPECTION – U.S. Coast Guard survey, conducted in a drydock every five years, of a vessel's hull, machinery and other components.

FLATBACK – Lakes slang for a non-self-unloader.

FOOTER – Lakes slang for 1,000-foot vessel.

FORECASTLE – (FOHK s'l) Area at the forward part of the ship and beneath the main cabins, often used for crew's quarters or storage.

FOREPEAK – The space below the forecastle.

FORWARD – Toward the front, or bow, of a ship.

FREEBOARD – The distance from the water line to the main deck.

GROSS TONNAGE – The internal space of a vessel, measured in units of 100 cubic feet (2.83 cubic meters) = a gross ton.

HATCH – An opening in the deck through which cargo is lowered or raised. A hatch is closed by securing a hatch cover over it.

HULL – The body of a ship, not including its superstructure, masts or machinery.

INTEGRATED TUG/BARGE (ITB) – Tug-barge combination in which the tug is rigidly mated to the barge. *Presque Isle* is one example.

IRON DECKHAND – Mechanical device that runs on rails on a vessel's main deck and is used to remove and replace hatch covers.

JONES ACT – A U.S. cabotage law that mandates that cargoes moved between American ports be carried by U.S.-flagged, U.S.-built and U.S.-crewed vessels.

KEEL – A ship's steel backbone. It runs along the lowest part of the hull.

LAID UP or **LAY UP** – Out of service.

MARITIME CLASS – Style of lake vessel built during World War II as part of the nation's war effort. *Mississagi* is one example.

NET REGISTERED TONNAGE – The internal capacity of a vessel available for carrying cargo. It does not include the space occupied by boilers, engines, shaft alleys, chain lockers or officers' and crew's quarters. Net registered tonnage is usually referred to as registered tonnage or net tonnage and is used to calculate taxes, tolls and port charges.

RIVER CLASS SELF-UNLOADER – Group of vessels built in the 1970s to service smaller ports and negotiate narrow rivers such as Cleveland's Cuyahoga. *Wolverine* is one example.

SELF-UNLOADER – Vessel able to discharge its own cargo using a system of conveyor belts and a movable boom.

SLAG – By-product of the steelmaking process which is later ground up and used for paving roads.

STEM – The extreme forward end of the bow.

STEMWINDER – Vessel with all cabins aft.

STERN – The back of the ship.

STRAIGHT-DECKER – A non-self-unloading vessel. *Edward L. Ryerson* is one example.

TACONITE – Processed, pelletized iron ore. Easy to load and unload, this is the primary type of ore shipped on the Great Lakes and St. Lawrence Seaway. Also known as pellets.

TRACTOR TUG – Highly maneuverable tug propelled by either a Z-drive or cycloidal system rather than the traditional screw propeller.

Vessel Index

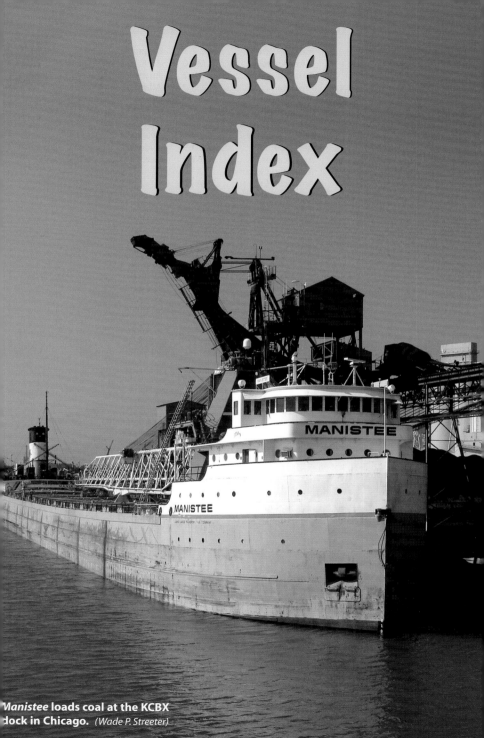

Manistee loads coal at the KCBX dock in Chicago. *(Wade P. Streeter)*

A

Vessel Name	Fleet #
A-390	A-12
A-397	A-12
A-410	A-12
Aachen	II-2
Abegweit	C-18
Acacia	A-8
Acquamarina	IF-4
Acushnet	M-8
Adamastos	IE-6
Adanac	P-12
Advent	C-3
Agawa Canyon	A-7
Agena	IR-4
Aggie C	I-2
Agios Minas	IH-3
Aird, John B.	A-7
Aivik	T-16
Alabama	G-18
Alam Sempurna	IP-1
Albert C	I-2
Alcona	R-9
Alder	U-3
Aldo H.	M-15
Aleksandrov, Grigoriy	IF-2
Alexandria Belle	U-1
Alexis-Simard	A-6
Algobay	A-7
Algocanada	A-7
Algocape	A-7
Algoeast	A-7
Algoisle	A-7
Algolake	A-7
Algomah	A-15
Algomarine	A-7
Algonorth	A-7
Algonova	A-7
Algontario	A-7
Algoport	A-7
Algorail	A-7
Algosar	A-7
Algoscotia	A-7
Algosea	A-7
Algosoo	A-7
Algosteel	A-7
Algoville	A-7
Algoway	A-7
Algowood	A-7
Alice E	A-9, E-5
Alkyon	II-4
Alouette	T-4
Alouette Spirit	M-15
Alpena	I-3
Altman, Anna Marie	Z-1
Altman, Victor J.	Z-1
Alton Andrew	M-10
Amalia	II-2
Amanda	II-2
Ambassador	IC-17
Amber Mae	R-9
AMC 100	A-9
AMC 200	A-9
AMC 300	A-9
Americaborg	IW-2
American Century	A-10
American Courage	A-10
American Fortitude	A-10
American Girl	S-23
American Integrity	A-10
American Mariner	A-10
American Republic	A-10
American Spirit	A-10
American Valor	A-10
American Victory	A-10
Amundsen	C-3
Anchor Bay	G-19
Anderson, Arthur M.	G-17
Andre H.	L-9
Andrea J.	E-4
Andrea Marie I	D-3
Andrew J.	E-4
Andrie, Barbara	A-12
Andrie, Candace	A-12
Andrie, Clara	A-12
Andrie, Karen	A-12
Andrie, Meredith	A-12
Andromeda	IB-1
Anglian Lady	P-12
Angus, D.J.	G-12
Anja	II-2
Ann Marie	L-16
Annalisa	II-2
Antalina	IT-1
Antikeri	IA-3
Apalachee	T-3
Apollon	IS-3
Appledore IV	B-5
Appledore V	B-5
Arabian Wind	IE-1
Arca	S-5
Arctic	F-2
Arizona	G-18
Arkansas	G-18
Asher, Chas.	R-5
Asher, John R.	R-5
Asher, Stephan M.	R-5
Ashland Bayfield Express	A-16
Askew, Henry	H-3
ASL Sanderling	IO-2
Astron	IC-3
Atigamayg	O-4
Atkinson, Arthur K.	S-2
Atlantic Erie	C-2
Atlantic Huron	C-2
Atlantic Superior	C-2
Atwell, Idus	M-18
Aurora Borealis	C-16
Avantage	L-9
Avdeevka	IC-11
Avenger IV	P-12

B

Vessel Name	Fleet #
Badger	L-5
Bagotville	M-18
Baird, Spencer F.	U-5
Balticland	IE-4
Barbara Rita	A-12
Barbro	IF-8
Barge Laviolette	U-13
Barker, James R.	I-6
Barker, Kaye E.	I-6
Barry J	K-7
Basse-Cote	L-9
Bavaria	IB-8
Bayfield	M-4
Bayridge Service	H-10
Bayship	B-4
BBC Asia	IB-8
BBC Atlantic	IB-8
BBC Australia	IB-8
BBC Campana	IW-1
BBC Elbe	IB-8
BBC Ems	IB-8
BBC England	IJ-2
BBC Finland	IB-8
BBC France	IB-8
BBC Iceland	IB-8
BBC India	IB-3
BBC Italy	IW-1
BBC Korea	II-3
BBC Mexico	IB-8
BBC Mississippi	IB-8
BBC Ontario	IK-2
BBC Peru	IW-1
BBC Plata	IW-1
BBC Russia	II-3
BBC Scandinavia	IB-8
BBC Scotland	IB-8
BBC Shanghai	IB-8
BBC Singapore	IB-8
BBC Spain	IW-1
BBC Venezuela	IB-8
Beaupre	A-4
Beaver	A-15

Vessel Name	Fleet #
Beaver D.	V-2
Beaver Delta II	M-18
Beaver Gamma	M-18
Beaver Islander	B-7
Beaver Kay	M-18
Beaver State	M-1
Bee Jay	G-4
Beeghly, Charles M.	I-6
Beluga Constitution	IB-3
Beluga Efficiency	IB-3
Beluga Elegance	IB-3
Beluga Emotion	IB-3
Beluga Endurance	IB-3
Beluga Energy	IB-3
Beluga Eternity	IB-3
Beluga Expectation	IB-3
Beluga Federation	IB-3
Beluga Formation	IB-3
Beluga Fusion	IB-3
Beluga Indication	IB-3
Beluga Legislation	IB-3
Beluga Recognition	IB-3
Beluga Recommendation	IB-3
Beluga Resolution	IB-3
Beluga Revolution	IB-3
Berdyansk	IC-11
Betsiamites	L-9
Bide-A-Wee	S-13
Billmaier, D.L.	U-2
Birchglen	C-2
Biscayne Bay	U-3
Black, Martha L.	C-3
Block, Joseph L.	C-7
Blough, Roger	G-17
Blue Heron	U-11
Blue Heron V	B-12
Bluebill	IN-1
Bluewing	IN-1
Boatman No. 3	M-15
Boatman No. 6	M-15
Bogdan	IN-2
Boland, John J.	A-10
Bonnie B. III	M-15
Bonnie G.	T-6
Borkum	IB-8
Bornholm	IH-7
Bowes, Bobby	D-4
Boyd, David	G-23
Boyer, Willis B.	M-32
Bramble	P-8
Brandon E.	E-5
Breaker	S-30
Brenda L.	F-5
Bright Laker	ID-1
Bristol Bay	U-3
Brutus I	T-12
Buckley	K-6
Buckthorn	U-3
Buffalo	A-10
Bunyan, Paul	U-2
Burns Harbor	A-10
Busch, Barbara Merry	B-20
Busch, Gregory J.	B-20
Busse, Fred A.	D-8
Buxton II	K-7

C

Vessel Name	Fleet #
C.T.C. No. 1	S-27
Cabot {2}	IO-2
Cadillac	S-29
California	G-18
Callaway, Cason J.	G-17
Callie M.	M-10
Calumet	I-7, L-15
Cameron O.	S-3
Canadian	M-18
Canadian Argosy	M-18
Canadian Empress	S-24
Canadian Enterprise	U-13
Canadian Jubilee	D-4
Canadian Leader	U-13
Canadian Miner	U-13
Canadian Navigator	U-13
Canadian Olympic	U-13
Canadian Progress	U-13
Canadian Prospector	U-13
Canadian Provider	U-13
Canadian Ranger	U-13
Canadian Transfer	U-13
Canadian Transport	U-13
Cantankerus	E-8

Canadian tanker *Algosar* upbound for Sault Ste. Marie, Ont. *(Roger LeLievre)*

***American Mariner* and *Canadian Provider*.** *(Brian Kimball)*

Vessel Name	Fleet #
Cap Charles	IE-8
Cap Diamant	IE-8
Cap Georges	IE-8
Cap Guillaume	IE-8
Cap Lara	IE-8
Cap Laurent	IE-8
Cap Leon	IE-8
Cap Philippe	IE-8
Cap Pierre	IE-8
Cap Streeter	S-11
Cape Discovery	C-3
Cape Dundas	C-3
Cape Hurd	C-3
Cape Storm	C-3
Capetan Michalis	IU-1
Capricorn	IB-1
Capt. Shepler	S-7
Carey, Emmett J.	O-7
Cargo Master	M-18
Caribou Isle	C-3
Carl M.	M-18
Carlee Emily	K-3
Carleton, George N.	G-13
Carol Ann	K-7
Carola	II-2
Carolina Borealis	C-16
Carrick, John J.	M-13
Carrol C. I	M-15
Catharina-C	IC-4
Cavalier des Mers	C-21
Cavalier Maxim	C-21
Cavalier Royal	C-21
CEC Fantasy	IC-8
CEC Fighter	IC-8
CEC Spring	IC-8
Cedarglen	C-2
Celebreeze, Anthony J.	C-15
Celine	IE-7
Cemba	C-6
CFL Prospect	IC-1
CGB-12000	U-3
CGB-12001	U-3
Challenge	G-21
Champion	C-8, D-14
Channahon	I-2
Channel Cat	M-21
Charles XX	M-19
Charlevoix	C-9
Charlie E.	I-7
Chem Bothnia	IC-6
Chemical Trader	IE-10
Cheraw	U-2
Chicago's First Lady	M-20
Chicago's Little Lady	M-20
Chi-Cheemaun	O-8
Chief Shingwauk	L-12
Chief Wawatam	P-12
Chippewa	A-15
Chippewa III	S-19
Chris Ann	H-9
Cinnamon	IN-1
City of Algonac	D-2
City of Milwaukee	S-20
Clark, Wilbur R.	H-4
Clarke, Philip R.	G-17
Claudia	IE-7
Cleanshores	H-3
Cleveland	L-7
Cleveland Rocks	L-7
Clipper Falcon	IL-4
Clipper Golfito	IC-9
Clipper Karen	IC-9
Clipper Kira	IC-9
Clipper Kristin	IC-9
Clipper Krystal	IC-9
Clipper Kylie	IC-9
Clipper Lancer	IC-9
Clipper Leader	IC-9
Clipper Leaner	IC-9
Clipper Legacy	IC-9
Clipper Legend	IC-9
Clipper Loyalty	IC-9
Clipper Tasmania	IC-9
Clipper Tobago	IC-9
Clipper Trinidad	IC-9
Clipper Trojan	IC-9
Clyde	G-8
Coastal Cruiser	T-5
Cobia	W-5
Cod	U-16
Cohen, Wilfred M.	P-12
Cojak	S-15
Coleman	B-9
Colombe, J.E.	Y-1
Colorado	G-18
Columbia	S-31
Columbia V (The)	A-11
Commodore Straits	U-13
Condarrell	M-15
Coo-Coo	L-9
Cooper, J.W.	C-19
Cooper, Wyn	F-4
Coriolis II	U-9
Cornelius, Adam E.	A-10
Corsair	A-15
Cort, Stewart J.	I-6
Cotter, Edward M.	B-18
Coucoucache	L-9
Covadonga	IA-2
Cove Isle	C-3
Crapo, S.T.	I-3
Cresswell, Peter R.	A-7
Croaker	B-15
Crystal Diamond	IC-16
Crystal Topaz	IC-16
CSL Assiniboine	C-2
CSL Laurentien	C-2
CSL Niagara	C-2
CSL Tadoussac	C-2
C.T.M.A.Vacancier	C-22
C.T.M.A. Voyageur	C-22
Cuyahoga	L-14

D

Vessel Name	Fleet #
Dagna	IW-2
Dahlke, Ronald J.	A-12
Daldean	B-13
Dalmig	H-7
Danicia	B-2
Daniel E.	E-5
Daniele M.	M-15
Daniella	IJ-3
Dapper Dan	M-18
Darrell, William	H-11
Dauntless	M-17
David Allen	N-9
David E.	E-5, H-4
David T.D.	L-9
Daviken	IV-2
Dawn Light	T-7
de Champlain, Samuel	L-2
Dean, Annie M.	D-4
Dean, Elmer	G-1
Debbie Lyn	M-3
Defiance	A-9
Delaware	G-18
Deltuva	IL-4
Demolen	U-2
Denis M	A-5
Denise E.	E-5
Derek E.	E-5
Des Groseilliers	C-3
Des Plaines	C-1
Deschenes, Jos.	S-12
Desgagnés, Amelia	T-15
Desgagnés, Anna	T-15
Desgagnés, Camilla	T-15
Desgagnés, Catherine	T-15
Desgagnés, Maria	T-15
Desgagnés, Melissa	T-15
Desgagnés, Petrolia	T-15
Desgagnés, Rosaire A.	T-15
Desgagnés, Sarah	T-15
Desgagnés, Thalassa	T-15
Desgagnés, Vega	T-15
Desgagnés, Zelada	T-15

Vessel Name	Fleet #
Desjardins, Alphonse	S-12
Detroit Princess	D-6
Devine, Barney	W-4
Diamond Belle	D-7
Diamond Jack	D-7
Diamond Queen	D-7
Diamond Star	R-3
Diezeborg	IW-2
Dilly, William B.	M-18
Ditte Theresa	IH-8
Dobrush	IC-11
Doc Morin	U-13
Doggersbank	IP-3
Donald Bert	M-3
Donald Mac	G-13
Dongeborg	IW-2
Donner, William H.	K-9
Dora	IT-2
Dorothea	IL-5
Dorothy Ann	I-6
Dover	M-3
Dover Light	E-1
Doxa D	IB-2
Doyle	C-1
Dr. Bob	T-1
Drechtborg	IW-2
Drummond Islander II	M-1
Drummond Islander III	E-2
Drummond Islander IV	E-2
Duc d'Orleans	F-6

Vessel Name	Fleet #
Duc d'Orleans II	D-11
Duga	L-9
Duluth	G-15
Durocher, Ray	D-14
Dutch Runner	IR-1
Dzintari	IL-1

E

Vessel Name	Fleet #
Eagle	S-10
Ebn El Waleed	IE-2
Ecosse	N-1
Edelweiss I	E-3
Edelweiss II	E-3
Edith J.	E-4
Edna G.	L-3
Edward H.	M-25
Eider	IP-2
Eileen C	I-2
Elikon	IH-6
Elizabeth	P-1
Elpida	IS-9
Elsie D.	R-7
Emerald Isle	B-7
Emerald Star	R-3
Empire Sandy	N-3
Empire State	T-6
Empress of Canada	E-6
Emsmoon	IM-1
Endurance	IH-2
Energy 5501	H-10
English River	L-1
Enterprise 2000	O-3
Environaut	G-6
Erich	M-17
Erie Explorer	O-4
Erie-West	M-15
Escort	B-2
Escorte	L-9
Esperanza	R-7
Essayons	C-5
Evans McKeil	M-15
Evening Star	S-11
Everlast	M-13
Eyrarbakki	W-1

F

Vessel Name	Fleet #
Fairlane	IJ-3
Fairlift	IJ-3
Fairload	IJ-3
Fairmast	IJ-3
Fairpartner	IJ-3
Fairplay XIV	IF-1
Fairplayer	IJ-3
Faith	D-13
Federal Agno	IF-3
Federal Asahi {2}	IF-3

American Integrity **downbound near the Soo on May 13, 2007.** *(Roger LeLievre)*

G

Edward E. Gillen's tug *Jullane J.* pushes a stone barge at Milwaukee. *(Peter Groh)*

Vessel Name	Fleet #
Gillen, Edward E. III	E-4
Gillmore, Q.A.	N-8
Glen	IE-3
Glenada	T-5
Glenora	O-5
Global Carrier	II-5
Glory	IC-5, IH-2
Goldeneye	IS-3
Goodtime I	G-9
Goodtime III	G-10
Gott, Edwin H.	G-17
Gouin, Lomer	S-12
Goviken	IV-2
Graham, H.E.	L-9
Graham, Sandy	B-6
Grand Fleuve	C-21
Grand Island	P-4
Grand Portal	P-4
Grande Baie	A-6
Grande Caribe	IA-4
Grande Mariner	IA-4
Grant, R.F.	L-9
Grayfox	U-7
Grayling	G-22
Great Blue Heron	B-11
Great Lakes	K-5
Great Lakes Trader	V-1
Green, Magdalena	IB-3
Green, Makiri	IB-3
Green, Margaretha	IB-3
Green, Marion	IB-3
Green, Marlene	IB-3
Greenstone II	U-6
Greenwing	IN-1
Greta V	M-18
Gretchen B.	L-16
Griffon	C-3
Grue des Iles	S-12
Gull Isle	C-3
Gulmar	IG-2

H

Vessel Name	Fleet #
Haida	H-6
Halandriani	IS-1
Halifax	C-2
Hamilton Energy	U-13
Hamilton Harbour Queen	H-2
Hammond Bay	L-11, U-2
Handy Andy	M-18
Hanlan II, Ned	T-13
Hannah 1801	H-4
Hannah 1802	H-4
Hannah 2901	H-4
Hannah 2902	H-4
Hannah 2903	H-4
Hannah 3601	H-4
Hannah 5101	H-4
Hannah 6301	H-4
Hannah 7701	H-4
Hannah, Daryl C.	H-4
Hannah, Donald C.	H-4
Hannah, Hannah D.	H-4
Hannah, James A.	H-4
Hannah, Kristen Lee	H-4
Hannah, Mark	H-4
Hannah, Mary E.	H-4
Hannah, Mary Page	S-3
Hannah, Peggy D.	H-4
Hannah, Susan W.	H-4
Happy Ranger	IB-5
Harbour Star	B-19
Harvey	U-2
Haskell	D-1
Hayden, Fischer	G-15
Helene	S-4
Henry, Alexander	M-9
Hiawatha	R-7, S-13
Highlander Sea	A-3
His Majesty's Ship Detroit	P-11
Hoey, Carolyn	G-2
Hoey, Patricia	G-2
Hoey, William	G-2
Hogan, Joseph J.	J-1
Holden, John	M-18
Holiday	S-13
Holly Ann	H-9
Hollyhock	U-3
Houghton	K-2
Howe Islander	C-20
Huron	A-15, P-8
Huron Belle	L-8
Huron Lady II	B-12
Huron Maid	L-8

I

Vessel Name	Fleet #
I.V. No. 10	D-10
I.V. No. 11	D-10
I.V. No. 13	D-10
I.V. No. 14	D-10
I.V. No. 8	D-10
I.V. No. 9	D-10
Ian Mac	M-3
Ida M.	R-4
Ida M. II	R-4
Idaho	G-18
Iglehart, J.A.W.	I-3
Illinois	G-18
Imbeau, Armand	S-12
Indian Maiden	B-6
Indiana	G-18
Indiana Harbor	A-10
Indock, W.B.	N-7
Inglis, William	T-11
Inland Seas	I-4
Innisfree	C-11
Innovation	L-2
Integrity	L-2
Intrepid III	N-1
Inviken	IV-2
Invincible	L-15
Iowa	G-18
Ira	IC-12
Irma	IP-4
Iroquois	M-28
Irvin, William A.,	D-12
Iryda	IP-4
Isa	IP-4
Isadora	IP-4
Isarstern	IR-3
Island Belle I	K-8
Island Clipper	V-6
Island Duchess	U-1
Island Express	A-15
Island Heritage	T-4
Island Princess	A-13
Island Queen	M-4
Island Queen III	K-8
Island Queen V	T-18
Island Skipper	IS-7
Island Star	K-8
Island Triangle	IS-7
Island Wanderer	U-1
Islander	B-3, M-27, R-8
Islay	N-8
Isle Royale Queen III	S-18
Isle Royale Queen IV	I-9
Isolda	IP-4
Ivi	IC-12

J

Vessel Name	Fleet #
Jackman, Capt. Henry	A-7
Jackson, Herbert C.	I-6
Jackson, W.G.	G-12
Jacquelyn Nicole	S-3
Jade Star	R-3
Jaguar II	C-16
Jamie L.	M-18
Jana	II-2
Jane Ann IV	T-2
Janice C. No. 1	C-19
Jarco 1402	R-9
Jarrett M.	M-15
Jeanette M	D-3
Jean-Raymond	M-15
Jerry G.	L-9

USCG *Katmai Bay* meets *Vancouverborg* in the Detroit River. *(Roger LeLievre)*

K

L

M

Vessel Name	Fleet #
Mackinaw City	M-1
Madeleine	C-22
Madeline	M-4
Mado-Ray	L-9
Magnetic	F-3
Maid of the Mist IV	M-5
Maid of the Mist V	M-5
Maid of the Mist VI	M-5
Maid of the Mist VII	M-5
Maine	G-18
Maineborg	IW-2
Maisonneuve	A-5
Makeevka	IC-11
Malden	P-12
Malyovitza	IN-2
Manatra	U-7
Mandarin	IN-1
Manistee	L-15
Manitou	M-6, M-14, T-17
Manitou Isle	M-7
Manitowoc	K-9, L-15, U-2
Manora Naree	IP-5
Maple	U-15
Maple City	T-12
Maple Grove	O-1
Marcoux, Camille	S-12
Margaret Ann	H-9
Margaret M.	H-4
Margot	N-6
Marie-Jeanne	IE-7
Marinus Green	IB-3
Mariposa Belle	M-11
Maritime Trader	V-7
Mariupol	IC-11
Market, Wm.	M-27
Marlyn	S-11
Marquette	C-11
Marquette II	S-29
Martin, Rt. Hon. Paul J.	C-2
Mary Ann	H-9
Marysville	G-2
Massachusetts	G-18
Mather, William G.	M-31
Matt Allen	K-7
Maumee	L-15
MBT 10	M-29
MBT 20	M-29
MBT 33	M-29
McAllister 132	A-1
McAsphalt 401	M-13
McBride, Sam	T-11
McCarthy Jr., Walter J.	A-10
McCauley	S-25
McCleary's Spirit	K-1
McCombs, Judge	H-3
McGrath, James E.	M-15
McKee Sons	L-15
McKeil, Jarrett	M-15
McKeil, Wyatt	H-7
McLane	G-20
McLeod, Norman	M-13
Medemborg	IW-2
Medill, Joseph	B-2
Menasha	G-4, M-19
Menier Consol	T-8
Menominee	L-6
Mermaid	R-6
Mesabi Miner	I-6
Meta	IO-7
Meteor	S-21
Metis	E-12
Michigan	K-5
Michiganborg	IW-2
Michipicoten	L-14
Middle Channel	C-8
Mighty Jake	G-8
Mighty Jessie	G-8
Mighty Jimmy	G-8
Mighty John III	G-8
Miles, Paddy	H-12
Milin Kamak	IN-2
Milo	IS-3
Miltiades	IS-3
Milwaukee	G-18
Milwaukee Clipper	G-14
Miners Castle	P-4
Minnesota	G-18
Miseford	T-5
Mishe-Mokwa	M-7
Misner, H. H.	B-10
Miss Buffalo II	B-16
Miss Edna	K-7
Miss Laura	M-10

***John J. Munson* under full steam in the lower St. Marys River.** *(Mark Whitney)*

Vessel Name	Fleet #
Miss Libby	T-1
Miss Midland	M-23
Miss Munising	S-8
Miss Olympia	N-4
Miss Superior	P-4
Mississagi	L-14
Mississauga Express	IH-2
Mississippi	G-18
Missouri	G-18
Mister Joe	M-18
Mljet	IA-8
Mobile Bay	U-3
Moby Dick	G-8
Moezelborg	IW-2
Mohawk	M-1
Molly M. 1	M-15
Montana	G-18
Montreal Express	IH-2
Montrealais	U-13
Moor	IE-3
Moore, Olive L.	K-9
Moore, William J.	K-1
Morgan	K-6
Mount Ace	IT-4
Mount McKay	N-8
Mountain Blossom	IL-3
Mrs. C.	C-19
Munson, John G.	G-17
Musky II	G-22

N

Vessel Name	Fleet #
Nadro Clipper	N-1
Namaycush	O-4
Nancy Anne	D-14
Nanticoke	C-2
Nassauborg	IW-2
Nathan S	C-1
Nautica Queen	N-2
Navcomar No. 1	L-9
Neah Bay	U-3
Nebraska	G-18
Neebish Islander II	E-2
Neeskay	U-11
Neptune III	D-4
New Beginnings	T-14
New Jersey	G-18
New York	G-18
Newberry, Jerry	M-18
Niagara	E-9
Niagara Prince	IA-4
Niagara Queen II	O-6
Nichevo II	M-4
Nicola	II-2
Nicole M.	M-15
Nicolet	U-2
Nida	IP-4
Niki S	C-1
Nils B.	IW-1
Nina	II-2
Nindawayma	P-12
Nipigon Osprey	O-4
No. 55	M-1
No. 56	M-1
Noble, Robert	W-1
Nogat	IP-4
Nokomis	S-13
Nordik Express	T-15
Norgoma	S-28
Norisle	S-22
Norma B.	F-3
Norris, James	U-13
North Carolina	G-18
North Channel	C-8
North Dakota	G-18
North Fighter	IE-3
Northern Spirit 1	S-16
Northwestern	G-19
Noyes, Hack	W-4

O

Vessel Name	Fleet #
Oatka	B-14
Ocean Abys	L-9
Ocean Bravo	L-9
Ocean Charlie	L-9
Ocean Delta	L-9
Ocean Echo II	L-9
Ocean Foxtrot	L-9
Ocean Golf	L-9
Ocean Hauler	M-15
Ocean Henry Bain	L-9
Ocean Hercule	L-9
Ocean Intrepide	L-9
Ocean Jupiter	L-9
Ocean K. Rusby	L-9
Ocean Pride	IF-4
Ocean Raymond Lemay	L-9
Oceanex Avalon	IO-2
Oconto	P-9
Odra	IP-4
Ohio	G-18
Oil Queen	S-23
Ojibway	L-14, M-1
Okapi	IF-5
Oklahoma	G-18
Okoltchitza	IN-2
Old Mission	K-6
Oldendorff, Elise	IO-3
Olympic Melody	IO-4
Olympic Mentor	IO-4
Olympic Merit	IO-4
Olympic Miracle	IO-4
Omni-Atlas	L-9
Omni-Richelieu	L-9
Omni St. Laurent	L-9
Onego Merchant	IO-6
Onego Trader	IO-6
Onego Traveller	IO-6
Ongiara	T-11
Ontamich	B-13
Orfea	IT-7
Oriental Kerria	IS-4
Oriole	S-16
Orla	IP-4
Orna	IS-3
Orsula	IA-8
Osborne, F.M.	O-7
OSC Vlistdiep	IH-5
Oshawa	M-18
Oshkosh #15	Y-1
Osprey	P-12
Ostrander, G.L.	L-2
Ottawa	A-15
Ottawa Express	IH-2
Ours Polaire	N-7
Outer Island	E-7

P

Vessel Name	Fleet #
P.M.L. 2501	P-12
P.M.L. 357	P-12
P.M.L. 9000	P-12
P.M.L. Alton	P-12
Pacific Standard	M-15
Palawan	IH-4
Palessa	IH-4
Pan Voyager	IS-11
Panam Atlantico	IC-15
Panam Felice	IC-15
Panam Flota	IC-15
Panam Oceanica	IC-15
Panam Sol	IC-14
Panam Trinity	IC-15
Panama	B-10
Pancaldo	IH-4
Panos G.	IG-1
Papoose III	K-8
Park State	M-26
Pathfinder	I-6
Patronicola, Calliroe	IO-4
Paula M.	M-18
Peach State	M-1
Pearkes, George R.	C-3
Pelee Islander	O-5
Peninsula	G-13
Pennsylvania	G-18
Pere Marquette 10	E-11

Vessel Name	Fleet #
Pere Marquette 41	P-2
Perelik	IN-2
Performance	S-25
Perrin, J.V.	L-9
Persenk	IN-2
Pete, C. West	B-1
Petite Forte	S-27
Pictured Rocks	P-4
Pierson, Robert S.	L-14
Pilica	IP-4
Pineglen	C-2
Pioneer	IC-17
Pioneer Princess	T-10
Pioneer Queen	T-10
Pioneerland	G-8
Platytera	IA-5
Pochard	IH-4
Point Valour	T-5
Point Viking	A-2
Polaris	I-8
Polydefkis P	IC-13
Pomorze Zachodnie	IP-4
Pontokratis	IO-1
Pontoporos	IO-1
Port City Princess	P-7
Port Mechins	D-10
Power	IH-2
Prairieland	G-8
Presque Isle	G-17
Pride of Michigan	U-7
Princess Wenonah	B-3
Prinsenborg	IW-2
Provmar Terminal	U-13
Provmar Terminal II	U-13
Puffin	IH-4
Purcell, Robert	A-12
Purha	IF-7
Purves, John	D-9
Purvis, W.I. Scott	P-12
Purvis, W.J. Ivan	P-12
Put-In-Bay	M-27
Pyrgos	IF-5

Q-R

Vessel Name	Fleet #
Quebecois	U-13
Quinte Loyalist	O-5
R.C.L. Tug II	M-18
Racine	U-2
Radisson	S-12, S-29
Radisson, Pierre	C-3
Radium Yellowknife	N-7
Randolph, Curtis	D-5
Ranger III	U-6
Rapide Blanc	L-9
Rebecca	II-2
Rebecca Lynn	A-12
Redhead	IP-2
Rega	IP-4
Reliance	P-12
Rennie, Thomas	T-11
Rest, Willliam	T-12
Rhode Island	G-18
Richter, Arni J.	W-1
Richter, C.G.	W-1
Risely, Samuel	C-3
Robert John	G-13
Robert W.	T-5
Robin E.	E-5
Robin Lynn	S-6
Robinson Bay	S-25
Rochelle Kaye	R-9
Rocket	P-12
Roman, Stephen B.	E-12
Rosaire	D-10
Rosalee D.	T-5
Rosemary	M-11
Rouble, J.R.	T-1
Roxane D.	L-9
Royal Pescadores	IS-5
Ryerson, Edward L.	C-7

S

Vessel Name	Fleet #
S Pacific	IJ-2
Sabina	IE-7
Sacre Bleu	S-7
Saginaw	L-14
Sagittarius	II-1
Salvage Monarch	N-7
Salvor	M-15
Sandpiper	H-5
Sandra Mary	M-18
Sandviken	IV-2
Santiago	IB-8
Sarah B	G-15
Sarah No. 1	T-1
Sault au Cochon	M-15
Sauniere	A-7
Savard, Felix Antione	S-12
Savard, Joseph	S-12
Scandrett, Fred	T-12
Schlaeger, Victor L.	C-10
Schwartz, H.J.	U-2
SCL Bern	IE-7
Sea Chief	B-2
Sea Eagle II	S-27
Sea Fox II	T-4
Sea Prince II	R-4
Sea Veteran	IV-1
Seaguardian II	IT-3
Seahound	N-1
Sealink	IT-3
Segwun	M-33
Selvick, Carla Anne	S-3
Selvick, John M.	C-1
Selvick, Kimberly	C-1
Selvick, Sharon M.	S-3
Selvick, William C.	S-3
Seneca	M-26, IA-3
Seram Wind	IE-1
Serena	II-2
Serendipity Princess	M-23
Service Boat No.1	L-9
Service Boat No.4	L-9
Seymour, Wilf	M-15
Shamrock	J-2
Shannon	G-2
Shark	C-3
Sheila P.	P-12
Shenandoah	R-2
Shenehon	G-16
Sherwin, John	I-6
Shipka	IN-2
Shipsands	T-14
Shirley Irene	K-3
Shoreline II	S-11
Showboat Royal Grace	M-11
Siam Star	IE-5
Sichem Aneline	IE-3
Sichem Beijing	IE-3
Sichem Challenge	IE-3
Sichem Defiance	IE-3
Sichem Manila	IE-3
Sichem Mumbai	IE-3
Sichem New York	IE-3
Sichem Padua	IE-3
Sichem Palace	IE-3
Sichem Peace	IE-3
Sichem Princess Marie-Chantal	IE-3
Sichem Singapore	IE-3
Silver Wind	IE-1
Silversides	G-20
Simcoe Islander	C-20
Simonsen	U-2
Simpson, Miss Kim	T-14
Sioux	M-1, Z-1
Sir Walter	IA-1
Siscowet	B-2
Skaftafell	IB-8
Skyline Princess	M-20
Skyline Queen	M-20
Smith Jr., L.L.	U-12
Smith, Dean R.	M-10
Smith, F.C.G.	C-3
Snohomish	S-1
Sofia	II-2
Songa Crystal	IB-6

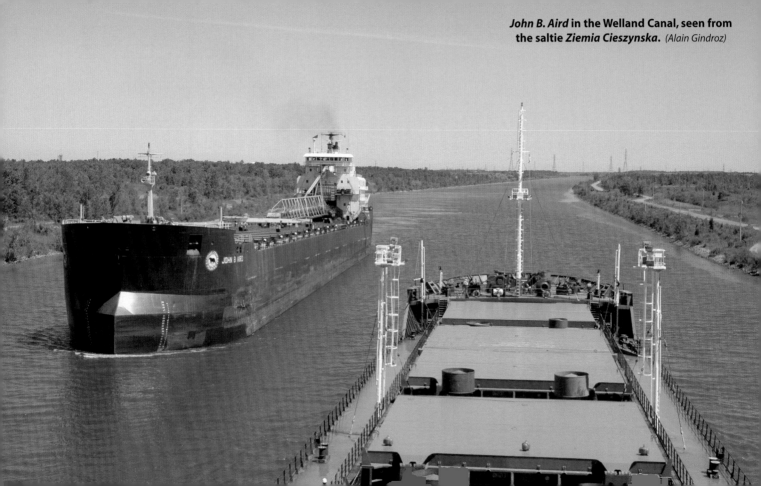

John B. Aird **in the Welland Canal, seen from the saltie *Ziemia Cieszynska*.** *(Alain Gindroz)*

Vessel Name	Fleet #
Soo River Belle	S-14
South Bass	M-27
South Carolina	G-18
South Channel	C-8
Spar Garnet	IS-8
Spar Jade	IS-8
Spar Opal	IS-8
Spar Ruby	IS-8
Spartan	L-5
Speer, Edgar B.	G-17
Spencer, Sarah	T-2
Spirit of Chicago	S-17
Spirit of LaSalle	S-18
Spruceglen	C-2
Spuds	R-5
St. Clair	A-10
St. John, J.S.	E-10
St. Marys Cement	S-27
St. Marys Cement II	S-27
St. Marys Cement III	S-27
St. Marys Challenger	S-27
St. Marys Conquest	S-27
Stacey Dawn	C-19
Star of Chicago	S-11
Staris	IL-4
Starlight	IO-5
State of Michigan	G-19
STC 2004	B-20
Ste. Claire	M-12
Ste. Claire V (The)	A-11
Steelhead	M-21
Stefania I	IF-8
Stella Borealis	C-16
Stellanova	IJ-3
Stellaprima	IJ-3
Stolt Aspiration	IS-10
Stolt Kite	IS-10
Stormont	M-15
Straits Express	A-15
Straits of Mackinac II	A-15
Strekalovskiy, Mikhail	IM-3
Sturgeon	G-22
Sugar Islander II	E-2
Sullivan, Denis	P-5
Sulu Wind	IE-1
Sundew	D-12
Sundstraum	IA-6
Sunliner	W-2
Superior	G-18
Susan L.	S-3
Susan Michelle	D-3
Suvorov, Aleksandr	IM-3
Swan Lake	IL-3
Sykes, Wilfred	C-7

T

Vessel Name	Fleet #
Tandem I	N-4
Tanner	K-6
Tatjana	II-2
TCCA 1	T-12
Techno-Venture	M-15
Tecumseh II	P-12
Tenacious	R-9
Tennessee	G-18
Texas	G-18
The Hope	S-7
The Shoreline	S-9
The Sullivans	B-15
The Welcome	S-7
Thekla	II-2
Thomas, Hamp	H-12
Thompson Jr., Joseph H.	U-14
Thompson, Joseph H.	U-14
Thompson, Maxine	F-5
Thor Sofia	IC-8
Thousand Islander	G-5
Thousand Islander II	G-5
Thousand Islander III	G-5
Thousand Islander IV	G-5
Thousand Islander V	G-5
Thunder Cape	C-3
Timberland	G-8
Timesaver II	T-1
Timmy A.	R-5
Toni D	V-2
Toronto Express	IH-2
Torontonian	M-11
Townsend, Paul H.	I-3
Tracer	IB-5
Tracy	C-3
Tradewind Service	H-10
Tradewind Union	IT-6
Tramper	IB-5
Transit	C-21, N-4
Transporter	IB-5
Traveller	IB-5
Tregurtha, Lee A.	I-6
Tregurtha, Paul R.	I-6
Trillium	T-11
Triumph	IH-2
Turchese	IF-4
Tuscarora	IA-3
Tuvaq	IC-10
Twolan, W.N.	A-1

U-V

Vessel Name	Fleet #
Umiak I	F-2
Umiavut	L-13
Uncle Sam 7	U-1
Undaunted	P-2
Upper Canada	L-6
Uta	II-2
Utviken	IV-2
Vaasaborg	IW-2
Vac	N-1
Valencia Express	IH-2
Valerie B.	D-14
Valley Camp	L-10
Vancouverborg	IW-2
VanEnkevort, Joyce L.	V-1
Vanessa-C	IC-4
Varnebank	IP-3
Vavilov, Pavel	IM-3
Vechtborg	IW-2
Veerseborg	IF-9
Veler	U-2
Vermont	G-18
Versluis, James J.	C-12
Viateur's Spirit	M-15
Victoria	II-2
Victoriaborg	IW-2
Victorian Princess	V-3
Victory	K-9, M-22, IH-2
Vida C.	C-17
Vigilant 1	N-1
Viking I	K-9
Vindemia	IS-6
Virginia	G-18
Virginiaborg	IW-2
Viscaya	IH-1
Vista King	V-5
Vista Queen	V-5
Vista Star	V-5
Vlistborg	IW-2
VM/S Hercules	S-26
VM/S Maisonneuve	S-26
VM/S St. Lambert	S-26
VM/S St. Louis III	S-26
Von Riedel, Franz A.	Z-1
Von Riedel, Gesine	Z-1
Von Riedel, Lacey	Z-1
Voorneborg	IW-2
Vossborg	IF-9
Voyager	S-11
Voyageur	M-28
Voyageur II	G-11
Vysotskiy, Vladimir	IN-3

W

Vessel Name	Fleet #
Wagenborg, Egbert	IW-2
Walpole Islander	D-2
Wanda III	M-33
Warner, William L.	H-4

Vessel Name	Fleet #
Warta	IP-4
Washington	G-18, W-1
Waub Nav. No. 1	P-12
Wayward Princess	N-3
Welland	D-3
Wendella	W-2
Wendella LTD	W-2
Wenonah	G-11
Wenonah II	M-33
Weserstern	IR-3
West Shore	B-3
West Wind	B-17
Westcott, J.W. II	J-1
Whistler	IP-2
Whitby	M-18
White, H. Lee	A-10
Whitefish Bay	U-2
William C	I-2
Willmac	M-15
Windmill Point	T-12
Windoc	A-7
Windy	W-3
Windy City	I-2
Windy II	W-3
Wing, Barbara	C-5
Winnebago	J-4
Winona	II-2
Wisconsin	G-18
Wolf River	G-13
Wolfe Islander III	O-5
Wolverine	T-6
Wonda Goldie	O-4
Woody	IS-3
Wyandot	S-7
Wyatt M.	M-15
Wyoming	G-18

X-Y-X

Vessel Name	Fleet #
Xenia	II-2
Yamaska	IE-1
Yankcanuck	P-12
Yankee Clipper	V-6
Yankton	Z-1
Yarmouth	IE-1
Yellowknife	IE-1
Yick Hua	IC-7
YM Jupiter	IY-3
Yosemite	IE-1
Ypermachos	IA-5
Yucatan	IE-1
Zanis Griva	IL-1
Zeus	IY-1
Ziemia Chelminska	IP-4
Ziemia Cieszynska	IP-4
Ziemia Gnieznienska	IP-4
Ziemia Gornoslaska	IP-4
Ziemia Lodzka	IP-4
Ziemia Suwalska	IP-4
Ziemia Tarnowska	IP-4
Ziemia Zamojska	IP-4

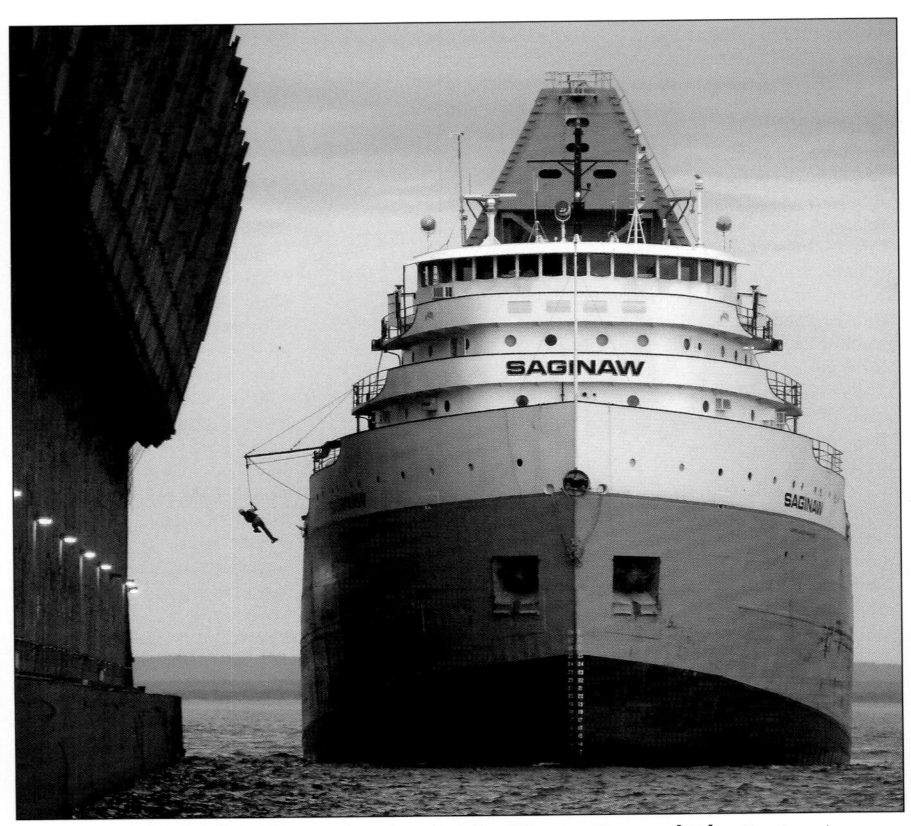

Saginaw **lands a crewman ashore at the Marquette ore dock.** *(Lee Rowe)*

Gordon C. Leitch **pours on the power leaving the Welland Canal's Lock 7.** *(Roger LeLievre)*

GORDON C. LEITCH
ST. CATHARINES

Fleet Listings

GREAT LAKES / SEAWAY FLEETS

Listed after each vessel in order are: Type of Vessel, Year Built, Type of Engine, Maximum Cargo Capacity (at midsummer draft in long tons) or Gross Tonnage*, Overall Length, Breadth and Depth (from the top of the keel to the top of the upper deck beam) or Draft*. Only vessels over 30 feet long are included. The figures given are as accurate as possible and are given for informational purposes only. Vessels and owners are listed alphabetically as per American Bureau of Shipping and Lloyd's Register of Shipping format. Builder yard and location, as well as other pertinent information, are listed for major vessels; former names of vessels and years of operation under the former names appear in parentheses. A number in brackets following a vessel's name indicates how many vessels, including the one listed, have carried that name.

KEY TO TYPE OF VESSEL

2B ... Brigantine
2S ... 2-Masted Schooner
3S ... 3-Masted Schooner
4S ... 4-Masted Schooner
AC ... Auto Carrier
AT ... Articulated Tug
ATB ... Articulated Tug/Barge
BC ... Bulk Carrier
BK ... Bulk Carrier/Tanker
BT ... Buoy Tender
CA ... Catamaran
CC ... Cement Carrier
CF ... Car Ferry
CO ... Container Vessel
CS ... Crane Ship
DB ... Deck Barge
DH ... Hopper Barge
DR ... Dredge
DS ... Spud Barge
DV ... Drilling Vessel
DW ... Scow
ES ... Excursion Ship
EV ... Environmental Response
FB ... Fireboat
FD ... Floating Dry Dock
FT ... Fishing Tug
GC ... General Cargo
GL ... Gate Lifter
GU ... Grain Self-Unloader
HL ... Heavy Lift Vessel
IB ... Ice Breaker
IT ... Integrated Tug
ITB ... Integrated Tug/Barge
MB ... Mailboat
MU ... Museum Vessel
PA ... Passenger Vessel
PB ... Pilot Boat
PF ... Passenger Ferry
PK ... Package Freighter
RR ... Roll On/Roll Off
RT ... Refueling Tanker
RV ... Research Vessel
SB ... Supply Boat
SC ... Sand Carrier
SR ... Search & Rescue
SU ... Self-Unloader
SV ... Survey Vessel
TB ... Tug Boat
TF ... Train Ferry
TK ... Tanker
TW ... Towboat
TT ... Tractor Tug Boat
TV ... Training Vessel

KEY TO PROPULSION

B ... Barge
D ... Diesel
DE ... Diesel Electric
Q ... Steam - Quad Exp. Compound Engine
R ... Steam - Triple Exp. Compound Engine
S ... Steam - Skinner "Uniflow" Engine
T ... Steam - Turbine Engine
W ... Sailing Vessel (Wind)

Fleet #	Fleet Name / Vessel Name	Type of Vessel	Year Built	Type of Engine	Cargo Cap. or Gross*	Overall Length	Breadth	Depth or Draft*
A-1	**A. B. M. MARINE, THUNDER BAY, ON**							
	McAllister 132	DB	1954	B	7,000	343' 00"	63' 00"	19' 00"
	Built: Burrard Dry Dock, N. Vancouver, BC (Powell No. 1 '54-'61, Alberni Carrier '61-'77, Genmar 132 '77-'79)							
	W. N. Twolan	TB	1962	D	299*	106' 00"	29' 05"	15' 00"
	Built: George T. Davie & Sons, Lauzon, QC							
A-2	**ABITIBI-CONSOLIDATED INC., MONTREAL, QC**							
	Point Viking	TB	1962	D	207*	98' 05"	27' 10"	13' 05"
	Built: Davie Shipbuilding Co., Lauzon, QC (Foundation Viking '62-'75)							
A-3	**ACHESON VENTURES LLC, PORT HURON, MI** *(achesonventures.com)*							
	Highlander Sea	ES/2S	1927	W/D	140*	154' 00"	25' 06"	14' 00"
	Built: A.D. Story Shipyard, Essex, MA (Pilot '27-'76, Star Pilot '76-'98, Caledonia '98-'98)							
A-4	**ADMINISTRATION PORTUAIRE DE QUÉBEC (QUEBEC PORT AUTHORITY), QUÉBEC, QC**							
	Beaupre	TB	1952	D	13*	37' 05"	10' 49"	4' 08"
A-5	**ADMINISTRATION PORTUAIRE DE MONTRÉAL (MONTREAL PORT AUTHORITY), MONTREAL, QC**							
	Denis M	TB	1942	D	21*	46' 07"	12' 08"	4' 01"
	Maisonneuve	TB	1972	D	103*	63' 10"	20' 07"	9' 03"

Fleet #	Fleet Name / Vessel Name	Type of Vessel	Year Built	Type of Engine	Cargo Cap. or Gross*	Overall Length	Breadth	Depth or Draft*
A-6	**ALCAN INC., MONTREAL, QC** *(alcan.com)*							
	Alexis-Simard	TT	1980	D	286*	92′ 00″	34′ 00″	13′ 07″
	Built: Georgetown Shipyards Ltd., Georgetown, PEI							
	Grande Baie	TT	1972	D	194*	86′ 06″	30′ 00″	12′ 00″
	Built: Prince Edward Island Lending Authority, Chalottetown, PEI							
A-7	**ALGOMA CENTRAL CORP., ST. CATHARINES, ON** *(algonet.com)*							
	**** VESSELS OPERATED & MANAGED BY SEAWAY MARINE TRANSPORT, ST. CATHARINES, ON, A PARTNERSHIP BETWEEN ALGOMA CENTRAL AND UPPER LAKES GROUP INC.***							
	Agawa Canyon*	SU	1970	D	23,400	647′ 00″	72′ 00″	40′ 00″
	Built: Collingwood Shipyards, Collingwood, ON							
	Algobay*	SU	1978	D	34,900	730′ 00″	75′ 10″	46′ 06″
	Built: Collingwood Shipyards, Collingwood, ON; last operated in 2002; laid up at Toronto, ON; expected to re-enter service in December 2009 with a new forebody (Algobay '78-'94, Atlantic Trader '94-'97)							
	Algocape* {2}	BC	1967	D	29,950	729′ 09″	75′ 04″	39′ 08″
	Built: Davie Shipbuilding Co., Lauzon, QC (Richelieu {3} '67-'94)							
	Algoisle*	BC	1963	D	26,700	730′ 00″	75′ 05″	39′ 03″
	Built: Verolme Cork Shipyard, Ltd., Cork, Ireland (Silver Isle '63-'94)							
	Algolake*	SU	1977	D	32,150	730′ 00″	75′ 06″	46′ 06″
	Built: Collingwood Shipyards, Collingwood, ON							
	Algomarine*	SU	1968	D	27,000	729′ 10″	75′ 04″	39′ 08″
	Built: Davie Shipbuilding Co., Lauzon, QC; converted to a self-unloader by Port Weller Dry Docks, St. Catharines, ON, in '89 (Lake Manitoba '68-'87)							
	Algonorth*	BC	1971	D	28,000	729′ 11″	75′ 02″	42′ 11″
	Built: Upper Clyde Shipbuilders, Govan, Scotland (Temple Bar '71-'76, Lake Nipigon '76-'84, Laketon {2} '84-'86, Lake Nipigon '86-'87)							
	Algontario*	BC	1960	D	29,100	730′ 00″	75′ 09″	40′ 02″
	*Built: Schlieker-Werft, Hamburg, West Germany; rebuilt and lengthened with new forebody at Davie Shipyard, Lauzon, QC, in '77 (**[Fore Section]** Cartiercliffe Hall '76-'88, Winnipeg {2} '88-'94 **[Stern Section]** Ruhr Ore '60-'76)*							
	Algoport*	SU	1979	D	32,000	658′ 00″	75′ 10″	46′ 06″
	Built: Collingwood Shipyards, Collingwood, ON; scheduled for forebody replacement in 2010							
	Algorail* {2}	SU	1968	D	23,750	640′ 05″	72′ 03″	40′ 00″
	Built: Collingwood Shipyards, Collingwood, ON							
	Algosoo* {2}	SU	1974	D	31,300	730′ 00″	75′ 05″	44′ 06″
	Built: Collingwood Shipyards, Collingwood, ON; last Great Lakes vessel built with cabins at the bow							
	Algosteel* {2}	SU	1966	D	27,000	729′ 11″	75′ 04″	39′ 08″
	Built: Davie Shipbuilding Co., Lauzon, QC; converted to a self-unloader by Port Weller Dry Docks, St. Catharines, ON, in '89 (A. S. Glossbrenner '66-'87, Algogulf {1} '87-'90)							
	Algoville*	BC	1967	D	31,250	730′ 00″	77′ 11″	39′ 08″
	Built: St. John Shipbuilding & Drydock Co., St. John, NB; widened by 3′ at Port Weller Dry Docks, St. Catharines, ON, in '96 (Senneville '67-'94)							
	Algoway* {2}	SU	1972	D	24,000	650′ 00″	72′ 00″	40′ 00″
	Built: Collingwood Shipyards, Collingwood, ON							
	Algowood*	SU	1981	D	31,750	740′ 00″	76′ 01″	46′ 06″
	Built: Collingwood Shipyards, Collingwood, ON; lengthened 10′ in '00 at Port Weller Dry Docks, St. Catharines, ON							
	Capt. Henry Jackman*	SU	1981	D	30,550	730′ 00″	76′ 01″	42′ 00″
	Built: Collingwood Shipyards, Collingwood, ON; converted to a self-unloader by Port Weller Dry Docks, St. Catharines, ON, in '96 (Lake Wabush '81-'87)							
	John B. Aird*	SU	1983	D	31,300	730′ 00″	76′ 01″	46′ 06″
	Built: Collingwood Shipyards, Collingwood, ON							
	Peter R. Cresswell*	SU	1982	D	31,700	730′ 00″	76′ 01″	42′ 00″
	Built: Collingwood Shipyards, Collingwood, ON; converted to a self-unloader by Port Weller Dry Docks, St. Catharines, ON, in '98 (Algowest '82-'01)							
	ALGOMA TANKERS LTD., ST. CATHARINES, ON – DIVISION OF ALGOMA CENTRAL CORP.							
	Algocanada	TK	2008	D	11,062	426′ 00″	65′ 00″	32′ 08″
	Built: Eregli Shipyard, Zonguldak, Turkey							
	Algoeast	TK	1977	D	9,750	431′ 05″	65′ 07″	35′ 05″
	Built: Mitsubishi Heavy Industries Ltd., Shimonoseki, Japan; converted from single to double hull by Port Weller Dry Docks, St. Catharines, ON, in '00 (Texaco Brave {2} '77-'86, Le Brave '86-'97, Imperial St. Lawrence {2} '97-'97)							

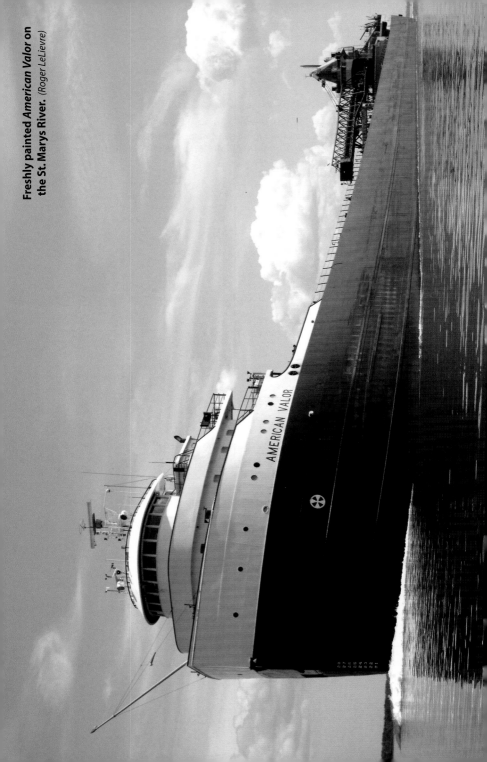

Freshly painted *American Valor* on the St. Marys River. *(Roger LeLievre)*

Fleet #.	Fleet Name Vessel Name	Type of Vessel	Year Built	Type of Engine	Cargo Cap. or Gross*	Overall Length	Breadth	Depth or Draft*
	Algonova {2}	TK	2007	D	11,062	426′ 00″	65′ 00″	32′ 08″
	Built: Eregli Shipyard, Zonguldak, Turkey (Eregli 04 '07-'08)							
	Algosar {2}	TK	1978	D	10,099	432′ 06″	65′ 00″	29′ 04″
	Built: Levingston Shipbuilding Co., Orange, TX (Gemini '78-'05)							
	Algoscotia	TK	2004	D	18,010	488′ 01″	78′ 00″	42′ 00″
	Built: Jiangnan Shipyard (Group) Co. Ltd., Shangahi, Peoples Republic of China							
	Algosea	TK	1998	D	16,775	472′ 04″	75′ 04″	41′09″
	Built: Alabama Shipyard Inc., Mobile, Ala. (Aggersborg '98-'05)							
	SOCIÉTÉ QUÉBECOISE D' EXPLORATION MINIÈRE, SAINTE-FOY, QC – CHARTERER							
	Sauniere	SU	1970	D	23,900	642′ 10″	74′ 10″	42′ 00″
	Built: Lithgows Ltd., East Yard, Glasgow, Scotland; lengthened 122′ by Swan Hunter Ship Repairers, Northshield, UK, in '75; converted to a self-unloader by Herb Fraser & Associates, Port Colborne, ON, in '76 (Bulknes '70-'70, Brooknes '70-'76, Algosea {1} '76-'82)							
	VESSEL IS JOINTLY OWNED BY ALGOMA CENTRAL MARINE AND UPPER LAKES SHIPPING LTD.							
	Windoc {2}	BC	1959	B	29,100	730′ 00″	75′ 09″	40′ 02″
	*Built: Schlicting-Werlt Willy H. Schlieker, East Germany; rebuilt and lengthened with new forebody at Davie Shipbuilding Co., Lauzon, QC, in '78; damaged by fire in 2001; laid up and awaiting a decision on its future at Port Colborne, ON (**[Stern Section]** Rhine Ore '59-'76, **[Fore Section]** Steelcliffe Hall '76-'88)*							
A-8	**AMERICAN ACADEMY OF INDUSTRY, CHICAGO, IL** *(aai-acacia.org)*							
	Acacia	MU	1944	DE	1,025*	180′ 00″	37′ 00″	17′ 04″
	Built: Marine Ironworks and Shipbuilding Corp., Duluth, MN; former U.S. Coast Guard bouy tender/ icebreaker was decommissioned in '06; scheduled to become a museum at Chicago, IL (Launched as USCGC Thistle [WAGL-406])							
A-9	**AMERICAN MARINE CONSTRUCTORS INC., BENTON HARBOR, MI** *(americanmarineconstructors.com)*							
	Alice E	TB	1944	T	146*	81′ 01″	24′ 00″	9′ 10″
	Built: George Lawley & Son Corp., Neponset, MA							
	AMC 100	DB	1979	B	2,273	200′ 00″	52′ 00″	14′ 00″
	AMC 200	DB	1979	B	2,273	200′ 00″	36′ 00″	11′ 08″
	AMC 300	DB	1977	B	1,048	180′ 00″	54′ 00″	12′ 00″
	Defiance	TW	1966	D	26*	44′ 08″	18′ 00″	6′ 00″
A-10	**AMERICAN STEAMSHIP CO., WILLIAMSVILLE, NY** *(americansteamship.com)*							
	Adam E. Cornelius {4}	SU	1973	D	28,200	680′ 00″	78′ 00″	42′ 00″
	Built: American Shipbuilding Co., Toledo, OH (Roger M. Kyes '73-'89)							
	American Century	SU	1981	D	78,850	1,000′ 00″	105′ 00″	56′ 00″
	Built: Bay Shipbuilding Co., Sturgeon Bay, WI (Columbia Star '81-'06)							
	American Courage	SU	1979	D	23,800	636′ 00″	68′ 00″	40′ 00″
	Built: Bay Shipbuilding Co., Sturgeon Bay, WI (Fred R. White Jr. '79-'06)							
	American Fortitude	SU	1953	T	22,300	690′ 00″	70′ 00″	37′ 00″
	Built: American Shipbuilding Co., Lorain, OH; converted to a self-unloader by Bay Shipbuilding, Sturgeon Bay, WI, in '81 (Ernest T. Weir {2} '53-'78, Courtney Burton '78-'06)							
	American Integrity	SU	1978	D	78,850	1,000′ 00″	105′ 00″	56′ 00″
	Built: Bay Shipbuilding Co., Sturgeon Bay, WI (Lewis Wilson Foy '78-'91, Oglebay Norton '91-'06)							
	American Mariner	SU	1980	D	37,200	730′ 00″	78′ 00″	45′ 00″
	Built: Bay Shipbuilding Co., Sturgeon Bay, WI (Laid down as Chicago {3})							
	American Republic	SU	1981	D	24,800	634′ 10″	68′ 00″	40′ 00″
	Built: Bay Shipbuilding Co., Sturgeon Bay, WI							
	American Spirit	SU	1978	D	59,700	1,004′ 00″	105′ 00″	50′ 00″
	Built: American Shipbuilding Co., Lorain, OH (George A. Stinson '78-'04)							
	American Valor	SU	1953	T	25,500	767′ 00″	70′ 00″	36′ 00″
	Built: American Shipbuilding Co., Lorain, OH; lengthened by 120' by Fraser Shipyard, Superior, WI, in '74, converted to a self-unloader in '82 (Armco '53-'06)							
	American Victory	SU	1942	T	26,300	730′ 00″	75′ 00″	39′ 03″
	Built: Bethlehem Shipbuilding and Drydock Co., Sparrows Point, MD; converted from saltwater tanker to a Great Lakes bulk carrier by Maryland Shipbuilding in '61; converted to a self-unloader by Bay Shipbuilding Co., Sturgeon Bay, WI, in '82 (Laid down as Marquette. USS Neshanic [AO-71] '42-'47, Gulfoil '47-'61, Pioneer Challenger '61-'62, Middletown '62-'06)							

Fleet #.	Fleet Name Vessel Name	Type of Vessel	Year Built	Type of Engine	Cargo Cap. or Gross*	Overall Length	Breadth	Depth or Draft*
	Buffalo {3}	SU	1978	D	23,800	634' 10"	68' 00"	40' 00"
	Built: Bay Shipbuilding Co., Sturgeon Bay, WI							
	Burns Harbor {2}	SU	1980	D	78,850	1,000' 00"	105' 00"	56' 00"
	Built: Bay Shipbuilding Co., Sturgeon Bay, WI							
	H. Lee White {2}	SU	1974	D	35,200	704' 00"	78' 00"	45' 00"
	Built: Bay Shipbuilding Co., Sturgeon Bay, WI							
	Indiana Harbor	SU	1979	D	78,850	1,000' 00"	105' 00"	56' 00"
	Built: Bay Shipbuilding Co., Sturgeon Bay, WI							
	John J. Boland {4}	SU	1973	D	33,800	680' 00"	78' 00"	45' 00"
	Built: Bay Shipbuilding Co., Sturgeon Bay, WI (Charles E. Wilson '73-'00)							
	Sam Laud	SU	1975	D	23,800	634' 10"	68' 00"	40' 00"
	Built: Bay Shipbuilding Co., Sturgeon Bay, WI							
	St. Clair {3}	SU	1976	D	44,000	770' 00"	92' 00"	52' 00"
	Built: Bay Shipbuilding Co., Sturgeon Bay, WI							
	Walter J. McCarthy Jr.	SU	1977	D	78,850	1,000' 00"	105' 00"	56' 00"
	Built: Bay Shipbuilding Co., Sturgeon Bay, WI (Belle River '77-'90)							
A-11	**AMHERSTBURG FERRY CO. INC, AMHERSTBURG, ON**							
	Columbia V (The)	PA/CF	1946	D	65*	65' 00"	28' 10"	8' 06"
	(Crystal O, St. Clair Flats)							
	Ste. Claire V (The)	PA/CF	1997	D	82*	86' 06"	32' 00"	6' 00"
	(Courtney O., M. Bourbonnais)							
A-12	**ANDRIE INC., MUSKEGON, MI** *(andrie.com)*							
	A-390	TK	1982	B	2,346*	310' 00"	60' 00"	19' 03"
	Built: St. Louis Shipbuilding & Steel Co., St. Louis, MO (Canonie 40 '82-'92)							
	A-397	TK	1962	B	2,928*	270' 00"	60' 00"	25' 00"
	Built: Dravo Corp., Pittsburgh, PA (Auntie Mame '62-'91, Iron Mike '91-'93)							
	A-410	TK	1955	B	3,793*	335' 00"	54' 00"	26' 06"
	Built: Ingalls Shipbuilding Corp., Birmingham, AL (Methane '55-'63, B-6400 '63-'71, Kelly '71-'86, Canonie 50 '86-'93)							
	Barbara Andrie	TB	1940	D	298*	121' 10"	29' 06"	16' 00"
	Built: Pennsylvania Shipyards, Inc., Beaumont, TX (Edmond J. Moran '40-'76)							
	Barbara Rita	TW	1981	D	15*	36' 00"	14' 00"	6' 00"
	Candace Andrie	CS	1958	B	1,000	150' 00"	52' 00"	10' 00"
	Built: Calumet Shipyard & Drydock Co., Chicago, IL (MCD '58-'73, Minnesota '73-'88)							
	Clara Andrie	DR	1930	B	1,000	110' 00"	30' 00"	6' 10"
	John Joseph	TB	1993	D	15*	40' 00"	14' 00"	5' 00"
	Karen Andrie {2}	TB	1965	D	433*	120' 00"	31' 06"	16' 00"
	Built: Gulfport Shipbuilding, Port Arthur, TX (Sarah Hays '65-'93)							
	Meredith Andrie	DS	1971	B	521*	140' 00"	50' 00"	9' 00"
	Built: Twin City Shipyard, St. Paul, MN (Illinois '71-'02)							
	Rebecca Lynn	TB	1964	D	433*	120' 00"	31' 08"	18' 09"
	Built: Gulfport Shipbuilding, Port Arthur, TX (Kathrine Clewis '64-'96)							
	Robert Purcell	TB	1943	D	29*	45' 02"	12' 08"	7' 09"
	Ronald J. Dahlke	TB	1903	D	58*	63' 03"	17' 05"	9' 03"
	Built: Johnston Bros., Ferrysburg, MI (Bonita '03-'14, Chicago Harbor No. 4 '14-'60, Eddie B. '60-'69, Seneca Queen '69-'70, Ludington '70-'96, Seneca Queen '96-'04)							
A-13	**APOSTLE ISLANDS CRUISE SERVICE, BAYFIELD, WI** *(apostleisland.com)*							
	Island Princess {2}	ES	1973	D	63*	65' 07"	20' 05"	7' 03"
A-14	**ARGEE BOAT CRUISES LTD., PENETANGUISHENE, ON** *(georgianbaycruises.com)*							
	Georgian Queen	ES	1918	D	249*	119' 00"	36' 00"	16' 06"
	Built: Port Arthur Shipbuilding, Port Arthur, ON (Victoria '18-'18, Murray Stewart '18-'48, David Richard '48-'79)							
A-15	**ARNOLD TRANSIT CO., MACKINAC ISLAND, MI** *(arnoldline.com)*							
	Algomah	PF/PK	1961	D	125	93' 00"	31' 00"	8' 00"
	Beaver	CF	1952	D	87*	64' 09"	30' 02"	8' 00"
	Chippewa {6}	PF/PK	1962	D	125	93' 00"	31' 00"	8' 00"
	Corsair	CF	1955	D	98*	94' 06"	33' 00"	8' 06"

Fleet #.	Fleet Name / Vessel Name	Type of Vessel	Year Built	Type of Engine	Cargo Cap. or Gross*	Overall Length	Breadth	Depth or Draft*
	Huron {5}	PF/PK	1955	D	80	91′06″	25′00″	10′01″
	Island Express	PF/CA	1988	D	90*	82′07″	28′06″	8′05″
	Mackinac Express	PF/CA	1987	D	90*	82′07″	28′06″	8′05″
	Mackinac Islander	CF	1947	D	99*	84′00″	30′00″	8′03″
	(Drummond Islander '47-'02)							
	Ottawa {2}	PF/PK	1959	D	125	93′00″	31′00″	8′00″
	Straits Express	PF/CA	1995	D	99*	101′00″	29′11″	6′08″
	Straits of Mackinac II	PF/PK	1969	D	89*	89′11″	27′00″	8′08″
A-16	**ASHLAND BAYFIELD CRUISE LINE INC., WASHBURN, WI**							
	Ashland Bayfield Express	PA	1995	D	13*	49′00″	18′05″	5′00″
B-1	**B & L TUG SERVICE, THESSALON, ON**							
	C. West Pete	TB	1958	D	29*	65′00″	17′05″	6′00″
B-2	**BASIC TOWING INC., ESCANABA, MI** *(basicmarine.com)*							
	Danicia	TB	1944	DE	382*	110′02″	27′03″	15′07″
	Built: Ira S. Bushy and Sons Inc., Brooklyn, NY (USCGC Chinook [WYT / WYTM-96] '44-'86, Tracie B '86-'98)							
	Erika Kobasic	TB	1939	DE	226*	110′00″	26′05″	15′01″
	Built: Texas-Gulfport Shipbuilding, Port Athur, TX (USCGC Arundel [WYT / WYTM-90] '39-'84, Karen Andrie {1} '84-'90)							
	Escort	TB	1969	D	26*	50′00″	13′00″	7′00″
	Joseph Medill	FB	1949	D	351*	92′00	23′00	7′06″
	Former Chicago fire boat; stripped and inactive at Escanaba, MI							
	Koziol	TB	1973	D	356*	109′00″	30′06″	16′03″
	Built: Marinette Marine Corp., Marinette, WI (USS Chetek [YTB-827] '73-'96, Chetek '96-'00)							
	Krystal	TB	1954	D	23*	45′02″	12′08″	6′00″
	(ST-2168 '54-'62, Thunder Bay '62-'02)							
	Lake Explorer	RV	1962	D	69*	82′10″	17′07″	5′11″
	Former EPA research vessel; inactive at Escanaba, MI (USCGC Point Roberts [WPB-82332] '62-'92)							
	Sea Chief	TB	1952	D	390*	107′00″	26′06″	14′10″
	Built: Avondale Marine Ways Inc., Westwego, LA; inactive at Escanaba, MI (U. S. Army LT-1944 '52-'62, USCOE Washington '62-'00)							
	Siscowet	RV	1946	D	54*	57′00″	14′06″	7′00″
	Former U.S. Department of the Interior research vessel; inactive at Escanaba, MI							
B-3	**BAY CITY BOAT LINES LLC, BAY CITY, MI** *(baycityboatlines.com)*							
	Islander {1}	ES	1946	D	39*	53′04″	21′00″	5′05″
	Princess Wenonah	ES	1954	D	96*	64′09″	32′09″	9′09″
	Built: Sturgeon Bay Shipbuilding, Sturgeon Bay, WI (William M. Miller '54-'98)							
	West Shore {2}	ES	1947	D	94*	64′10″	30′00″	9′03″
B-4	**BAY SHIPBUILDING CO., STURGEON BAY, WI** *(manitowocmarine.com)*							
	Bayship	TB	1943	D	19*	45′00″	12′06″	6′00″
	Built: Sturgeon Bay Shipbuilding Co., Sturgeon Bay, WI (Sturshipco)							
B-5	**BAYSAIL, BAY CITY, MI** *(baysailbaycity.org)*							
	Appledore IV	2S/ES	1989	W/D	72*	85′00″	19′00″	9′06″
	Appledore V	2S/ES	1992	W/D	34*	65′00″	16′00″	8′06″
B-6	**BEAUSOLEIL FIRST NATION TRANSPORTATION, CHRISTIAN ISLAND, ON** *(chimnissing.ca)*							
	Indian Maiden	PA/CF	1987	D	91.5*	73′06″	23′00″	8′00″
	Sandy Graham	PA/CF	1957	D	212*	125′07″	39′09″	8′00″
	Built: Barbour Boat Works Inc., New Bern, NC							
B-7	**BEAVER ISLAND BOAT CO., CHARLEVOIX, MI** *(www.bibco.com)*							
	Beaver Islander	PF/CF	1963	D	95*	96′03″	27′05″	9′09″
	Built: Sturgeon Bay Shipbuilding, Sturgeon Bay, WI							
	Emerald Isle {2}	PF/CF	1997	D	95*	130′00″	38′08″	12′00″
	Built: Washburn & Doughty Associates, Inc., East Boothbay, ME							
B-8	**BEST OF ALL TOURS LTD., ERIE, PA** *(piboattours.com)*							
	Lady Kate {2}	ES	1952	D	11*	59′03″	15′00″	4′00″
	(G. A. Boeckling II '52-?, Cedar Point III ?-'89, Island Trader '89-'97)							

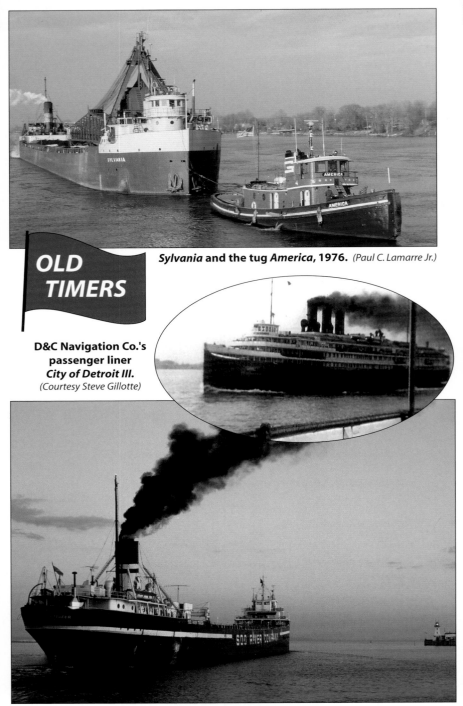

***Sylvania* and the tug *America*, 1976.** *(Paul C. Lamarre Jr.)*

OLD TIMERS

D&C Navigation Co.'s passenger liner *City of Detroit III.* *(Courtesy Steve Gillotte)*

***Soo River Trader* departing Port Colborne in 1982.** *(Paul C. Lamarre Jr.)*

Fleet #.	Fleet Name Vessel Name	Type of Vessel	Year Built	Type of Engine	Cargo Cap. or Gross*	Overall Length	Breadth	Depth or Draft*
B-9	**BILLINGTON CONTRACTING INC., DULUTH, MN**							
	Col. D.D. Gaillard	DB	1916	B		116′ 00″	40′ 00″	11′ 06″
	Long-inactive former U.S. Army Corps of Engineers dipper dredge is for sale at Duluth							
	Coleman	CS	1923	B	502*	153′ 06″	40′ 06″	10′ 06″
	Lake Superior	TB	1943	D	248*	114′ 00″	26′ 00″	13′ 08″
	Built: Tampa Marine Corp., Tampa, FL (Major Emil H. Block '43-'47, U. S. Army LT-18 '47-'50)							
	Panama	DS	1942	B		210′ 01″	44′ 01″	10′ 01″
B-10	**BLACK CREEK CONSTRUCTION CO., NANTICOKE, ON**							
	H. H. Misner	TB	1946	D	28*	66′ 09″	16′ 04″	4′ 05″
	Built: George Gamble, Port Dover, ON							
B-11	**BLUE HERON CO., TOBERMORY, ON** *(blueheronco.com)*							
	Blue Heron V	ES	1983	D	24*	54′ 06″	17′ 05″	7′ 02″
	Great Blue Heron	ES	1994	D	112*	79′ 00″	22′ 00″	6′ 05″
B-12	**BLUEWATER EXCURSIONS INC., FORT GRATIOT, MI** *(huronlady.com)*							
	Huron Lady II	ES	1993	D	82*	65′ 00″	19′ 00″	10′ 00″
	(Lady Lumina '93-'99)							
B-13	**BLUEWATER FERRY, SOMBRA, ON** *(bluewaterferry.com)*							
	Daldean	CF	1951	D	145*	75′ 00″	35′ 00″	7′ 00″
	Ontamich	CF	1939	D	55*	65′ 00″	28′ 10″	8′ 06″
B-14	**BRUCE VON RIEDEL, KNIFE RIVER, MN**							
	Oatka	TB	1935	D	10*	40′ 00″	10′ 00″	4′ 06″
B-15	**BUFFALO AND ERIE COUNTY NAVAL & MILITARY PARK, BUFFALO, NY** *(buffalonavalpark.org)*							
	Croaker	MU	1944	D	1,526*	311′ 07″	27′ 02″	33′ 09″
	Former U. S. Navy "Gato" class submarine IXSS-246; open to the public at Buffalo, NY							
	Little Rock	MU	1945	T	10,670*	610′ 01″	66′ 04″	25′ 00″
	Former U. S. Navy "Cleveland / Little Rock" class guided missile cruiser; open to the public at Buffalo, NY							
	The Sullivans	MU	1943	T	2,500*	376′ 06″	39′ 08″	22′ 08″
	Former U. S. Navy "Fletcher" class destroyer; open to the public at Buffalo, NY (Launched as USS Putnam)							
B-16	**BUFFALO CHARTERS INC., BUFFALO, NY** *(missbuffalo.com)*							
	Miss Buffalo II	ES	1972	D	88*	81′ 09″	24′ 00″	6′ 00″
B-17	**BUFFALO INDUSTRIAL DIVING CO. (BIDCO), BUFFALO, NY** *(bidcomarine.com)*							
	West Wind	TB	1941	D	54*	60′ 04″	17′ 01″	7′ 07″
	Built: Lester F. Alexander Co., New Orleans, LA (West Wind '41-'46, Russell 2 '61-'97)							
B-18	**BUFFALO DEPARTMENT OF PUBLIC WORKS, BUFFALO, NY**							
	Edward M. Cotter	FB	1900	D	208*	118′ 00″	24′ 00″	11′ 06″
	Built: Crescent Shipbuilding, Elizabeth, NJ (W. S. Grattan 1900-'53, Firefighter '53-'54)							
B-19	**BUS & BOAT COMPANY, TORONTO, ON** *(thebusandboatcompany.com)*							
	Harbour Star	ES	1978	D	45*	63′ 06″	15′ 09″	3′ 09″
	(K. Wayne Simpson '78-'95)							
B-20	**BUSCH MARINE INC., CARROLLTON, MI**							
	Barbara Merry Busch	TB	1938	DE	158*	89′ 04″	25′ 02″	10 00″
	Built: Defoe Shipbuilding Co., Bay City, MI (Thomas E. Moran 38-'40, USS Namontack YTB 738 '40-'47, Thomas E. Moran '47-'47, Harriet Moran '47-'75, Viking '75-'93, Georgetown '93-'99, Sharon Elizabeth '99-'05, Statesboro '05-'07)							
	Gregory J. Busch	TB	1919	D	299*	151′ 00″	28′ 00″	16′ 09″
	Built: Whitney Bros. Co., Superior, WI (Humaconna '19-'77)							
	STC 2004	TK	1986	B	2,364	240′ 00″	50′ 00″	9′ 05″
	Built: St. Louis Shipbuilding & Steel Co., St. Louis, MO							
C-1	**CALUMET RIVER FLEETING INC., CHICAGO, IL**							
	Des Plaines	TW	1956	D	175*	98′ 00″	28′ 00″	8′ 04″
	Built: St. Louis Shipbuilding & Steel Co., St. Louis, MO							
	Doyle	TB	1932	D	36*	62′ 00″	16′ 01″	8′ 00″
	Built: Hans Hansen Welding Co., Toledo, OH (G. F. Becker, Baldy B. ?-'08)							

Fleet #.	Fleet Name Vessel Name	Type of Vessel	Year Built	Type of Engine	Cargo Cap. or Gross*	Overall Length	Breadth	Depth or Draft*
	John M. Selvick	TB	1898	D	256*	118′ 00″	24′ 00″	12′ 07″
	Built: Chicago Shipbuilding Co., Chicago, IL (Illinois {1} 1898-'41, John Roen III '41-'74)							
	Kimberly Selvick	TW	1975	D	93*	51′ 10″	28′ 00″	10′ 00″
	Built: Grafton Boat Co., Grafton, IL (Scout '75-'02)							
	Krista S	TB	1954	D	95*	72′ 00″	22′ 00″	8′ 00″
	Built: Pascagoula, MS (Sea Wolf '54-'01, Jimmy Wray '01-'08)							
	M/V Zuccolo	TB	1954	D	76*	66′ 00″	19′ 00″	9′ 00″
	(Sanita '54-'77, Soo Chief '77-'81, Susan M. Selvick '81-'96, Nathan S. '96-'02, John M. Perry '02-'08)							
	Nathan S	TB	1951	D	144*	90′ 00″	24′ 00″	12′00″
	Built: Ira S. Bushey & Sons Inc., Brooklyn, NY (Huntington '51-'05, Spartacus '05-'06, Huntington '06-'08)							
	Niki S	TW	1971	D	39*	42′ 00″	18′ 00″	6′ 00″
	(Miss Josie '71-'79, Matador VI '79-'08))							
C-2	**CANADA STEAMSHIP LINES INC., MONTREAL, QC** *(csl.ca)*							
	(VESSELS MANAGED BY V.SHIPS CANADA INC., MONTREAL, QC)							
	Atlantic Erie	SU	1985	D	37,411	736′ 07″	75′ 10″	50′ 00″
	Built: Collingwood Shipyards, Collingwood, ON (Hon. Paul Martin '85-'88)							
	Atlantic Huron {2}	SU	1984	D	34,800	736′ 07″	78′ 01″	46′ 06″
	Built: Collingwood Shipyards, Collingwood, ON; converted to a self-unloader in '89 and widened by 3′ in '03 at Port Weller Dry Docks, St. Catharines, ON (Prairie Harvest '84-'89, Atlantic Huron {2} '89-'94, Melvin H. Baker II {2} '94-'97)							
	Atlantic Superior	SU	1982	D	36,219	730′ 00″	75′ 10″	50′ 00″
	Built: Collingwood Shipyards, Collingwood, ON (Atlantic Superior '82-'97, M. H. Baker III '97-'03)							
	Birchglen {2}	BC	1983	D	33,824	730′ 01″	75′ 09″	48′ 00″
	Built: Govan Shipyards, Glasgow, Scotland (Canada Marquis '83-'91, Federal Richelieu '91-'91, Federal MacKenzie '91-'01, MacKenzie '01-'02)							
	Cedarglen {2}	BC	1959	D	29,510	730′ 00″	75′ 09″	40′ 02″
	*Built: Schlieker-Werft, Hamburg, West Germany; rebuilt, lengthened with a new forebody at Davie Shipbuilding, Co., Lauzon, QC, in '77 (**[Stern Section]** Ems Ore '59-'76, **[Fore Section]** Montcliffe Hall '76-'88, Cartierdoc '88-'02)*							
	CSL Assiniboine	SU	1977	D	36,768	739′ 10″	78′ 01″	48′ 05″
	Built: Davie Shipbuilding Co., Lauzon, QC; rebuilt with a new forebody at Port Weller Dry Docks, St. Catharines, ON, in '05 (Jean Parisien '77-'05)							
	CSL Laurentien	SU	1977	D	37,795	739′ 10″	78′ 01″	48′ 05″
	Built: Collingwood Shipyards, Collingwood; ON; rebuilt with new forebody in '01 at Port Weller Dry Docks, St. Catharines, ON (Stern section: Louis R. Desmarais '77-'01)							
	CSL Niagara	SU	1972	D	37,694	739′ 10″	78′ 01″	48′ 05″
	Built: Collingwood Shipyards, Collingwood, ON; rebuilt with a new forebody in '99 at Port Weller Dry Docks, St. Catharines, ON (Stern section: J. W. McGiffin '72-'99)							
	CSL Tadoussac	SU	1969	D	30,051	730′ 00″	78′ 00″	42′ 00″
	Built: Collingwood Shipyards, Collingwood, ON; rebuilt with new midbody, widened by 3′ at Port Weller Dry Docks, St. Catharines, ON, in '01 (Tadoussac {2} '69-'01)							
	Frontenac {5}	SU	1968	D	26,822	729′ 07″	75′ 03″	39′ 08″
	Built: Davie Shipbuilding Co., Lauzon, QC; converted to a self-unloader by Collingwood Shipyards, Collingwood, ON, in '73							
	Halifax	SU	1963	T	29,283	730′ 02″	75′ 00″	39′ 03″
	Built: Davie Shipbuilding Co., Lauzon, QC; converted to a self-unloader, deepened 6′ at Port Arthur Shipbuilding, Thunder Bay, ON, in '80 (Frankcliffe Hall {2} '63-'88)							
	Nanticoke	SU	1980	D	35,123	729′ 10″	75′ 08″	46′ 06″
	Built: Collingwood Shipyards, Collingwood, ON							
	Pineglen {2}	BC	1985	D	33,197	736′ 07″	75′ 10″	42′ 00″
	Built: Collingwood Shipyards, Collingwood, ON (Paterson '85-'02)							
	Rt. Hon. Paul J. Martin	SU	1973	D	37,694	739′ 10″	78′ 01″	48′ 05″
	Built: Collingwood Shipyards, Collingwood, ON; rebuilt with a new forebody in '00 at Port Weller Dry Docks, St. Catharines, ON (Stern section: H. M. Griffith '73-'00)							
	Spruceglen {2}	BC	1983	D	33,824	730′ 01″	75′ 09″	48′ 00″
	Built: Govan Shipyards, Glasgow, Scotland (Selkirk Settler '83-'91, Federal St. Louis '91-'91, Federal Fraser {2} '91-2001, Fraser '01-'02)							
C-3	**CANADIAN COAST GUARD (FISHERIES AND OCEANS CANADA), OTTAWA, ON** *(ccg-gcc.gc.ca)*							
	CENTRAL AND ARCTIC REGION, SARNIA, ON							
	Advent	RV	1972	D	72*	77′ 01″	18′ 05″	5′ 03″
	Cape Discovery	SR	2004	D	34*	47′ 09″	14′ 00″	4′ 05″

***Herbert C. Jackson* passes under the Duluth Aerial Bridge.** *(Sam Lapinski)*

Fleet #.	Fleet Name Vessel Name	Type of Vessel	Year Built	Type of Engine	Cargo Cap. or Gross*	Overall Length	Breadth	Depth or Draft*
	Cape Hurd	SR	1982	D	55*	70' 10"	18' 00"	8' 09"
	(CG 126 '82-'85)							
	Caribou Isle	BT	1985	D	92*	75' 06"	19' 08"	7' 04"
	Cape Dundas	SR	2004	D	39*	47' 09"	14' 00"	4' 05"
	Cape Storm	SR	1999	D	34*	47' 09"	14' 00"	4' 05"
	Cove Isle	BT	1980	D	92*	65' 07"	19' 08"	7' 04"
	Griffon	IB	1970	D	2,212*	234' 00"	49' 00"	21' 06"
	Built: Davie Shipbuilding Co., Lauzon, QC							
	Gull Isle	BT	1980	D	80*	65' 07"	19' 08"	7' 04"
	Limnos	RV	1968	D	460*	147' 00"	32' 00"	12' 00"
	Built: Port Weller Dry Docks, St. Catharines, ON							
	Samuel Risley	IB	1985	D	1,988*	228' 09"	47' 01"	21' 09"
	Built: Vito Steel Boat & Barge Construction Ltd., Delta, BC							
	Shark	RV	1971	D	30*	52' 06"	14' 09"	7' 03"
	Thunder Cape	SR	2000	D	34*	47' 09"	14' 00"	4' 05"
	LAURENTIAN REGION, QUÉBEC, QC *(Vessels over 100' only have been listed)*							
	Amundsen	RV	1978	D	5,910*	295' 09"	63' 09"	31' 04"
	Built: Burrard Dry Dock Co., N. Vancouver, BC (Sir John Franklin '78-'03)							
	Des Groseilliers	IB	1983	D	5,910*	322' 07"	64' 00"	35' 06"
	Built: Port Weller Dry Docks, St. Catharines, ON							
	F. C. G. Smith	SV	1985	D	439*	114' 02"	45' 11"	11' 02"
	Built: Georgetown Shipyard, Georgetown, PEI							
	George R. Pearkes	IB	1986	D	3,809*	272' 04"	53' 02"	25' 02"
	Built: Versatile Pacific Shipyards, Victoria, BC							
	Louisbourg	RV	1977	D	295*	124' 00"	26' 11"	11' 06"
	Built: Breton Industrial & Machinery, Port Hawkesbury, NS							
	Martha L. Black	IB	1986	D	3,818*	272' 04"	53' 02"	25' 02"
	Built: Versatile Pacific Shipyards, Victoria, BC							
	Pierre Radisson	IB	1978	D	5,910*	322' 00"	62' 10"	35' 06"
	Built: Burrard Dry Dock Co., N. Vancouver, BC							
	Tracy	BT	1968	D	963*	181' 01"	38' 00"	16' 00"
	Built: Port Weller Dry Docks, St. Catharines, ON							
C-4	**CAUSLEY CONTRACTING, BAY CITY, MI**							
	Jill Marie	TB	1891	D	24*	60' 00"	12' 06"	6' 00"
	Built: Cleveland Shipbuilding Co., Cleveland, OH (Cisco 1891-'52, Capama-S '52-'07)							
C-5	**CELEST BAY TIMBER & MARINE, DULUTH, MN**							
	Barbara Wing	TW	1942	D	11*	36' 00"	9' 08"	3' 05"
	(Blake '42-'62, John V. II '62-'06)							
	Essayons	TB	1908	R	117*	85' 06"	21' 02"	11' 09"
C-6	**CEMBA MOTOR SHIPS LTD., PELEE ISLAND, ON**							
	Cemba	TK	1960	D	17*	50' 00"	15' 06"	7' 06"
C-7	**CENTRAL MARINE LOGISTICS INC., GRIFFITH, IN** *(centralmarinelogistics.com)*							
	Edward L. Ryerson	BC	1960	T	27,500	730' 00"	75' 00"	39' 00"
	Built: Manitowoc Shipbuilding Co., Manitowoc, WI; last U.S.-flag non-self-unloader built on the lakes							
	Joseph L. Block	SU	1976	D	37,200	728' 00"	78' 00"	45' 00"
	Built: Bay Shipbuilding Co., Sturgeon Bay, WI							
	Wilfred Sykes	SU	1949	T	21,500	678' 00"	70' 00"	37' 00"
	Built: American Shipbuilding Co., Lorain, OH; converted to a self-unloader by Fraser Shipyards, Superior, WI, in '75							
C-8	**CHAMPION'S AUTO FERRY INC., ALGONAC, MI** *(harsensisland.com/champion.html)*							
	Champion {1}	CF	1941	D	65*	65' 00"	29' 00"	8' 06"
	Middle Channel	CF	1997	D	97*	79' 00"	31' 00"	8' 03"
	North Channel	CF	1967	D	67*	75' 00"	30' 00"	8' 00"
	South Channel	CF	1973	D	94*	79' 00"	31' 00"	8' 03"
C-9	**CHARLEVOIX COUNTY TRANSPORTATION AUTHORITY, CHARLEVOIX, MI**							
	Charlevoix {1}	CF	1926	D	43*	50' 00"	32' 00"	3' 09"

Fleet #.	Fleet Name Vessel Name	Type of Vessel	Year Built	Type of Engine	Cargo Cap. or Gross*	Overall Length	Breadth	Depth or Draft*
C-10	**CHICAGO FIRE DEPARTMENT, CHICAGO, IL**							
	Victor L. Schlaeger	FB	1949	D	350*	92' 06"	24' 00"	11' 00"
C-11	**CHICAGO LINE CRUISES LLC, CHICAGO, IL** *(www.chicagoline.com)*							
	Ft. Dearborn	ES	1985	D	72*	64' 10"	22' 00"	7' 04"
	Innisfree	ES	1980	D	35*	61' 09"	15' 06"	5' 07"
	Marquette {6}	ES	1957	D	29*	50' 07"	15' 00"	4' 00"
C-12	**CHICAGO WATER PUMPING STATION, CHICAGO, IL**							
	James J. Versluis	TB	1957	D	126*	83' 00"	22' 00"	11' 02"
C-13	**CITY OF KEWAUNEE, KEWAUNEE, WI** *(cityofkewaunee.org)*							
	Ludington	MU	1943	D	249*	115' 00"	26' 00"	13' 08"
	Built: Jacobson Shipyard, Oyster Bay, NY; former U.S. Army Corps of Engineers tug is open to the public as a marine museum at Kewaunee, WI (Major Wilbur F. Browder [LT-4] '43-'47)							
C-14	**CLAYTON FIRE DEPARTMENT, CLAYTON, NY**							
	Last Chance	FB	2003	D		36' 00"	13' 00"	2' 04"
C-15	**CLEVELAND FIRE DEPARTMENT, CLEVELAND, OH**							
	Anthony J. Celebrezze	FB	1961	D	42*	66' 00"	17' 00"	5' 00"
C-16	**CLUB CANAMAC CRUISES, TORONTO, ON**							
	Aurora Borealis	ES	1983	D	277*	101' 00"	24' 00"	6' 00"
	Carolina Borealis	ES	1943	D	182*	84' 06"	20' 00"	10' 04"
	Rebuilt from a tug in '02 (HMCS Glenmont [W-27] '43-'45, Glenmont '43-'02)							
	Jaguar II	ES	1968	D	142*	95' 03"	20' 00"	9' 00"
	(Jaguar '68-'86)							
	Stella Borealis	ES	1989	D	356*	118' 00"	26' 00"	7' 00"
C-17	**COBBY MARINE (1985) INC., KINGSVILLE, ON**							
	Vida C.	TB	1960	D	17*	46' 03"	15' 05"	3' 02"
C-18	**COLUMBIA YACHT CLUB, CHICAGO, IL** *(columbiayachtclub.com)*							
	Abegweit	CF	1947	D	6,694*	372' 06"	61' 00"	24' 09"
	Built: Marine Industries Ltd., Sorel, QC; former CN Marine Inc. vessel last operated in 1981; in use as a private, floating clubhouse in Chicago, IL (Abegweit '47- 81, Abby '81- '97)							
C-19	**COOPER MARINE LTD., SELKIRK, ON**							
	J.W. Cooper	PB	1984	D	25*	48' 00"	14' 07"	5' 00"
	Janice C. No. 1	TB	1980	D	33*	56' 10"	20' 02"	5' 07"
	Juleen I	PB	1972	D	23*	46' 00"	14' 01"	4' 05"
	Lady Kim	PB	1974	D	20*	44' 00"	13' 00"	4' 00"
	Mrs. C.	PB	2006	D	26*	50' 00"	14' 05"	4' 05"
	Stacey Dawn	TB	1993	D	14*	35' 09"	17' 04"	3' 05"
C-20	**CORPORATION OF THE TOWNSHIP OF FRONTENAC ISLANDS, WOLFE ISLAND, ON**							
	Howe Islander	CF	1946	D	13*	53' 00"	12' 00"	3' 00"
	Simcoe Islander	PF	1964	D	24*	47' 09"	18' 00"	3' 06"
C-21	**CROISIÈRES AML INC., QUÉBEC, QC** *(croisieresaml.com)*							
	Cavalier des Mers	ES	1974	D	161*	91' 08"	21' 03"	8' 05"
	(Marine Sprinter '74-'84)							
	Cavalier Maxim	ES	1962	D	752*	191' 02"	42' 00"	11' 07"
	(Osborne Castle '62-'78, Le Gobelet D' Argent '78-'88, Gobelet D' Argent '88-'89, Le Maxim '89-'93)							
	Cavalier Royal	ES	1971	D	283*	125' 00"	24' 00"	5' 00"
	Grand Fleuve	ES	1987	D	499*	145' 00"	30' 00"	5' 06"
	Louis Jolliet	ES	1938	R	2,436*	170' 01"	70' 00"	17' 00"
	Transit	ES	1992	D	102*	66' 00"	22' 00"	2' 08"
C-22	**CTMA GROUP, CAP-AUX-MEULES, QC** *(ctma.ca)*							
	C.T.M.A. Vacancier	PA/RR	1973	D	11,481*	388' 04"	70' 02"	43' 06"
	(Aurella '80-'82, Saint Patrick II '82-'98, Egnatia II '98-'00, Ville de Sete '00-'01, City of Cork '01-'02)							
	C.T.M.A. Voyageur	PA/RR	1972	D	4,526*	327' 09"	52' 06"	31' 07"
	Built: Trosvik Versted A/S., Brevik, Norway (Anderida)							

Fleet #.	Fleet Name Vessel Name	Type of Vessel	Year Built	Type of Engine	Cargo Cap. or Gross*	Overall Length	Breadth	Depth or Draft*
	Madeleine	PA	1981	D	10,024*	381′ 04″	60′ 06″	41′ 00″
	Built: Verolme Cork Dockyard Ltd., Cobh, Ireland (Isle of Inishturk)							
D-1	**D. K. CONSTRUCTION INC., HOLLAND, MI**							
	Haskell	TB	1936	D	19*	40′ 00″	10′ 00″	4′ 06″
D-2	**DALE T. DEAN / WALPOLE-ALGONAC FERRY LINE, PORT LAMBTON, ON** *(walpolealgonacferry.com)*							
	City of Algonac	CF	1990	D	82*	62′ 06″	27′ 09″	5′ 09″
	Walpole Islander	CF	1986	D	72*	54′ 05″	27′ 09″	6′ 03″
D-3	**DAN MINOR & SONS INC., PORT COLBORNE, ON**							
	Andrea Marie I	TB	1963	D	87*	75′ 02″	24′ 07″	7′ 03″
	Jeanette M	TB	1981	D	31*	62′ 09″	20 01″	4′ 05″
	Susan Michelle	TB	1995	D	89*	79′ 10″	20′ 11″	6′ 02″
	Welland	TB	1954	D	94*	86′ 00″	20′ 00″	8′ 00″
D-4	**DEAN CONSTRUCTION CO. LTD., BELLE RIVER, ON** *(deanconstructioncompany.com)*							
	Annie M. Dean	TB	1981	D	58*	50′ 00″	19′ 00″	5′ 00″
	Bobby Bowes	TB	1944	D	11*	37′ 04″	10′ 02″	3′ 06″
	Canadian Jubilee	DR	1978	D	896*	149′ 09″	56′ 01″	11′ 01″
	Neptune III	TB	1939	D	23*	53′ 10″	15′ 06″	5′ 00″
D-5	**DETROIT CITY FIRE DEPARTMENT, DETROIT, MI**							
	Curtis Randolph	FB	1979	D	85*	77′ 10″	21′ 06″	9′ 03″
D-6	**DETROIT PRINCESS LLC, DETROIT, MI** *(detroitprincess.com)*							
	Detroit Princess	PA	1993	D	1,430*	190′ 09″	60′ 00″	11′ 01″
	Built: Leevac Shipyards Inc., Jennings, LA (Players Riverboat Casino II '93-'04)							
D-7	**DIAMOND JACK'S RIVER TOURS, DETROIT, MI** *(diamondjack.com)*							
	Diamond Belle	ES	1958	D	93*	93′ 06″	25′ 10″	10′ 01″
	Built: Hans Hansen Welding Co., Toledo, OH (Mackinac Islander {2} '58-'90, Sir Richard '90-'91)							
	Diamond Jack	ES	1955	D	82*	72′ 00″	25′ 00″	8′ 00″
	Built: Christy Corp, Sturgeon Bay, WI (Emerald Isle {1} '55-'91)							
	Diamond Queen	ES	1956	D	94*	92′ 00″	25′ 00″	10′ 00″
	Built: Marinette Marine Corp., Marinette, WI (Mohawk '56-'96)							
D-8	**DOOR COUNTY CRUISES LLC, STURGEON BAY, WI** *(doorcountycruises.com)*							
	Fred A. Busse	ES	1937	D	99*	92′ 00″	22′ 04″	11′ 00″
	Built: Defoe Boat & Motor Works, Bay City, MI; former Chicago fireboat offers cruises at Sturgeon Bay, WI							
D-9	**DOOR COUNTY MARITIME MUSEUM & LIGHTHOUSE PRESERVATION SOCIETY INC., STURGEON BAY, WI** *(dcmm.org)*							
	John Purves	MU	1919	D	436*	150′ 00″	27′ 06″	16′ 08″
	Built: Bethlehem Steel Co., Elizabeth, NJ; former Roen/Andrie Inc. tug has been refurbished as a museum display (Butterfield '19-'42, LT-145 '42-'57)							
D-10	**DRAGAGE VERREAULT INC., LES MÉCHINS, QC** *(dragageverreault.com)*							
	I.V. No. 8	DR	1967	B	348*	96′ 03″	36′ 00″	8′ 05″
	Built: Verreault Navigation Inc., Les Mechins, QC							
	I.V. No. 9	GC	1936	D	148*	106′ 08″	23′ 10″	8′ 05″
	Built: Geo. T. Davie & Sons, Lauzon, QC (A.C.D. '36-'69)							
	I.V. No. 10	GC	1936	D	320*	110′ 00″	23′ 10″	8′ 05″
	Built: Geo. T. Davie & Sons, Lauzon, QC (G.T.D. '36-'69)							
	I.V. No. 11	GC	1935	D	144*	106′ 08″	24′ 00″	8′ 00″
	Built: Geo. T. Davie & Sons, Lauzon, QC (Donpaco '35-'72)							
	I.V. No. 13	GC	1936	D	148*	106′ 08″	24′ 00″	8′ 00″
	Built: Geo. T. Davie & Sons, Lauzon, QC (Newscarrier '36-'72)							
	I.V. No. 14	GC	1937	D	229*	113′ 00″	22′ 05″	8′ 06″
	Built: Geo. T. Davie & Sons, Lauzon, QC (Kermic '37-'74)							
	Port Mechins	DR	1949	R	1,321*	200′ 00″	40′ 02″	18′ 00″
	Built: Lobnitz & Co., Renfrew, Scotland (Haffar '49-'88, Lockeport '88-'92)							
	Rosaire	DR	1952	B	714*	137′ 07″	44′ 06″	9′ 01″
	Built: Saint John Drydock Co., Saint John, NB							

Fleet #.	Fleet Name Vessel Name	Type of Vessel	Year Built	Type of Engine	Cargo Cap. or Gross*	Overall Length	Breadth	Depth or Draft*
D-11	**DUC D' ORLEANS CRUISE BOAT, CORUNNA, ON** *(ducdorleans.com)*							
	Duc d' Orleans II	ES	1987	D	120*	71' 03		7' 07"
	Built: Blount Marine Corp., Warren, RI (Spirit of Newport '87-'06)							
D-12	**DULUTH ENTERTAINMENT CONVENTION CENTER, DULUTH, MN** *(decc.org/attractions/irvin)*							
	Sundew	MU	1944	DE	1,025*	180' 00"	37' 00"	17' 04"
	Built: Marine Ironworks and Shipbuilding Corp., Duluth, MN; former U.S. Coast Guard cutter WLB-404 was decommissioned in 2004; open to the public at Duluth, MN							
	William A. Irvin	MU	1938	T	14,050	610' 09"	60' 00"	32' 06"
	Built: American Shipbuilding Co., Lorain, OH; former United States Steel Corp. bulk carrier last operated Dec. 16, 1978; open to the public at Duluth, MN							
D-13	**DULUTH TIMBER CO., DULUTH, MN**							
	Faith	CS	1906	B	705*	120' 00"	38' 00"	10' 03"
D-14	**DUROCHER MARINE, DIV. OF KOKOSING CONSTRUCTION CO., CHEBOYGAN, MI** *(durocher.biz)*							
	Champion {3}	TB	1974	D	125*	75' 00"	24' 00"	9' 06"
	Built: Service Machine & Shipbuilding Co., Amelia, LA							
	General {2}	TB	1954	D	119*	71' 00"	19' 06"	9' 06"
	Built: Missouri Valley Bridge & Iron Works, Leavenworth, KY (U. S. Army ST-1999 '54-'61, USCOE Au Sable '61-'84, Challenger {3} '84-'87)							
	Joe Van	TB	1955	D	32*	57' 09"	16' 06"	9' 00"
	Built: W.J. Hingston, Buffalo, NY							
	Nancy Anne	TB	1969	D	73*	60' 00"	20' 00"	6' 00"
	Built: Houma Shipbuilding Co., Houma, LA							
	Ray Durocher	TB	1943	D	20*	45' 06"	12' 05"	7' 06"
	Valerie B.	TB	1981	D	101*	65' 00"	24' 06"	10' 00"
	Built: Rayco Shipbuilders & Repairers, Bourg, LA (Mr. Joshua '81-?, Michael Van ?-'03)							
E-1	**EASTERN CANADA RESPONSE CORP., OTTAWA, ON**							
	Dover Light	EV	1968	B	7,870	146' 05"	50' 00"	13' 07"
	Built: Nashville Bridge Co., Nashville, TN (Jackson Purchase '68-'83, Eliza S-1877 '83-'86)							
E-2	**EASTERN UPPER PENINSULA TRANSIT AUTHORITY, SAULT STE. MARIE, MI**							
	Drummond Islander III	CF	1989	D	96*	108' 00"	37' 00"	12' 03"
	Built: Moss Point Marine Inc., Escatawpa, MS							
	Drummond Islander IV	CF	2000	D	377*	148' 00"	40' 00"	12' 00"
	Built: Basic Marine Inc., Escanaba, MI							
	Neebish Islander II	CF	1946	D	90*	89' 00"	29' 06"	6' 09"
	Built: Lock City Machine/Marine, Sault Ste. Marie, MI (Sugar Islander '46-'95)							
	Sugar Islander II	CF	1995	D	223*	114' 00"	40' 00"	10' 00"
	Built: Basic Marine Inc., Escanaba, MI							
E-3	**EDELWEISS CRUISE DINING, MILWAUKEE, WI** *(edelweissboats.com)*							
	Edelweiss I	ES	1988	D	87*	64' 08"	18' 00"	6' 00"
	Edelweiss II	ES	1989	D	89*	73' 08"	20' 00"	7' 00"
E-4	**EDWARD E. GILLEN CO., MILWAUKEE, WI** *(gillenco.com)*							
	Andrea J.	PA	1958	D	24*	39' 00"	11' 00"	6' 05"
	(Kayla D. Kadinger '58-'06)							
	Andrew J.	TB	1950	D	25*	47' 00"	15' 07"	8' 00"
	Edith J.	TB	1962	D	19*	45' 03"	13' 00"	8' 00"
	Edward E. Gillen III	TB	1988	D	95*	75' 00"	26' 00"	9' 06"
	Built: Terrebonne Shipbuilders Inc., Houma, LA							
	Jullane J.	TB	1969	D	98*	65' 06"	22' 00"	8' 06
	Built: Bollinger Shipyards, Lockport, LA (N. F. Candies, Connie Guidry ?-'89, David J. Kadinger '89-'06)							
	Kristin J.	TB	1963	D	60*	52' 06"	19' 01"	7' 04"
	Built: St. Charles Steel Works, Thibodaux, LA (Jason A. Kadinger '63-'06)							
E-5	**EGAN MARINE CORP., LEMONT, IL**							
	Alice E.	TB	1950	D	183*	100' 00"	26' 00"	9' 00"
	Built: St. Louis Shipbuilding, St. Louis, MO (L. L. Wright '50-'55, Martin '55-'74, Mary Ann '74-'77, Judi C. '77-'94)							

CUYAHOGA

Vessel Spotlight

Launched May 15, 1943, this Maritime-class steel bulk freighter was built at an approximate cost of $1.97 million as the *Mesabi* for the United States Maritime Commission under an arrangement whereby obsolete tonnage was traded for new hulls.

The vessel was the 10th of 16 similarly designed lakers built during World War II to carry much needed iron ore. The *Mesabi*, built with a new, cruiser stern design, was powered by a four-cylinder, double-compound, Lentz-Poppet steam engine with two coal-fired water-tube boilers. The power plant was German-designed, rather ironic for the World War II era, and was basically two separate engines placed end to end and sending power to a common shaft.

Mesabi was delivered to the Great Lakes Steamship Co. and renamed *J. Burton Ayers.* Later owners included the Northwestern Mutual Life Insurance Co. of Milwaukee and the Wilson Marine Transit Co. of Cleveland.

Kinsman Marine Transit Co. of Cleveland acquired the *J. Burton Ayers* in 1973 and sold her in 1974 to Oglebay Norton's Columbia Transportation Division. During winter 1973-74, the straight-decker was converted to a self-unloader, and during the next winter's layup, the vessel's boilers were converted to oil. In December 1990, the *Ayers* laid up at Toledo's Frog Pond, and she was formally deactivated Aug. 5, 1991.

In 1995, the *J. Burton Ayers* was sold to Lower Lakes Towing Ltd., Port Dover, Ont. The new owner had the vessel towed from Toledo to Sarnia for repainting and refit, and she became the first laker for the relatively new company. The by-then-classic lake boat was renamed *Cuyahoga* (her first rename in 52 years) and formally registered Canadian that November. The *Cuyahoga* left Sarnia shortly after on her maiden voyage to Meldrum Bay, Ont., for a load of limestone for delivery to Cleveland.

During the 1999-2000 winter layup at Sarnia, the *Cuyahoga* had her original Lentz-Poppet engine replaced with a new Caterpillar diesel. On Aug. 30, 2002, the *Cuyahoga* delivered the first cargo of wheat by a self-unloader to the General Mills Frontier Elevator at Buffalo, N.Y. The *Cuyahoga* is the second oldest Canadian-registered lake boat still in active service on the Great Lakes, preceded only by her fleet-mate, *Mississagi*. **– George Wharton**

J. Burton Ayers as part of the Wilson fleet. *(Tom Manse)*

***Cuyahoga* upbound in the Detroit River in 2007.** *(Wade P. Streeter)*

Fleet #.	Fleet Name Vessel Name	Type of Vessel	Year Built	Type of Engine	Cargo Cap. or Gross*	Overall Length	Breadth	Depth or Draft*
	Brandon E.	TB	1945	D	21*	45′ 00″	12′ 08″	6′ 00″
	Built: Sturgeon Bay Shipbuilding & Drydock Co., Sturgeon Bay, WI (ST-929 '45-'45, Heron '46-'62, Heidi '62-'64, James Edward '64-?, David E. ?-'96)							
	Daniel E.	TW	1967	D	70*	70′ 00″	18′ 06″	6′ 08″
	Built: River Enterprises Inc., Morris, IL (Foster M. Ford '67-'84)							
	David E.	TW	1952	D	236*	95′ 00″	30′ 00″	8′ 06″
	Built: Sturgeon Bay Shipbuilding & Drydock Co., Sturgeon Bay, WI (Irving Crown '52-'01)							
	Denise E.	TB	1889	D	123*	84′ 09″	19′ 00″	9′ 00″
	Built: Dialogue & Son, Camden, NJ (Asa W. Hughes 1889-'13, Triton {1} '13-'81, Navajo {2} '81-'92, Robin E. '92-'06)							
	Derek E.	TB	1907	D	85*	72′ 06″	20′ 01″	10′ 06″
	Built: Benjamin T. Cowles, Buffalo, NY (John Kelderhouse '07-'13, Sachem '13-'90)							
	Lisa E.	TB	1963	D	75*	65′ 06″	20′ 00″	8′ 06″
	Built: Main Iron Works Inc., Houma, LA (Dixie Scout '63-'90)							
	Robin E.	TB	1912	D	138*	80′ 07″	21′ 06″	10′ 03″
	Built: Dialogue & Son, Camden, NJ (Caspian '12-'48, Trojan '48-'81, Cherokee {1} '81-'93, Denise E. '93-'06)							
E-6	**EMPRESS OF CANADA ENTERPRISES LTD., TORONTO, ON**							
	Empress of Canada	ES	1980	D	399*	116′ 00″	28′ 00″	6′ 06″
	Built: Hike Metal Products, Wheatley, ON (Island Queen V {2} '80-'89)							
E-7	**ERICKSON MARINE FREIGHT INC., BAYFIELD, WI**							
	Outer Island	PK	1942	D	136*	103′ 05″	32′ 00″	5′ 00″
	(LCT 203 '42-'46, Pluswood '46-'53)							
E-8	**ERIE ISLANDS PETROLEUM INC., PUT-IN-BAY, OH**							
	Cantankerus	TK	1955	D	43*	53′ 02″	14′ 00″	7′ 00″
	Built: Marinette Marine Corp., Marinette, WI							
E-9	**ERIE MARITIME MUSEUM, ERIE, PA** *(brigniagara.org)*							
	Niagara	MU/2B	1988	W	295*	198′ 00″	32′ 00″	10′ 06″
	Reconstruction of Oliver Hazard Perry's U. S. Navy brigantine from the War of 1812							
E-10	**ERIE SAND AND GRAVEL CO., ERIE, PA**							
	J. S. St. John	SC	1945	D	680	174′ 00″	32′ 02″	15′ 00″
	Built: Smith Shipyards & Engineering Corp., Pensacola, FL (USS YO-178 '45-'51, Lake Edward '51-'67)							
E-11	**ESCANABA & LAKE SUPERIOR RAILROAD, WELLS, MI** *(elsrr.com)*							
	Pere Marquette 10	TF	1945	B	27 rail cars	400′ 00″	53′ 00″	22′ 00″
	Built: Manitowoc Shipbuilding Co., Manitowoc, WI; last operated Oct. 7, 1994; laid up at Toledo, OH							
E-12	**ESSROC CANADA INC., NORTH YORK, ON** *(essroc.com)* ***(VESSELS MANAGED BY UPPER LAKES GROUP INC.)***							
	Metis	CC	1956	B	5,800	331′ 00″	43′ 09″	26′ 00″
	Built: Davie Shipbuilding Co., Lauzon, QC; lengthened 72', deepened 3'06" in '59 and converted to a self-unloading cement barge in '91 by Kingston Ship Building & Dry Dock Co., Kingston, ON							
	Stephen B. Roman	CC	1965	D	7,600	488′ 09″	56′ 00″	35′ 06″
	Built: Davie Shipbuilding Co., Lauzon, QC; converted to a self-unloading cement carrier by Collingwood Shipyards, Collingwood, ON, in '83 (Fort William '65-'83)							
F-1	**FAUST CORP., GROSSE POINTE FARMS, MI**							
	Linnhurst	TB	1930	D	11*	37′ 06″	10′ 06″	4′ 08″
F-2	**FEDNAV LTD., MONTREAL, QC** *(fednav.com)* ***CANARCTIC SHIPPING CO. LTD. - DIVISION OF FEDNAV LTD. (SEE ALSO SALTWATER FLEET IF-3)***							
	Arctic	GC	1978	D	26,440	692′ 04″	75′ 05″	49′ 05″
	Built: Port Weller Dry Docks, Port Weller, ON							
	Umiak I	BC	2006	D	31,992	619′ 04″	87′ 02″	51′ 50″
	Built: Universal Shipbuilding Corp., Kawasaki, Japan							
F-3	**FERRISS MARINE CONTRACTING, DETROIT, MI**							
	Magnetic	TB	1925	D	30*	55′ 00″	14′ 00″	6′ 06″
	Built: Spedden Shipbuilding Co., Baltimore, MD (Col. J.D. Graham '24-'65, Nicholson '65-'83)							
	Norma B.	TB	1940	D	14*	43′ 00″	15′ 00″	4′ 00″

Fleet #.	Fleet Name / Vessel Name	Type of Vessel	Year Built	Type of Engine	Cargo Cap. or Gross*	Overall Length	Breadth	Depth or Draft*
F-4	**FITZ SUSTAINABLE FORESTRY MANAGEMENT LTD., SARATOGA SPRINGS, NY**							
	Wyn Cooper	TB	1973	D	25*	48′ 00″	13′ 00″	4′ 00″
F-5	**FRASER SHIPYARDS INC., SUPERIOR, WI** *(frasershipyards.com)*							
	Brenda L.	TB	1941	D	11*	36′ 00″	10′ 00″	3′ 08″
	(Harbour I '41-'58, Su-Joy III '58 -'78)							
	Maxine Thompson	TB	1959	D	30*	47′ 04″	13′ 00″	6′ 06″
	(Susan A. Fraser '59-'78)							
	Reuben Johnson	TB	1912	D	71*	78′ 00″	17′ 00″	11′ 00″
	Built: Great Lakes Towing Co., Cleveland, OH (Buffalo '12-'28, Churchill '28-'48, Buffalo '48-'74, Todd Fraser '74-'78)							
	Wally Kendzora	TB	1956	D	24*	43′ 00″	12′ 00″	5′ 06″
F-6	**FRIENDS OF THE Q105, SARNIA, ON**							
	Duc d' Orleans	ES	1943	D	112*	112′ 00″	17′ 10″	6′ 03″
	World War II sub chaser is undergoing restoration at Sarnia, ON (HMCS ML-105 '43-'48)							
G-1	**GABRIEL MARINE, ALGONAC, MI**							
	Elmer Dean	TB	1998	D	45*	68′ 00″	16′ 08″	6′ 00″
G-2	**GAELIC TUGBOAT CO., DETROIT, MI** *(gaelictugboat.com)*							
	Carolyn Hoey	TB	1951	D	146*	88′ 06″	25′ 06″	11′ 00″
	Built: Alexander Shipyard Inc., New Orleans, LA (Atlas '51-'84, Susan Hoey {1} '84-'85, Atlas '85-'87)							
	LSC 236	TK	1943	B	584*	195′ 06″	35′ 01″	10′ 01
	Marysville	TK	1973	B	1,136*	200′ 00″	50′ 00″	12′ 06″
	(N.M.S. No. 102 '73-'81)							
	Patricia Hoey {2}	TB	1949	D	146*	88′ 06″	25′ 06″	11′ 00″
	Built: Alexander Shipyard, Inc., New Orleans, LA (Propeller '49-'82, Bantry Bay '82-'91)							
	Shannon	TB	1944	D	145*	101′ 00″	28′ 00″	13′ 00″
	Built: Consolidated Shipbuilding Corp., Morris Heights, NY (USS Connewango [YT / YTB / YTM-388] '44-'77)							
	William Hoey {2}	TB	1924	D	99*	85′ 00″	21′ 06″	10′ 09″
	Built: Manitowoc Shipbuilding Co., Manitowoc, WI (Martha C. '24-'52, Langdon C. Hardwicke '52-'82, Wabash {2} '82-'93, Katie Ann {1} '93-'99)							

***Algoway,* with the tug *South Dakota* assisting, at South Chicago.** *(Mike Sipper)*

Fleet #	Fleet Name Vessel Name	Type of Vessel	Year Built	Type of Engine	Cargo Cap. or Gross*	Overall Length	Breadth	Depth or Draft*
G-3	**GALCON MARINE LTD., TORONTO, ON**							
	Kenteau	TB	1937	D	15*	54′07″	16′04″	4′02″
G-4	**GALLAGHER MARINE CONSTRUCTION CO. INC., ESCANABA, MI**							
	Bee Jay	TB	1939	D	19*	45′00″	13′00″	7′00″
	Menasha	CS	1926	B	168*	94′04″	20′00″	5′00″
G-5	**GANANOQUE BOAT LINE, GANANOQUE, ON** *(ganboatline.com)*							
	Thousand Islander	ES	1972	D	200*	96′11″	22′01″	5′05″
	Thousand Islander II	ES	1973	D	200*	99′00″	22′01″	5′00″
	Thousand Islander III	ES	1975	D	376*	118′00″	28′00″	6′00″
	Thousand Islander IV	ES	1976	D	347*	110′09″	28′04″	10′08″
	Thousand Islander V	ES	1979	D	246*	88′00″	24′00″	5′00″
	(Concordia '79-'97)							
G-6	**GANNON UNIVERSITY, ERIE, PA** *(www.gannon.edu)*							
	Environaut	RV	1950	D	13*	36′05″	12′00″	5′00″
G-7	**GARDINER MARINE, RICHARD'S LANDING, ON**							
	Joyce B. Gardiner	TB	1962	D	71*	72′00″	19′00″	12′00″
	Built: McNamara Marine Ltd., Toronto, ON (Angus M. '62-'92, Omni Sorel '92-'02)							
G-8	**GEO. GRADEL CO., TOLEDO, OH** *(georgegradelco.tripod.com)*							
	Clyde	DB	1922	B	704*	134′00″	41′00″	12′00″
	John Francis	TB	1965	D	99*	75′00″	22′00″	9′00″
	Built: Bollinger Shipbuilding Inc., Lockport, LA (Dad '65-'98, Creole Eagle '98-'03)							
	Josephine	TB	1957	D	103*	86′09″	20′06″	7′09″
	(Wambrau '57-'87, Sea Diver II '87-'03)							
	Mighty Jake	TB	1969	D	15*	36′00″	12′03″	7′03″
	Mighty Jessie	TB	1954	D	57*	61′02″	18′00″	7′03″
	Mighty Jimmy	TB	1945	D	27*	56′00″	15′10″	7′00″
	Mighty John III	TB	1962	D	24*	45′00″	15′00″	5′10″
	(Niagara Queen '62-'99)							
	Moby Dick	DB	1952	B	835	121′00″	33′02″	10′06″
	Pioneerland	TB	1943	D	53*	58′00″	16′08″	8′00″
	Prairieland	TB	1955	D	35*	49′02″	15′02″	6′00″
	Timberland	TB	1946	D	20*	41′03″	13′01″	7′00″
G-9	**GOODTIME LAKE ERIE ISLAND CRUISES LLC, SANDUSKY, OH** *(goodtimeboat.com)*							
	Goodtime I	ES	1960	D	81*	111′00″	29′08″	9′05″
	Built: Blount Marine Corp., Warren, RI							
G-10	**GOODTIME TRANSIT BOATS INC., CLEVELAND, OH** *(goodtimeiii.com)*							
	Goodtime III	ES	1990	D	95*	161′00″	40′00″	11′00″
	Bulit: Leevac Shipyards Inc., Jennings, LA							
G-11	**GRAND PORTAGE / ISLE ROYALE TRANSPORTATION LINE, SUPERIOR, WI** *(isleroyaleboats.com)*							
	Voyageur II	ES	1970	D	40*	63′00″	18′00″	5′00″
	Wenonah	ES	1960	D	91*	70′07″	19′04″	9′07″
	Built: Dubuque Boat & Boiler Works, Dubuque, IA (Jamaica '60-'64)							
G-12	**GRAND VALLEY STATE UNIVERSITY, ANNIS WATER RESOURCES, MUSKEGON, MI** *(gvsu.edu/wri)*							
	D. J. Angus	RV	1986	D	16*	45′00″	14′00″	4′00″
	W. G. Jackson	RV	1996	D	80*	64′10″	20′00″	5′00″
G-13	**GRAVEL AND LAKE SERVICES LTD., THUNDER BAY, ON**							
	Donald Mac	TB	1914	D	69*	71′00″	17′00″	10′00″
	Built: Thor Iron Works Ltd., Toronto, ON							
	George N. Carleton	TB	1943	D	97*	82′00″	21′00″	11′00″
	Built: Russel Brothers, Owen Sound, ON (HMCS Glenlea [W-25] '43-'45, Bansaga '45-'64)							
	Peninsula	TB	1944	D	261*	111′00″	27′00″	13′00″
	Built: Montreal Drydock Ltd., Montreal, QC (HMCS Norton [W-31] '44-'45, W.A.C. 1 '45-'46)							
	Robert John	TB	1945	D	98*	82′00″	20′01″	11′00″
	Built: Canadian Dredge & Dock Co., Kingston, ON (HMCS Gleneagle [W-40] '45-'46, Bansturdy '46-'65)							

Kaye E. Barker **unloading coal at the B.C. Cobb plant Muskegon.** *(Mike Sipper)*

Fleet #	Fleet Name Vessel Name	Type of Vessel	Year Built	Type of Engine	Cargo Cap. or Gross*	Overall Length	Breadth	Depth or Draft*
	Wolf River	BC	1956	D	5,880	349' 02"	43' 07"	25' 04"
	Built: Port Weller Dry Docks, Port Weller, ON; last operated in 1998; laid up at Thunder Bay, ON (Tecumseh {2} '56-'67, New York News {3} '67-'86, Stella Desgagnes '86-'93, Beam Beginner '94-'95)							
G-14	**GREAT LAKES CLIPPER PRESERVATION ASSOCIATION, MUSKEGON, MI** *(milwaukeeclipper.com)*							
	Milwaukee Clipper	MU	1904	Q	4,272	361' 00"	45' 00"	28' 00"
	Built: American Shipbuilding Co., Cleveland, OH; rebuilt in '40 at Manitowoc Shipbuilding Co., Manitowoc, WI; former Wisconsin & Michigan Steamship Co. passenger/auto carrier last operated in 1970; undergoing restoration and open to the public at Muskegon, MI (Juniata '04-'41)							
G-15	**GREAT LAKES DOCK & MATERIALS LLC, MUSKEGON, MI** *(greatlakesdock.com)*							
	Duluth	TB	1954	D	87*	70' 01"	19' 05"	9' 08"
	Built: Missouri Valley Bridge & Iron Works, Leavenworth, KS (U. S. Army ST-2015 '54-'62)							
	Fischer Hayden	TB	1967	D	64*	54' 00"	22' 1"	7' 1"
	Built: Main Iron Works Inc., Houma, LA (Gloria G. Cheramie, Joyce P. Crosby)							
	Sarah B	TB	1953	D	23*	45' 00"	13' 00"	7' 00"
	Built: Nashville Bridge Co., Nashville, TN (ST-2161 '53-'63, Tawas Bay '63-'03)							
G-16	**GREAT LAKES ENVIRONMENTAL RESEARCH LABORATORY, MUSKEGON, MI** *(www.glerl.noaa.gov)*							
	Laurentian	RV	1974	D	129*	80' 00"	21' 06"	11' 00"
	Shenehon	SV	1953	D	90*	65' 00"	17' 00"	6' 00"
	GREAT LAKES FEEDER LINES INC., BURLINGTON, ON *(glfeederlines.com)* ***SEE SALTWATER FLEET IR-1***							
G-17	**GREAT LAKES FLEET INC./KEY LAKES INC., DULUTH, MN (MANAGER)** *(www.keyship.com)*							
	CANADIAN NATIONAL RAILWAY, MONTREAL, QC – OWNER *(www.cn.ca)*							
	Arthur M. Anderson	SU	1952	T	25,300	767' 00"	70' 00"	36' 00"
	Built: American Shipbuilding Co., Lorain, OH; lengthened 120' in '75 and converted to a self-unloader in '82 at Fraser Shipyards, Superior, WI							
	Cason J. Callaway	SU	1952	T	25,300	767' 00"	70' 00"	36' 00"
	Built: Great Lakes Engineering Works, River Rouge, MI; lengthened 120' in '74 and converted to a self-unloader in '82 '82 at Fraser Shipyards, Superior, WI							
	Edgar B. Speer	SU	1980	D	73,700	1,004' 00"	105' 00"	56' 00"
	Built: American Shipbuilding Co., Lorain, OH							
	Edwin H. Gott	SU	1979	D	74,100	1,004' 00"	105' 00"	56' 00"
	Built: Bay Shipbuilding Co., Sturgeon Bay, WI; converted from shuttle self-unloader to deck-mounted self-unloader at Bay Shipbuilding, Sturgeon Bay, WI, in '96							
	John G. Munson {2}	SU	1952	T	25,550	768' 03"	72' 00"	36' 00"
	Built: Manitowoc Shipbuilding Co., Manitowoc, WI; lengthened 102' at Fraser Shipyards, Superior, WI, in '76							
	Philip R. Clarke	SU	1952	T	25,300	767' 00"	70' 00"	36' 00"
	Built: American Shipbuilding Co., Lorain, OH; lengthened 120' in '74 and converted to a self-unloader in '82 at Fraser Shipyards, Superior, WI							
	Presque Isle {2}	IT	1973	D	1,578*	153' 03"	54' 00"	31' 03"
	Built: Halter Marine Services, New Orleans, LA							
	Presque Isle {2}	SU	1973	B	57,500	974' 06"	104' 07"	46' 06"
	Built: Erie Marine Inc., Erie, PA							
	[ITB Presque Isle OA dimensions together]					1,000' 00"	104' 07"	46' 06"
	Roger Blough	SU	1972	D	43,900	858' 00"	105' 00"	41' 06"
	Built: American Shipbuilding Co., Lorain, OH							
G-18	**THE GREAT LAKES GROUP, CLEVELAND, OH** *(thegreatlakesgroup.com)*							
	THE GREAT LAKES TOWING CO., CLEVELAND, OH – DIVISION OF THE GREAT LAKES GROUP							
	Alabama {2}	TB	1916	DE	98*	81' 00"	21' 03"	12' 05"
	Arizona	TB	1931	D	98*	84' 04"	20' 00"	12' 06"
	Arkansas {2}	TB	1909	D	98*	81' 00"	21' 03"	12' 05"
	(Yale '09-'48)							
	California	TB	1926	DE	98*	81' 00"	20' 00"	12' 06"
	Colorado	TB	1928	D	98*	84' 04"	20' 00"	12' 06"
	Delaware {4}	TB	1924	DE	98*	81' 00"	20' 00"	12' 06"
	Florida	TB	1926	D	99*	81' 00"	20' 00"	12' 06"
	(Florida '26-'83, Pinellas '83-'84)							

Fleet #.	Fleet Name / Vessel Name	Type of Vessel	Year Built	Type of Engine	Cargo Cap. or Gross*	Overall Length	Breadth	Depth or Draft*
	Idaho	TB	1931	DE	98*	84′ 00″	20′ 00″	12′ 06″
	Illinois {2}	TB	1914	D	99*	81′ 00″	20′ 00″	12′ 06″
	Indiana	TB	1911	DE	97*	81′ 00″	20′ 00″	12′ 06″
	Iowa	TB	1915	D	98*	81′ 00″	20′ 00″	12′ 06″
	Kansas	TB	1927	D	98*	81′ 00″	20′ 00″	12′ 06″
	Kentucky {2}	TB	1929	D	98*	84′ 04″	20′ 00″	12′ 06″
	Louisiana	TB	1917	D	98*	81′ 00″	20′ 00″	12′ 06″
	Maine {1}	TB	1921	D	96*	81′ 00″	20′ 00″	12′ 06″
	(Maine {1} ′21-′82, Saipan ′82-′83, Hillsboro ′83-′84)							
	Massachusetts	TB	1928	D	98*	84′ 04″	20′ 00″	12′ 06″
	Milwaukee	DB	1924	B	1,095	172′ 00″	40′ 00″	11′ 06″
	Minnesota {1}	TB	1911	D	98*	81′ 00″	20′ 00″	12′ 06″
	Mississippi	TB	1916	DE	98*	81′ 00″	20′ 00″	12′ 06″
	Missouri {2}	TB	1927	D	149*	88′ 04″	24′ 06″	12′ 03″
	(Rogers City {1} ′27-′56, Dolomite {1} ′56-′81, Chippewa {7} ′81-′90)							
	Montana	TB	1929	DE	98*	84′ 04″	20′ 00″	12′ 06″
	Nebraska	TB	1929	D	98*	84′ 04″	20′ 00″	12′ 06″
	New Jersey	TB	1924	D	98*	81′ 00″	20′ 00″	12′ 06″
	(New Jersey ′24-′52, Petco-21 ′52-′53)							
	New York	TB	1913	D	98*	81′ 00″	20′ 00″	12′ 06″
	North Carolina {2}	TB	1952	DE	145*	87′ 09″	24′ 01″	10′ 07″
	(Limestone ′52-′83, Wicklow ′83-′90)							
	North Dakota	TB	1910	D	97*	81′ 00″	20′ 00″	12′ 06″
	(John M. Truby ′10-′38)							
	Ohio {3}	TB	1903	D	194*	118′ 00″	24′ 00″	13′ 06″
	Built: Great Lakes Towing Co., Chicago, IL (M.F.D. No. 15 ′03-′52, Laurence C. Turner ′52-′73)							
	Oklahoma	TB	1913	DE	97*	81′ 00″	20′ 00″	12′ 06″
	(T. C. Lutz {2} ′13-′34)							
	Pennsylvania {3}	TB	1911	D	98*	81′ 00″	20′ 00″	12′ 06″
	Rhode Island	TB	1930	D	98*	84′ 04″	20′ 00″	12′ 06″
	South Carolina	TB	1925	D	102*	86′ 00″	21′ 00″	11′ 00″
	(Welcome {2} ′25-′53, Joseph H. Callan ′53-′72, South Carolina ′72-′82, Tulagi ′82-′83)							
	Superior {3}	TB	1912	D	147*	97′ 00″	22′ 00″	12′ 00″
	(Richard Fitzgerald ′12-′46)							
	Tennessee	TB	1917	D	98*	81′ 00″	20′ 00″	12′ 06″
	Texas	TB	1916	DE	97*	81′ 00″	20′ 00″	12′ 06″
	Vermont	TB	1914	D	98*	81′ 00″	20′ 00″	12′ 06″
	Virginia {2}	TB	1914	DE	97*	81′ 00″	20′ 00″	12′ 06″
	Washington {1}	TB	1925	DE	97*	81′ 00″	20′ 00″	12′ 06″
	Wisconsin {4}	TB	1897	D	105*	90′ 03″	21′ 00″	12′ 03″
	(America {3}, Midway)							
	Wyoming	TB	1929	D	104*	84′ 04″	20′ 00″	12′ 06″
G-19	**GREAT LAKES MARITIME ACADEMY – NORTHWESTERN MICHIGAN COLLEGE, TRAVERSE CITY, MI**							
	(nmc.edu/maritime)							
	Anchor Bay	TV	1953	D	23*	45′ 00″	13′ 00″	7′ 00″
	Built: Roamer Boat Co., Holland, MI (ST-2158 ′53-′62)							
	Northwestern {2}	TV	1969	D	12*	55′ 00″	15′ 00″	6′ 06″
	Built: Paasch Marine Services Inc., Erie, PA (USCOE North Central ′69-′98)							
	State of Michigan	TV	1986	D	1,914*	224′ 00″	43′ 00″	20′ 00″
	(USS Persistent ′86-′98, USCG Persistent ′98-′02)							
G-20	**GREAT LAKES NAVAL MEMORIAL & MUSEUM, MUSKEGON, MI** *(silversides.org)*							
	LST-393	MU	1942	D	2,100	328′ 00″	50′ 00″	25′ 00″
	Built: Newport News Shipbuilding and Dry Dock Co., Newport News, VA; former U.S. Navy / Wisconsin & Michigan Steamship Co. vessel last operated July 31, 1973; on display at Muskegon, MI (USS LST-393 ′42-′47, Highway 16 ′47-′99)							
	McLane	MU	1927	D	289*	125′ 00″	24′ 00″	12′ 06″
	Built: American Brown Boveri Electric Co., Camden, NJ; former U.S. Coast Guard Buck & A Quarter class medium endurance cutter; on display at Muskegon, MI (USCGC McLane [WSC / WMEC-146] ′27-′70, Manatra II ′70-′93)							

Fleet #	Fleet Name Vessel Name	Type of Vessel	Year Built	Type of Engine	Cargo Cap. or Gross*	Overall Length	Breadth	Depth or Draft*
	Silversides	MU	1941	D/V	1,526*	311′08″	27′03″	33′09″
	Built: Mare Island Naval Yard, Vallejo, CA; former U.S. Navy Albacore (Gato) class submarine AGSS-236; open to the public at Muskegon, MI							
G-21	**GREAT LAKES SCHOONER CO., TORONTO, ON** *(greatlakesschooner.com)*							
	Challenge	ES	1980	W/D	76*	96′00″	16′06″	8′00″
	Kajama	ES	1930	W/D	263*	128′09″	22′09″	11′08″
G-22	**GREAT LAKES SCIENCE CENTER, ANN ARBOR, MI** *(www.glsc.usgs.gov)*							
	Grayling	RV	1977	D	198*	75′00″	22′00″	9′10″
	Kaho	RV	1961	D	83*	64′10″	17′10″	9′00″
	Kiyi	RV	1999	D	290*	107′00″	27′00″	12′02″
	Musky II	RV	1960	D	25*	45′00″	14′04″	5′00″
	Sturgeon	RV	1977	D	325*	100′00″	25′05″	10′00″
G-23	**GREAT LAKES SHIPWRECK HISTORICAL SOCIETY, SAULT STE. MARIE, MI** *(shipwreckmuseum.com)*							
	David Boyd	RV	1982	D	26*	47′00″	17′00″	3′00″*
H-1	**H. LEE WHITE MARINE MUSEUM, OSWEGO, NY** *(hleewhitemarinemuseum.com)*							
	LT-5	MU	1943	D	305*	115′00″	28′00″	14′00″
	Built: Jakobson Shipyard, Oyster Bay, NY; former U.S. Army Corps of Engineers tug last operated in 1989; open to the public at Oswego, NY (Major Elisha K. Henson '43-'47, U.S. Army LT-5 '47-'47, Nash '47-'95)							
H-2	**HAMILTON HARBOUR QUEEN CRUISES, HAMILTON, ON**							
	Hamilton Harbour Queen	ES	1956	D	252*	100′00″	22′00″	4′05″
	Built: Russel-Hipwell Engines, Owen Sound, ON (Johnny B. '56-'89, Garden City '89-'00, Harbour Princess '00-'05)							
H-3	**HAMILTON PORT AUTHORITY, HAMILTON, ON** *(hamiltonport.ca)*							
	Cleanshores	TB	1979	D	10*	33′08″	11′03″	4′05″
	Henry Askew	TB	1947	Gas	10*	31′00″	14′05″	2′09″
	Judge McCombs	TB	1948	D	10*	36′00″	10′03″	4′00″
	Built: Northern Shipbuilding & Repair Co., Ltd., Bronte, ON (Bronte Sue '48-'50)							
H-4	**HANNAH MARINE CORP., LEMONT, IL** *(hannahmarine.com)*							
	Daryl C. Hannah {2}	TW	1956	D	268*	102′00″	28′00″	8′00″
	Built: Calumet Shipyard & Drydock Co., Chicago, IL (Cindy Jo '56-'66, Katherine L. '66-'93)							
	David E.	TB	1944	D	602*	149′00″	33′00″	16′00″
	Built: Marietta Manufacturing, Marietta, GA (LT 815 '44-'64, Henry Foss '64-'84, Kristin Lee '84-'93, Kristin Lee Hannah' 93-'00)							
	Donald C. Hannah	TB	1962	D	191*	91′00″	29′00″	11′06″
	Built: Main Iron Works, Inc., Houma, LA							
	Hannah 1801	TK	1967	B	2,695	240′00″	50′00″	12′00″
	Hannah 1802	TK	1967	B	2,695	240′00″	50′00″	12′00″
	Hannah 2901	TK	1962	B	2,768	264′00″	52′06″	12′06″
	Hannah 2902	TK	1962	B	2,768	264′00″	52′06″	12′06″
	Hannah 2903	TK	1962	B	2,768	264′00″	52′06″	12′06″
	Hannah 3601	TK	1972	B	5,035	290′00″	60′00″	18′03″
	Hannah 5101	TK	1978	B	8,050	360′00″	60′00″	22′06″
	Hannah 6301	TK	1980	B	8,050	407′01″	60′00″	21′00″
	Hannah 7701	DB	1981	B	7,143	340′00″	64′00″	21′02″
	Hannah D. Hannah	TB	1955	D	134*	86′00″	24′00″	10′00″
	Built: Sturgeon Bay Shipbuilding, Sturgeon Bay, WI (Harbor Ace '55-'61, Gopher State '61-'71, Betty Gale '71-'93)							
	James A. Hannah	TB	1945	D	593*	149′00″	33′00″	16′00″
	Built: Marietta Manufacturing, Marietta, GA (U. S. Army LT-820 '45-'65, Muskegon {1} '65-'71)							
	Kristin Lee Hannah	TW	1953	D	397*	111′10″	35′00″	8′04″
	Built: Sturgeon Bay Shipbuilding, Sturgeon Bay, WI (Inwaco '53-'61, Carrie S. '61-'68, Clark Frame '68-'96, Cheri Conway '96-'96, David E '96-'00)							
	Margaret M.	TB	1956	D	167*	89′06″	24′00″	10′00″
	Built: Sturgeon Bay Shipbuilding, Sturgeon Bay, WI (Shuttler '56-'60, Margaret M. Hannah '60-'84)							
	Mark Hannah	ATB	1969	D	191*	127′05″	32′01″	14′03″
	Built: Burton Shipyard, Bridge City, TX (Lead Horse '69-'73, Gulf Challenger '73-'80, Challenger {2} '80-'93)							
	Mary E. Hannah	TB	1945	D	612*	149′00″	33′00″	16′00″
	Built: Marietta Manufacturing, Marietta, GA (U. S. Army LT-821 '45-'47, Brooklyn '47-'66, Lee Reuben '66-'75)							

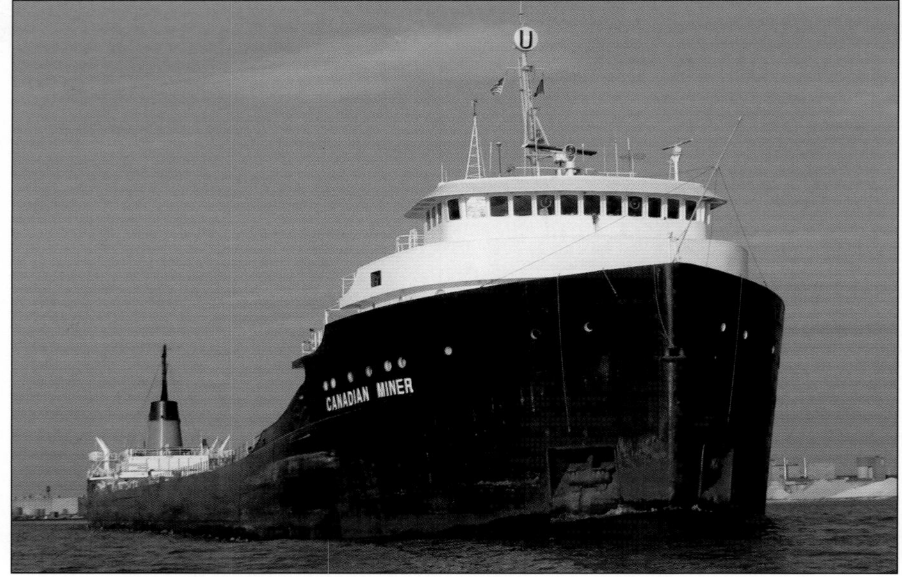

***Canadian Miner* downbound on the Detroit River in 2007.** *(Wade P. Streeter)*

CANADIAN MINER

Vessel Spotlight

The *Canadian Miner* is a fine example of the classic Great Lakes straight-deck bulk carrier, one of a series of such 730-footers built in the late 1950s and early 1960s to take advantage of the new size allowances permitted with the opening of the St. Lawrence Seaway in 1959. Built in two sections by two shipyards in Quebec, and joined by a third, the diesel-powered bulk carrier was launched April 25, 1966, at Montreal as the *Maplecliffe Hall* for the Hall Corp. of Canada.

Although cargoes for the *Maplecliffe Hall* were focused in the iron ore and grain trades, the bulk carrier set a coal record on June 11, 1971, loading 27,927 tons at Sandusky. In 1984, the vessel was used to carry CAST containers from Montreal to Windsor and Detroit. Only three trips were made, with the containers carried in the hold and stored on the deck. The venture proved unsuccessful and was discontinued. Later, with no loads, the laker laid up at Montreal in the summer of 1987 and was opened for public tours before being used to store cement over the winter.

With the dissolution of the Halco fleet, the *Maplecliffe Hall* joined Canada Steamship Lines in 1988, becoming the second boat in that fleet to bear the name *Lemoyne*. The *Lemoyne* began sailing for her new owners in spring 1988, her cargoes again concentrated in the grain and iron ore trades. In 1991, the *Lemoyne*, with her bulker fleet mates, began sailing under the Great Lakes Bulk Carriers' banner, a partnership formed from the bulker fleets of Canada Steamship Lines, Misener Holdings and Pioneer Shipping.

The *Lemoyne* made history on Dec. 18, 1992, at Cleveland as the last ship unloaded by a giant Hulett unloading machine. Shortly after, on Dec. 23, 1992, the laker laid up at Hamilton with a load of canola seed, never to sail for CSL again.

With the demise of Great Lakes Bulk Carriers, CSL and its other partners sold off their bulker fleets, with the *Lemoyne* going to Upper Lakes Shipping in early 1994. Renamed *Canadian Miner*, the bulker returned to service in October 1994, sailing under the management of Seaway Bulk Carriers.

The *Canadian Miner* continues to actively sail for the Upper Lakes fleet, now operated and managed by Seaway Marine Transport, a partnership consisting of the combined bulker and self-unloader fleets of Upper Lakes and Algoma Central. – ***George Wharton***

Fleet #	Fleet Name Vessel Name	Type of Vessel	Year Built	Type of Engine	Cargo Cap. or Gross*	Overall Length	Breadth	Depth or Draft*
	Peggy D. Hannah	TB	1920	D	145*	108' 00"	25' 00"	14' 00"
	Built: Whitney Brothers Co., Superior, WI (William A. Whitney '20-'92)							
	Susan W. Hannah	ATB	1977	D	174*	121' 06"	34' 06"	18' 02"
	Built: Toche Enterprises, Inc., Ocean Springs, MS (Lady Elda '77-'78, Kings Challenger '78-'78, ITM No. 1 '78-'81, Kings Challenger '81-'86)							
	Wilbur R. Clark	TB	1945	D	275*	151' 05"	33' 00"	18' 08"
	Built: Marietta Manufacturing, Marietta, GA (LT-789, Polar Challenger, Marine Challenger, Petro Challenger, Pacific Victory)							
	HMC SHIP MANAGEMENT LTD., LEMONT, IL – AFFILIATE OF HANNAH MARINE CORP.							
	William L. Warner	RT	1973	D	492*	120' 00"	40' 00"	14' 00"
	Built: Halter Marine, New Orleans, LA (Jos. F. Bigane '73-'04)							
H-5	**HARBOR LIGHT CRUISE LINES, TOLEDO, OH** *(sandpiperboat.com)*							
	Sandpiper	ES	1984	D	19*	65' 00"	16' 00"	4' 00"
H-6	**HCMS HAIDA NATIONAL HISTORICAL SITE, HAMILTON, ON** *(hmcshaida.ca)*							
	Haida	MU	1943	T	2,744*	377' 00"	37' 06"	15' 02"
	Former Royal Canadian Navy Tribal-class destroyer G-63 / DDE-215; open to the public at Hamilton, ON							
H-7	**HEDDLE MARINE SERVICE INC., HAMILTON, ON** *(heddlemarine.com)*							
	Dalmig	CF	1957	D	538*	175' 10"	40' 01"	11' 10"
	Built: Marine Industries Inc., Sorel, QC; vessel laid up at Hamilton, ON (Pierre de Saurel '57-'87)							
	King Fish 1	TB	1955	D	24*	47' 09"	12' 09"	5' 03"
	Wyatt McKeil	TB	1950	D	237*	102' 06"	26' 00"	13' 06"
	Built: Davie Shipbuilding Co., Lauzon, QC; vessel laid up at Hamilton, ON (Otis Wack '50-'97)							
H-8	**HERITAGE CRUISE LINES, ST. CATHARINES, ON**							
	Georgian Clipper	PA	1967	D	170*	78' 08"	12' 06"	6' 00"
H-9	**HOLLY MARINE TOWING, CHICAGO, IL**							
	Chris Ann	TB	1981	D	45*	51' 09"	17' 00"	6' 01"
	Built: Hudson Shipbuilders Inc., Pascagoula, MS (Captain Robbie '81-'90, Philip M. Pearse '90-'97)							
	Holly Ann	TB	1926	D	220*	108' 00"	26' 06"	15' 00"
	Built: Manitowoc Shipbuilding Co., Manitowoc, WI (Wm. A. Lydon '26-'92)							
	Katie Ann {3}	TB	1962	D	84*	60' 04"	24' 00"	8' 06"
	Margaret Ann	TB	1954	D	131*	82' 00"	24' 06"	11' 06"
	Built: Defoe Shipbuilding Co., Bay City, MI (John A. McGuire '54-'87, William Hoey {1} '87-'94)							
	Mary Ann	TW	1946	D	46*	52' 02"	18' 00"	5' 00"
H-10	**HORNBECK OFFSHORE SERVICES, COVINGTON, LA** *(hornbeckoffshore.com)*							
	Bayridge Service	TB	1981	D	194*	100' 00"	30' 00"	14' 05"
	Built: Bollinger Shipyard, Inc., Lockport, LA							
	Energy 5501	TK	1969	B	2,878*	341' 00"	54' 00"	17' 09"
	Tradewind Service	TB	1975	D	183*	104' 07"	30' 00"	12' 08"
	Built: Bollinger Shipyard Inc., Lockport, LA							
H-11	**HORNE TRANSPORTATION LTD., WOLFE ISLAND, ON** *(wolfeisland.com)*							
	William Darrell	CF	1952	D	66*	66' 00"	28' 00"	6' 00"
	Built: Harry Gamble, Port Dover, ON							
H-12	**HUFFMAN EQUIPMENT RENTAL INC., EASTLAKE, OH**							
	Hamp Thomas	TB	1968	D	22*	43' 00"	13' 00"	4' 00"
	Paddy Miles	TB	1934	D	16*	45' 04"	12' 04"	4' 07"
I-1	**ICEBREAKER MACKINAW MARITIME MUSEUM INC., MACKINAW CITY, MI** *(icebreakermackinawmuseum.org)*							
	Mackinaw **[WAGB-83]**	MU	1944	D	5,252*	290' 00"	74' 00"	29' 00"
	Built: Toledo Shipbuilding Co., Toledo, OH; former U.S. Coast Guard icebreaker wasdecomissioned 2006; open to the public at Mackinaw City, MI (Launched as USCGC Manitowoc [WAG-83])							
I-2	**ILLINOIS MARINE TOWING INC., LEMONT, IL** *(imtowing.com)*							
	Aggie C	TW	1977	D	134*	81' 00"	26' 00"	9' 00"

Fleet #.	Fleet Name Vessel Name	Type of Vessel	Year Built	Type of Engine	Cargo Cap. or Gross*	Overall Length	Breadth	Depth or Draft*
	Albert C	TW	1971	D	65*	61′ 02″	18′ 00″	5′ 07″
	Channahon	TW	2000	D	67*	52′ 00″	22′ 00″	7′ 00″
	Eileen C	TW	1982	D	145*	75′ 00″	26′ 00″	9′ 00″
	William C	TW	1968	D	143*	76′ 06″	24′ 00″	8′ 00″
	Windy City	TW	1979	D	141*	61′ 03″	26′ 00″	9′ 02″
I-3	**INLAND LAKES MANAGEMENT INC., ALPENA, MI**							
	Alpena {2}	CC	1942	T	15,550	519′ 06″	67′ 00″	35′ 00″
	Built: Great Lakes Engineering Works, River Rouge, MI; shortened by 120′ and converted to a self-unloading cement carrier at Fraser Shipyards, Superior, WI, in '91 (Leon Fraser '42-'91)							
	E. M. Ford	CC	1898	Q	7,100	428′ 00″	50′ 00″	28′ 00″
	Built: Cleveland Shipbuilding Co., Cleveland, OH; converted to a self-unloading cement carrier at Christy Corp., Sturgeon Bay, WI, in '56; last operated Sept. 16, 1996; in use as a cement storage and transfer vessel at Saginaw, MI (Presque Isle {1} 1898-'56)							
	J. A. W. Iglehart	CC	1936	T	12,500	501′ 06″	68′ 03″	37′ 00″
	Built: Sun Shipbuilding and Drydock Co., Chester, PA; converted from a saltwater tanker to a self-unloading cement carrier at American Ship Building Co., South Chicago, IL , in '65; last operated Oct. 29, 2006; in use as a cement storage/transfer vessel at Superior, WI (Pan Amoco '36-'55, Amoco '55-'60, H. R. Schemm '60-'65)							
	Paul H. Townsend	CC	1945	D	7,850	447′ 00″	50′ 00″	29′ 00″
	Built: Consolodated Steel Corp., Wilmington, DE; converted from a saltwater cargo vessel to a self-unloading cement carrier at Bethlehem Steel Co., Shipbuilding Div., Hoboken, NJ, & Calumet Shipyard, Chicago, IL, in '52 / '53; lengthened at Great Lakes Engineering Works, Ashtabula, OH, in '58; last operated Dec. 5, 2005; in use as a cement storage/transfer vessel at Muskegon, MI (USNS Hickory Coll '45-'46, USNS Coastal Delegate '46-'52)							
	S. T. Crapo	CC	1927	B	8,900	402′ 06″	60′ 03″	29′ 00″
	Built: Great Lakes Engineering Works, River Rouge, MI; last operated Sept. 4, 1996; in use as a cement storage and transfer vessel at Green Bay, WI							
I-4	**INLAND SEAS EDUCATION ASSOCIATION, SUTTONS BAY, MI** *(schoolship.org)*							
	Inland Seas	RV	1994	W	41*	61′ 06″	17′ 00″	7′ 00″
I-5	**INLAND TUG & BARGE LTD., BROCKVILLE, ON**							
	Katanni	TB	1991	D	19*	34′ 08″	14′ 05″	5′ 05″
I-6	**INTERLAKE STEAMSHIP CO., RICHFIELD, OH** *(interlakesteamship.com)*							
	Charles M. Beeghly	SU	1959	T	31,000	806′ 00″	75′ 00″	37′ 06″
	Built: American Shipbuilding Co., Lorain, OH; lengthened 96′ in '72; converted to a self-unloader in '81 at Fraser Shipyards, Superior, WI (Shenango II '59-'67)							
	Herbert C. Jackson	SU	1959	T	24,800	690′ 00″	75′ 00″	37′ 06″
	Built: Great Lakes Engineering Works, River Rouge, MI; converted to a self-unloader at Defoe Shipbuilding Co., Bay City, MI, in '75							
	James R. Barker	SU	1976	D	63,300	1,004′ 00″	105′ 00″	50′ 00″
	Built: American Shipbuilding Co., Lorain, OH							
	Mesabi Miner	SU	1977	D	63,300	1,004′ 00″	105′ 00″	50′ 00″
	Built: American Shipbuilding Co., Lorain, OH							
	Paul R. Tregurtha	SU	1981	D	68,000	1,013′ 06″	105′ 00″	56′ 00″
	Built: American Shipbuilding Co., Lorain, OH (William J. DeLancey '81-'90)							
	Stewart J. Cort	SU	1972	D	58,000	1,000′ 00″	105′ 00″	49′ 00″
	Built: Erie Marine Inc., Erie, PA; the Cort was the first 1,000-footer to enter Great Lakes service							
	INTERLAKE TRANSPORTATION INC., RICHFIELD, OH – DIVISION OF INTERLAKE STEAMSHIP CO.							
	Dorothy Ann	AT/TT	1999	D	1,600*	124′ 03″	44′ 00″	24′ 00″
	Built: Bay Shipbuilding Co., Sturgeon Bay, WI							
	Pathfinder {3}	SU	1953	B	26,700	606′ 02″	70′ 00″	36′ 00″
	Built: Great Lakes Engineering Works, River Rouge, MI; converted from a powered vessel to a self-unloading barge at Bay Shipbuilding, Sturgeon Bay, WI, in '98 (J. L. Mauthe '53-'98)							
	[ATB Dorothy Ann / Pathfinder {3} OA dimensions together]					700′ 00″	70′ 00″	36′ 00″
	LAKES SHIPPING CO. INC., RICHFIELD, OH – DIVISION OF INTERLAKE STEAMSHIP CO.							
	John Sherwin {2}	BC	1958	T	31,500	806′ 00″	75′ 00″	37′ 06″
	Built: American Steamship Co., Lorain, OH; lengthened 96′ at Fraser Shipyards, Superior, WI, in '73; last operated Nov. 16, 1981; in use as a grain storage hull at South Chicago, IL							

Fleet #	Fleet Name Vessel Name	Type of Vessel	Year Built	Type of Engine	Cargo Cap. or Gross*	Overall Length	Breadth	Depth or Draft*
	Kaye E. Barker	SU	1952	T	25,900	767′ 00″	70′ 00″	36′ 00″
	Built: American Shipbuilding Co., Toledo, OH; lengthened 120′ at Fraser Shipyards, Superior, WI, in '76; converted to a self-unloader at American Shipbuilding Co., Toledo, OH, in '81 (Edward B. Greene '52-'85, Benson Ford {3} '85-'89)							
	Lee A. Tregurtha	SU	1942	D	29,360	826′ 00″	75′ 00″	39′ 00″
	Built: Bethlehem Shipbuilding and Drydock Co., Sparrows Point, MD; converted from a saltwater tanker to a Great Lakes bulk carrier in '61; lengthened 96′ in '76 and converted to a self-unloader in '78, all at American Shipbuilding Co., Lorain, OH; repowered in '06 (Laid down as Mobiloil; launched as Samoset. USS Chiwawa [AO-68] '42-'46, Chiwawa '46-'61, Walter A. Sterling '61-'85, William Clay Ford {2} '85-'89)							
I-7	**INTERNATIONAL MARINE SALVAGE INC., PORT COLBORNE, ON** *(rawmaterials.com)*							
	Calumet	SU	1929	D	12,450	603′ 09″	60′ 00″	32′ 00″
	Built: Great Lakes Engineering Works, River Rouge, MI; converted to a self-unloader in 56; repowered in '68; awaiting scrapping at Port Colborne, ON (Myron C. Taylor '29-'01)							
	Kristin	TB	1944	D	261*	111′ 00″	27′ 00″	13′ 00″
	Awaiting scrapping at Port Colborne, ON (HMCS Riverton [W-47 / ATA-528] '44-'79, Techno St-Laurent '79-'02)							
	Charlie E.	TB	1943	D	32*	63′ 00″	16′ 06″	7′ 06″
	(Kolbe '43-'86, Lois T. '86-'02)							
I-8	**ISLAND FERRY SERVICES CORP., CHEBOYGAN, MI**							
	Polaris	PF	1952	D	99*	60′ 02″	36′ 00″	8′ 06″
I-9	**ISLE ROYALE LINE INC., COPPER HARBOR, MI** *(isleroyale.com)*							
	Isle Royale Queen IV	PA/PK	1980	D	93*	98 09″	22′ 01″	7′ 00″
	(American Freedom, John Jay, Shuttle V, Danielle G, Harbor Commuter V)							
J-1	**J. W. WESTCOTT CO., DETROIT, MI** *(jwwestcott.com)*							
	J. W. Westcott II	MB	1949	D	11*	46′ 01″	13′ 04″	4′ 06″
	Built: Paasch Marine Service, Erie, PA; floating post office has its own U.S. zip code, 48222							
	Joseph J. Hogan	MB	1957	D	16*	40′ 00″	12′ 06″	5′ 00″
	Backup mailboat and water taxi for vessels docked at Great Lakes Steel / Zug Island (USCOE Ottawa '57-'95)							
J-2	**JOSEPH B. MARTIN, BEAVER ISLAND, MI**							
	Shamrock {1}	TB	1933	D	60*	64′ 00″	18′ 00″	7′ 04″
	Built: Pennsylvania Shipyard Inc., Beaumont, TX							
J-3	**JUBILEE QUEEN CRUISES, TORONTO, ON** *(jubileequeencruises.ca)*							
	Jubilee Queen	ES	1986	D	269*	122′ 00″	23′ 09″	5′ 05″
	(Pioneer Princess III '86-'89)							
J-4	**JULIO CONTRACTING CO., HANCOCK, MI**							
	Winnebago	TW	1945	D	14*	40′ 00″	10′ 02″	4′ 06″
K-1	**K-SEA CANADA CORP., HALIFAX, NS** *(k-sea.com)*							
	VESSELS CHARTERED TO PETRO-NAV INC., MONTREAL, QC							
	McCleary's Spirit	TK	1969	B	6,888*	379′ 09″	63′ 03″	33′ 08″
	Built: Boelwerf, Belgium (LeVent '69-'02)							
	William J. Moore	TB	1970	D	564*	135′ 00″	34′ 09″	19′ 04″
	Built: Adelaide Ship Construction Pty Ltd., Port Adelaide, S. Australia (Warrawee '70-'76, Seaspan Raider '76-'87, Raider '87-'87, Raider IV '87-'88, Alice A. '88-'02)							
K-2	**KEHOE MARINE CONSTRUCTION CO., LANSDOWNE, ON**							
	Houghton	TB	1944	D	15*	45′ 00″	13′ 00″	6′ 00″
K-3	**KELLEYS ISLAND BOAT LINES, MARBLEHEAD, OH** *(kelleysislandferry.com)*							
	Carlee Emily	PA/CF	1987	D	98*	101′ 00″	34′ 06″	10′ 00″
	Built: Blount Marine Corp., Warren, RI (Endeavor '87-'02)							
	Kayla Marie	PA/CF	1975	D	93*	122′ 00″	40′ 00″	8′ 00″
	Built: New Bern Shipyard, New Bern, NC (R. Bruce Etherige '75-'97)							
	Shirley Irene	PA/CF	1991	D	68*	160′ 00″	46′ 00″	9′ 00″
K-4	**KEWEENAW EXCURSIONS INC., HOUGHTON, MI** *(keweenawexcursions.com)*							
	Keweenaw Star	ES	1981	D	97*	110′ 00″	23′ 04″	6′ 03″
	Built: Camcraft Inc., Crown Point, LA (Atlantic Star, Privateer, De De Bruce)							

Mission Point, in the St. Marys River, seen from the *Indiana Harbor*. *(Sam Lapinski)*

Fleet #	Fleet Name Vessel Name	Type of Vessel	Year Built	Type of Engine	Cargo Cap. or Gross*	Overall Length	Breadth	Depth or Draft*
K-5	**KEYSTONE GREAT LAKES INC., BALA CYNWYD, PA** *(keyship.com)*							
	Great Lakes {2}	TK	1982	B	5,024*	414′ 00″	60′ 00″	30′ 00″
	Built: Bay Shipbuilding Co., Sturgeon Bay, WI (Amoco Great Lakes '82-'85)							
	Michigan {10}	AT	1982	D	293*	107′ 08″	34′ 00″	16′ 00″
	Built: Bay Shipbuilding Co., Sturgeon Bay, WI (Amoco Michigan '82-'85)							
	[ATB Michigan / Great Lakes {2} OA dimensions together]					454′ 00″	60′ 00″	30′ 00″
K-6	**KINDRA LAKE TOWING LP, DOWNERS GROVE, IL** *(kindralake.com)*							
	Buckley	TW	1958	D	94*	95′ 00″	26′ 00″	11′ 00″
	Built: Parker Bros. Shipyard, Houston, TX (Linda Brooks '58-'67, Eddie B. {2} '67-'95)							
	Morgan	TB	1974	D	134*	90′ 00″	30′ 00″	10′ 06″
	Built: Peterson Builders Inc., Sturgeon Bay, WI (Donald O'Toole '74-'86, Bonesey B. '86-'95)							
	Old Mission	TB	1945	D	94*	85′ 00″	23′ 00″	10′ 04″
	Built: Sturgeon Bay Shipbuilding, Sturgeon Bay, WI (U. S. Army ST-880 '45-'47, USCOE Avondale '47-'64, Adrienne B. '64-'95)							
	Tanner	TB	1976	D	62*	56′ 06″	22′ 00″	7′ 05″
K-7	**KING CO. INC., HOLLAND, MI**							
	Barry J	TB	1943	D	26*	46′ 00″	13′ 00″	7′ 00″
	Buxton II	DR	1976	B	147*	130′ 02″	28′ 01″	7′ 00″
	Built: Barbour Boat Works Inc., Holland, MI							
	Carol Ann	TB	1981	D	86*	61′ 05″	24′ 00″	8′ 07″
	Built: Rodriguez Boat Builders, Bayou La Batre, AL							
	John Henry	TB	1954	D	66*	65′ 04″	19′ 04″	9′ 06″
	Built: Missouri Valley Steel, Leavenworth, KS (U. S. Army ST-2013 '54-'80)							
	Julie Dee	TB	1937	D	64*	68′ 08″	18′ 01″	7′ 06″
	Built: Herbert Slade, Beaumont, TX (Bonita {1} '03-'16, Chicago Harbor No. 4 '16-'60, Eddie B. {1} '60-'69, Seneca Queen '69-'70, Ludington '70 -?)							
	Matt Allen	TB	1961	D	146*	80′ 04″	24′ 00″	11′ 03″
	Built: Nolty Theriot Inc., Golden Meadow, LA (Gladys Bea '61-'73, American Viking '73-'83, Maribeth Andrie '83-'05)							
	Miss Edna	TB	1935	D	13*	36′ 08″	11′ 02″	4′ 08″
K-8	**KINGSTON & THE ISLANDS BOAT LINES LTD., KINGSTON, ON** *(1000islandscruises.on.ca)*							
	Island Belle I	ES	1988	D	150*	65′ 00″	22′ 00″	8′ 00″
	(Spirit of Brockville '88-'91)							
	Island Queen III	ES	1975	D	300*	96′ 00″	26′ 00″	11′ 00″
	Island Star	ES	1994	D	220*	97′ 00″	30′ 00″	10′ 00″
	(Le Bateau-Mouche II '94-'98)							
	Papoose III	ES	1968	D	110*	64′ 08″	23′ 03″	7′ 03″
K-9	**KK INTEGRATED LOGISTICS, MENOMINEE, MI** *(kkwarehousing.com)*							
	William H. Donner	CS	1914	B	9,400	524′ 00″	54′ 00″	30′ 00″
	Built: Great Lakes Engineering Works, Ashtabula, OH; last operated in 1969; in use as a cargo transfer vessel at Marinette, WI							
	KK INTEGRATED SHIPPING LLC, MENOMINEE, MI							
	James L. Kuber	SU	1953	B	25,500	767′ 00″	70′ 00″	36′ 00″
	Built: Great Lakes Engineering Works, River Rouge, MI; lengthened 120′ by Fraser Shipyards, Superior, WI, in '75; converted to a self-unloader by Bay Shipbuilding, Sturgeon Bay, WI, in '83, converted to a barge by the owners in '07 (Reserve '53-'08)							
	Lewis J. Kuber	SU	1952	B	22,300	698′ 00″	70′ 00″	37′ 00″
	Built: Bethlehem Steel Corp., Sparrows Point, MD; lengthened by 72′ by American Shipbuilding, South Chicago, IL, in '58; converted to a self-unloader by Fraser Shipyards, Superior, WI, in '80; converted to a barge by Erie Shipbuilding, Erie, PA, in '06; operated by VanEnkevort Tug & Barge Inc. (Sparrows Point '52-'90, Buckeye {3} '90-'06)							
	Manitowoc	DB	1926	B	3,080*	371′ 03″	67′ 03″	22′ 06″
	Built: Manitowoc Shipbuilding Co., Manitowoc, WI; laid up at Marinette, WI							
	Olive L. Moore	AT	1928	D	301*	125′ 00″	27′ 01″	13′ 09″
	Built: Manitowoc Shipbuilding Co., Manitowoc, WI (John F. Cushing '28-'66, James E. Skelly '66-'66)							
	Victory	TB	1980	D	194*	129′ 00″	43′ 01″	18′ 00″
	Built: McDermott Shipyard Inc., Amelia, LA							
	Viking I	CF	1925	D	2,713*	360′ 00″	56′ 03″	21′ 06″
	Built: Manitowoc Shipbuilding Co, Manitowoc, WI; laid up at Marinette, WI (Ann Arbor No. 7 '25-'64, Viking {2} '64-'96)							

Fleet #.	Fleet Name / Vessel Name	Type of Vessel	Year Built	Type of Engine	Cargo Cap. or Gross*	Overall Length	Breadth	Depth or Draft*
L-1	**LAFARGE CANADA INC., MONTREAL, QC**							
	(THE FOLLOWING VESSEL MANAGED BY CANADA STEAMSHIP LINES INC.)							
	English River	CC	1961	D	7,450	404′ 03″	60′ 00″	36′ 06″
	Built: Canadian Shipbuilding and Engineering Ltd., Collingwood, ON; converted to a self-unloading cement carrier by Port Arthur Shipbuilding, Port Arthur (now Thunder Bay), ON, in '74							
L-2	**LAFARGE NORTH AMERICA INC., SOUTHFIELD, MI** *(lafargenorthamerica.com)*							
	J. B. Ford	CC	1904	R	8,000	440′ 00″	50′ 00″	28′ 00″
	Built: American Ship Building Co., Lorain, OH; converted to a self-unloading cement carrier in '59; last operated Nov. 15, 1985; most recently used as a cement storage and transfer vessel at Superior, WI, and now laid up at that port (Edwin F. Holmes '04-'16, E. C. Collins '16-'59)							
	THE FOLLOWING VESSELS MANAGED BY ANDRIE INC., MUSKEGON, MI *(andrie.com)*							
	G. L. Ostrander	AT	1976	D	198*	140′ 02″	40′ 01″	22′ 03″
	Built: Halter Marine, New Orleans, LA (Andrew Martin '76-'90, Robert L. Torres '90-'94, Jacklyn M '94-'04)							
	Integrity	CC	1996	B	14,000	460′ 00″	70′ 00″	37′ 00″
	Built: Bay Shipbuilding Co., Sturgeon Bay, WI							
	[ATB G.L. Ostrander / Integrity OA dimensions together]					543′ 00″	70′ 00″	37′ 00″
	Innovation	CC	2006	B	7,320*	460′ 00″	70′ 00″	37′ 00″
	Built: Bay Shipbuilding Co., Sturgeon Bay, WI							
	Samuel de Champlain	AT	1975	D	299*	140′ 02″	39′ 02″	20′ 00″
	Built: Mangone Shipbuilding, Houston, TX (Musketeer Fury '75-'78, Tender Panther '78-'79, Margarita '79-'83, Vortice '83-'99, Norfolk '99-'06)							
L-3	**LAKE COUNTY HISTORICAL SOCIETY, TWO HARBORS, MN** *(northshorehistory.com)*							
	Edna G.	MU	1896	R	154*	102′ 00″	23′ 00″	14′ 06″
	Built: Cleveland Shipbuilding Co., Cleveland, OH; former Duluth, Missabe & Iron Range Railroad tug last operated in 1981; open to the public at Two Harbors, MN							
L-4	**LAKE EXPRESS LLC, MILWAUKEE, WI** *(lake-express.com)*							
	Lake Express	PA/CF	2004	D	96*	179′ 02″	57′ 07″	16′ 00″
	Built: Austal USA, Mobile, AL; high-speed ferry in service from Milwaukee, WI, to Muskegon, MI							
L-5	**LAKE MICHIGAN CARFERRY SERVICE INC., LUDINGTON, MI** *(ssbadger.com)*							
	Badger	PA/CF	1953	S	4,244*	410′ 06″	59′ 06″	24′ 00″
	Built: Christy Corp, Sturgeon Bay, WI; traditional ferry in service from Ludington, MI, to Manitowoc, WI							
	Spartan	PA/CF	1952	S	4,244*	410′ 06″	59′ 06″	24′ 00″
	Built: Christy Corp, Sturgeon Bay, WI; last operated Jan. 20, 1979; in long-term layup at Ludington, MI							
L-6	**LAKE TOWING INC., CLEVELAND, OH**							
	Menominee	TB	1967	D	235*	108′ 00″	29′ 00″	14′ 00″
	Upper Canada	PA/CF	1949	D	165*	143′ 00″	36′ 00″	11′ 00″
	Vessel laid up in Lorain, OH (Romeo and Annette '49-'66)							
L-7	**LAKEN SHIPPING CORP., CLEVELAND, OH** *(www.seawaymarinetransport.com)*							
	VESSELS CHARTERED AND COMMERCIALLY MANAGED BY SMT (USA) INC.							
	Cleveland	TB	1999	D	392*	105′ 02″	34′ 01″	15′ 00″
	Built: C & G Boat Works, Bayou La Batre, AL (James Palladino '99-'04)							
	Cleveland Rocks	SU	1957	B	6,280*	390′ 00″	71′ 00″	27′ 00″
	Built: Todd Shipyards Corp., Houston, TX (M-211 '57-'81, Virginia '81-'88, C-11 '88-'93, Kellstone 1 '93-'04)							
L-8	**LAKES PILOTS ASSOCIATION, PORT HURON, MI** *(lakespilots.com)*							
	Huron Belle	PB	1979	D	21*	50′ 00″	16′ 00″	7′ 09″
	Built: Gladding-Hearn Shipbuilding, Somerset, MA; vessel offers pilot service at Port Huron, MI							
	Huron Maid	PB	1976	D	26*	46′ 00″	16′ 00″	3′ 05″
	Built: Hans Hansen Welding Co., Toledo, OH; vessel offers pilot service at Detroit, MI							
L-9	**LE GROUPE OCÉAN INC., QUÉBEC, QC** *(groupocean.com)*							
	Basse-Cote	DB	1932	B	400	201′ 00″	40′ 00″	12′ 00″
	Betsiamites	SU	1969	B	11,600	402′ 00″	75′ 00″	24′ 00″
	Coo-Coo	TB	1956	D	11*	35′ 00″	10′ 00″	4′ 04″
	Coucoucache	TB	1934	D	95*	34′ 01″	9′ 05″	4′ 02″
	David T. D.	TB	1947	D	22*	42′ 01″	12′ 03″	5′ 08″

Fleet #	Fleet Name Vessel Name	Type of Vessel	Year Built	Type of Engine	Cargo Cap. or Gross*	Overall Length	Breadth	Depth or Draft*
	H. E. Graham	TB	1964	D	7*	32′09″	9′05″	3′05″
	J. V. Perrin	TB	1958	D	8*	34′01″	10′00″	3′09″
	Jerry G.	TB	1960	D	202*	91′06″	27′03″	12′06″
	Built: Davie Shipbuilding Co., Lauzon, QC							
	Kim R. D.	TB	1954	D	30*	48′07″	14′01″	5′08″
	La Croche	TB	1940	D	7*	32′07″	9′05″	3′05″
	La Prairie	TB	1975	D	110*	73′09″	25′09″	11′08″
	Built: Georgetown Shipyard, Georgetown, PEI							
	Lac St-Francois	BC	1979	B	1,200	195′00″	35′00″	12′00″
	Built: Nashville Bridge Co., Nashhville, TN							
	Le Phil D.	TB	1961	D	38*	56′01″	16′00″	5′08″
	Mado-Ray	TB	1954	D	12*	38′00″	12′01″	3′03″
	Navcomar No. 1	DB	1955	B	500	135′00″	35′00″	9′00″
	Ocean Abys	DB	1948	B	1,000	140′00″	40′00″	9′00″
	Ocean Bravo	TB	1970	D	320*	110′00″	28′06″	17′00″
	Built: Davie Shipbuilding Co., Lauzon, QC (Takis V. '70-'80, Donald P '80-'80, Nimue '80-'83, Donald P. '83-'98)							
	Ocean Delta	TB	1973	D	722*	136′08″	35′08″	22′00″
	Built: Ulstein Mek. Verksted A.S., Ulsteinvik, Norway (Sistella '73-'78, Sandy Cape '78-'80, Captain Ioannis S. '80-'99)							
	Ocean Golf	TB	1959	D	159*	103′00″	25′10″	11′09″
	Built: P.K. Harris & Sons, Appledore, England (Launched as Stranton. Helen M. McAllister '59-'97)							
	Ocean Henry Bain	TB	2006	D	402*	94′08″	30′01″	14′09″
	Built: East Isle Shipyard, Georgetown, PEI							
	Ocean Hercule	TB	1976	D	448*	120′00″	32′00″	19′00″
	(Stril Pilot '76-'81, Spirit Sky '81-'86, Ierland '86-'89, Ierlandia '89-'95, Charles Antoine '95-'97)							
	Ocean Intrepide	TT	1998	D	302*	80′00″	30′01″	14′09″
	Built: Industries Ocean Inc., Ile-Aux-Coudres, QC							
	Ocean Jupiter {2}	TT	1999	D	302*	80′00″	30′00″	13′04″
	Built: Industries Ocean Inc., Ile-Aux-Coudres, QC							
	Ocean K. Rusby	TB	2005	D	402*	94′08″	30′01″	14′09″
	Built: East Isle Shipyard, Georgetown, PEI							
	Ocean Raymond Lemay	TB	2006	D	402*	94′08″	30′01″	14′09″
	Built: East Isle Shipyard, Georgetown, PEI							
	Omni-Atlas	CS	1913	B	479*	133′00″	42′00″	10′00″
	Omni-Richelieu	TB	1969	D	144*	83′00″	24′06″	13′06″
	Built: Pictou Industries Ltd., Pictou, NS (Port Alfred II '69-'82)							
	Omni St. Laurent	TB	1957	D	161*	99′02″	24′09″	12′06″
	Built: P.K. Harris & Sons, Appledore, England (Diligent '57-'89)							
	Rapide Blanc	TB	1951	D	10*	34′00″	10′00″	4′03″
	Roxane D.	TB	1945	D	50*	60′06″	16′06″	6′07″
	OCÉAN REMORQUAGE TROIS-RIVIÈRES INC. – SUBSIDIARY OF LE GROUPE OCÉAN INC.							
	Andre H.	TB	1963	D	317*	126′00″	28′06″	15′06″
	Built: Davie Shipbuilding Co., Lauzon, QC (Foundation Valiant '63-'73, Point Valiant {1} '73-'95)							
	Avantage	TB	1969	D	367*	116′10″	32′09″	16′03″
	Built: J. Boel En Zonen, Temse, Belgium (Sea Lion '69-'97)							
	Duga	TB	1977	D	403*	111′00″	33′00″	16′01″
	Escorte	TT	1964	D	120*	85′00″	23′08″	11′00″
	Built: Jakobson Shipyard, Oyster Bay, NY (USS Menasha [YTB / YTM-773, YTM-761] '64-'92, Menasha {1} '92-'95)							
	Josee H.	PB	1961	D	66*	63′50″	16′02″	9′50″
	Ocean Charlie	TB	1973	D	448*	123′02″	31′06″	18′09″
	Built: Davie Shipbuilding Co., Lauzon, QC (Leonard W. '73-'98)							
	Ocean Echo II	AT	1969	D	438*	104′08″	35′05″	18′00″
	Built: Port Weller Dry Docks, Port Weller, ON (Atlantic '69-'75, Laval '75-'96)							
	Ocean Foxtrot	TB	1971	D	700*	184′05″	38′05″	16′07″
	Built: Cochrane & Sons Ltd., Selby, England (Polar Shore '71-'77, Canmar Supplier VII '77-'95)							
	R. F. Grant	TB	1969	D	78*	71′00″	17′00″	8′00″
	Built: Canadian Vickers Ltd., Montreal, QC							
	Service Boat No. 1	PB	1965	D	55*	57′08″	16′01″	7′06″
	Service Boat No. 4	PB	1959	D	26*	39′01″	14 02″	6′03″

Fleet #.	Fleet Name Vessel Name	Type of Vessel	Year Built	Type of Engine	Cargo Cap. or Gross*	Overall Length	Breadth	Depth or Draft*
L-10	**LE SAULT DE SAINTE MARIE HISTORIC SITES INC., SAULT STE. MARIE, MI** *(saulthistoricsites.com)*							
	Valley Camp {2}	MU	1917	R	12,000	550′ 00″	58′ 00″	31′ 00″
	Built: American Shipbuilding Co., Lorain, OH; former Hanna Mining Co./Wilson Marine Transit Co./Republic Steel Corp. bulk carrier last operated in 1966; open to the public at Sault Ste. Marie, MI (Louis W. Hill '17-'55)							
L-11	**LEE MARINE LTD., SOMBRA, ON** *(hammondbaycruises.com)*							
	Hammond Bay	ES	1992	D	43*	54′ 00″	16′ 00″	3′ 00″
	Built: Donald Mummery, Port Dover, ON (Scrimp & Scrounge '92-'95)							
	Nancy A. Lee	TB	1939	D	9*	40′ 00″	12′ 00″	3′ 00″
L-12	**LOCK TOURS CANADA BOAT CRUISES, SAULT STE. MARIE, ON** *(locktours.com)*							
	Chief Shingwauk	ES	1965	D	109*	70′ 00″	24′ 00″	4′ 06″
L- 13	**LOGISTEC CORP., MONTREAL, QC**							
	Umiavut	GC	1988	D	9,682	371′ 02″	63′ 01″	37′ 00″
	Built: Miho Shipbuilding Co. Ltd., Shimizu Shizuoka Prefecture, Japan; operated by Spliethoff's, Amsterdam, Netherlands (Completed as Newca; Kapitan Silin '88-'92, Lindengracht '92-'00)							
L-14	**LOWER LAKES TOWING LTD., PORT DOVER, ON** *(lowerlakes.com)*							
	Cuyahoga	SU	1943	D	15,675	620′ 00″	60′ 00″	35′ 00″
	Built: American Shipbuilding Co., Lorain, OH; converted to a self-unloader by Manitowoc Shipbuilding Co., Manitowoc, WI, in 74; repowered in '01 (J. Burton Ayers '43-'95)							
	Kaministiquia	BC	1983	D	33,824	730′ 00″	75′ 09″	48′ 00″
	Built: Govan Shipyards, Glasgow, Scotland (Saskatchewan Pioneer '83-'95, Lady Hamilton '95-'06, Voyageur Pioneer '06-'08)							
	Michipicoten {2}	SU	1952	T	22,300	698′ 00″	70′ 00″	37′ 00″
	Built: Bethlehem Shipbuilding & Drydock Co., Sparrows Point, MD; lengthened 72′ by American Shipbuilding, S. Chicago, IL, in '57; converted to a self-unloader by American Shipbuilding, Toledo, OH, in '80 (Elton Hoyt 2nd '52-'03)							
	Mississagi	SU	1943	D	15,800	620′ 06″	60′ 00″	35′ 00″
	Built: Great Lakes Engineering Works, River Rouge, MI; converted to a self-unloader by Fraser Shipyards, Superior, WI, in '67; repowered in '85 (Hill Annex '43-'43, George A. Sloan '43-'01)							
	Ojibway	BC	1952	D	20,668	642′ 03″	67′ 00″	35′ 00″
	Built: Defoe Shipbuilding Co., Bay City, MI; repowered in '05 (Charles L. Hutchinson {3} '52-'62, Ernest R. Breech '62-'88, Kinsman Independent '88-'05, Voyageur Independent '05-'08)							
	Robert S. Pierson	SU	1974	D	19,650	630′ 00″	68′ 00″	36′ 11″
	Built: American Shipbuilding Co., Lorain, OH (Wolverine {2} '74- '08)							
	Saginaw {3}	SU	1953	D	20,200	639′ 03″	72′ 00″	36′ 00″
	Built: Manitowoc Shipbuilding Co., Manitowoc, WI, repowered in '08 (John J. Boland {3} '53-'99)							
L-15	**LOWER LAKES TRANSPORTATION CO., WILLIAMSVILLE, NY, A DIVISION OF LOWER LAKES TOWING LTD.** *(lowerlakes.com)*							
	GRAND RIVER NAVIGATION CO., CLEVELAND, OH – OWNER – AFFILIATE OF LOWER LAKES TOWING LTD.							
	Manitowoc	SU	1973	D	19,650	630′ 00″	68′ 00″	36′ 11″
	Built: American Shipbuilding Co., Lorain, OH (William R. Roesch '73-'95, David Z. Norton {3} '95-'07, David Z. '07-'08)							
	Calumet {2}	SU	1973	D	19,650	630′ 00″	68′ 00″	36′ 11″
	Built: American Shipbuilding Co., Lorain, OH (Paul Thayer '73-'95, Earl W. Oglebay '95-'07, Earl W. '07-'08)							
	Invincible	ATB	1979	D	180*	100′ 00″	35′ 00″	22′ 06″
	Built: Atlantic Marine Inc., Fort George Island, FL (R. W. Sesler '79-'91)							
	Manistee	SU	1943	D	14,900	620′ 06″	60′ 03″	35′ 00″
	Built: Great Lakes Engineering Works, River Rouge, MI; converted to a self-unloader by Manitowoc Shipbuilding Co., Manitowoc, WI, in '64; repowered in '76 (Launched as Adirondack. Richard J. Reiss {2} '43-'86, Richard Reiss '86-'05)							
	Maumee	SU	1929	D	12,650	604′ 09″	60′ 00″	32′ 00″
	Built: American Shipbuilding Co., Lorain, OH; converted to a self-unloader by Manitowoc Shipbuilding Co., Manitowoc, WI, in '61; repowered in '64 (William G. Clyde '29-'61, Calcite II '61-'01)							
	LAKE SERVICE SHIPPING CO., GROSSE POINTE FARMS, MI – OWNER							
	McKee Sons	SU	1945	B	19,900	579′ 02″	71′ 06″	38′ 06″
	Built: Sun Shipbuilding and Drydock Co., Chester, PA; converted from saltwater vessel to a self-unloading Great Lakes bulk carrier by Maryland Drydock, Baltimore, MD, in '52; completed as a self-unloader by Manitowoc Shipbuilding Co., Manitowoc, WI, in '53; engine removed and converted to a self-unloading barge by Upper Lakes Towing, Escanaba, MI, in '91 (USNS Marine Angel '45-'52)							
	[ATB McKee Sons / Invincible OA dimensions together]					615′ 00″	71′ 06″	38′ 06″

Fleet #	Fleet Name / Vessel Name	Type of Vessel	Year Built	Type of Engine	Cargo Cap. or Gross*	Overall Length	Breadth	Depth or Draft*
L-16	**LUEDTKE ENGINEERING CO., FRANKFORT, MI** *(luedtke-eng.com)*							
	Alan K. Luedtke	TB	1944	D	149*	86′ 04″	23′ 00″	10′ 03″
	Built: Allen Boat Co., Harvey, LA (U. S. Army ST-527 '44-'55, USCOE Two Rivers '55-'90)							
	Ann Marie	TB	1954	D	119*	71′ 00″	19′ 06″	9′ 06″
	Built: Smith Basin & Drydock, Pensacola, FL (ST-9684 '54- '80, Lewis Castle '80-'97, Apache '97-'01)							
	Chris E. Luedtke	TB	1936	D	18*	42′ 05″	11′ 09″	5′ 00″
	Erich R. Luedtke	TB	1939	D	18*	42′ 05″	11′ 09″	5′ 00″
	Gretchen B.	TB	1943	D	18*	41′ 09″	12′ 05″	6′ 00″
	Karl E. Luedtke	TB	1928	D	32*	55′ 02″	14′ 09″	6′ 00″
	Buit: Leathem D. Smith Dock Co., Sturgeon Bay, WI							
	Kurt R. Luedtke	TB	1956	D	96*	72′ 00″	22′ 06″	7′ 06″
	Built: Lockport Shipyard, Lockport, LA (Jere C. '56-'90)							
M-1	**M. C. M. MARINE INC., SAULT STE. MARIE, MI** *(mcmmarine.com)*							
	Beaver State	TB	1935	D	18*	43′ 07″	12′ 00″	5′ 02″
	Drummond Islander II	CF	1961	D	97*	65′ 00″	36′ 00″	9′ 00″
	Built: Marinette Marine Corp., Marinette, WI							
	Mackinaw City	TB	1943	D	23*	38′ 00″	11′ 05″	4′ 07″
	Mohawk	TB	1945	D	46*	65′ 00″	19′ 00″	10′ 06″
	Built: Robert Jacob Inc., City Island, NY							
	No. 55	DR	1927	DE	721*	165′ 00″	42′ 08″	12′ 00″
	No. 56	DR	1927	DE	721*	165′ 00″	42′ 08″	12′ 00″
	Ojibway	SB	1945	D	65*	53′ 00″	28′ 00″	7′ 00″
	Built: Great Lakes Engineering Works, Ashtabula, OH							
	Peach State	TB	1961	D	19*	42′ 01″	12′ 04″	5′ 03″
	Sioux	DS	1954	B	504*	120′ 00″	50′ 00″	10′ 00″

Tug *LaPrairie* and the *Spruceglen* departing Hamilton. *(John McCreery)*

Fleet #.	Fleet Name Vessel Name	Type of Vessel	Year Built	Type of Engine	Cargo Cap. or Gross*	Overall Length	Breadth	Depth or Draft*
	William C. Gaynor	TB	1956	D	146*	94' 00"	27' 00"	11' 09"
	Built: Defoe Shipbuilding Co., Bay City, MI (William C. Gaynor '56-'88, Captain Barnaby '88-'02)							
M-2	**MACASSA BAY LIMITED, CORUNNA, ON** *(macassabay.com)*							
	Macassa Bay	ES	1986	D	200*	93' 07"	29' 07"	10' 04"
	Built: Boiler Pump & Marine Works Ltd., Hamilton, ON							
M-3	**MacDONALD MARINE LTD., GODERICH, ON** *(mactug.com)*							
	Debbie Lyn	TB	1950	D	10*	45' 00"	14' 00"	10' 00"
	Built: Mathieson Boat Works, Goderich, ON (Skipper '50-'60)							
	Donald Bert	TB	1953	D	11*	45' 00"	14' 00"	10' 00"
	Built: Mathieson Boat Works, Goderich, ON							
	Dover	TB	1931	D	70*	84' 00"	17' 00"	6' 00"
	Built: Canadian Mead-Morrison Co. Ltd., Welland, ON (Earleejune, Iveyrose)							
	Ian Mac	TB	1955	D	12*	45' 00"	14' 00"	10' 00"
	Built: Mathieson Boat Works, Goderich, ON							
M-4	**MADELINE ISLAND FERRY LINE INC., LaPOINTE, WI** *(madferry.com)*							
	Bayfield {2}	PA/CF	1952	D	83*	120' 00"	43' 00"	10' 00"
	Built: Chesapeake Marine Railway, Deltaville, VA (Charlotte '52-'99)							
	Island Queen {2}	PA/CF	1966	D	90*	75' 00"	34' 09"	10' 00"
	Madeline	PA/CF	1984	D	97*	90' 00"	35' 00"	8' 00"
	Nichevo II	PA/CF	1962	D	89*	65' 00"	32' 00"	8' 09"
M-5	**MAID OF THE MIST STEAMBOAT CO. LTD., NIAGARA FALLS, ON** *(maidofthemist.com)*							
	Maid of the Mist IV	ES	1976	D	74*	72' 00"	16' 00"	7' 00"
	Maid of the Mist V	ES	1983	D	74*	72' 00"	16' 00"	7' 00"
	Maid of the Mist VI	ES	1990	D	155*	78' 09"	29' 06"	7' 00"
	Maid of the Mist VII	ES	1997	D	160*	80' 00"	30' 00"	7' 00"
M-6	**MALCOLM MARINE, ST. CLAIR, MI**							
	Manitou {2}	TB	1942	D	491*	110' 00"	26' 05"	11' 06"
	Built: U.S. Coast Guard, Curtis Bay, MD (USCGC Manitou [WYT-60] '43-'84)							
M-7	**MANITOU ISLAND TRANSIT, LELAND, MI** *(leelanau.com/manitou)*							
	Manitou Isle	PA/PK	1946	D	39*	52' 00"	14' 00"	8' 00"
	(Namaycush '46-'59)							
	Mishe-Mokwa	PA/CF	1966	D	49*	65' 00"	17' 06"	8' 00"
M-8	**MARINE ONE TOWING & SALVAGE LTD., DETROIT, MI** *(marineonetowing.com)*							
	Acushnet	TB	1943	D	58*	65' 00"	18' 00"	7' 03"
	Built: Sturgeon Bay Shipbuilding & Dry Dock Co., Sturgeon Bay, WI (LaSalle '66-'80)							
M-9	**MARINE MUSEUM OF THE GREAT LAKES AT KINGSTON, KINGSTON, ON** *(marmuseum.ca)*							
	Alexander Henry	MU	1959	D	1,674*	210' 00"	44' 00"	17' 09"
	Built: Port Arthur Shipbuilding Co., Port Arthur, ON; former Canadian Coast Guard icebreaker was retired in 1985; open to the public at Kingston, ON							
M-10	**MARINE TECH LLC, DULUTH, MN** *(marinetechduluth.com)*							
	Alton Andrew	CS	1958	B		70' 00"	50' 00	6' 00"
	(No. 1 '58-'01)							
	Callie M.	TB	1910	D	51*	64' 03"	16' 09"	8' 06"
	Built: Houma Shipbuilding Co., Houma, LA (Chattanooga '10-'79, Howard T. Hagen '79-'94, Nancy Ann '94-'01)							
	Dean R. Smith	DR	1985	B	338*	120' 00"	48' 00"	7' 00"
	(No. 2 '85-'94, B. Yetter '94-'01)							
	Miss Laura	TB	1943	D	146*	81' 01"	24' 00"	9' 10"
	Built: Lawley & Son Corp., Neponset, MA (DPC-3 '43-'46, DS-43 '46-'50, Fresh Kills '50-'69, Richard K. '69-'93, Leopard '93-'03)							
M-11	**MARIPOSA CRUISE LINE LTD., TORONTO, ON** *(mariposacruises.com)*							
	Capt. Matthew Flinders	ES	1982	D	696*	144' 00"	40' 00"	8' 06"
	Built: North Arm Slipway Pty. Ltd., Port Adelaide, Australia							
	Mariposa Belle	ES	1970	D	195*	93' 00"	23' 00"	8' 00"
	Built: Hike Metal Products, Wheatley, ON (Niagara Belle '70-'73)							

Algosteel **greets the sunrise anchored off Marquette.** *(Rod Burdick)*

Fleet #.	Fleet Name Vessel Name	Type of Vessel	Year Built	Type of Engine	Cargo Cap. or Gross*	Overall Length	Breadth	Depth or Draft*
	Rosemary	ES	1960	D	52*	68′ 00″	15′ 06″	6′ 08″
	Showboat Royal Grace	ES	1988	D	135*	58′ 00″	18′ 00″	4′ 00″
	Torontonian	ES	1962	D	68*	68′ 00″	18′ 06″	6′ 08″
	(Shiawassie '62-'82)							
M-12	**MAXIMUS CORP., BLOOMFIELD HILLS, MI** *(boblosteamers.com)*							
	Ste. Claire	PA	1910	R	870*	197′ 00″	65′ 00″	14′ 00″
	Built: Detroit Dry Dock Co, Detroit, MI; former Detroit to Bob-Lo Island passenger steamer last operated Sept. 2, 1991; undergoing restoration at Detroit, MI							
M-13	**McASPHALT MARINE TRANSPORTATION LTD., SCARBOROUGH, ON** *(mcasphalt.com)*							
	Everlast	ATB	1976	D	1,361*	143′ 04″	44′ 04″	21′ 04″
	Built: Hakodate Dock Co., Hakodate, Japan (Bilibino '77-'96)							
	John J. Carrick	TK	2008	B	11,613	407′ 06″	71′ 07″	30′ 00″
	Built: Penglai Bohai Shipyard Co., Ltd., Penglai, China							
	McAsphalt 401	TK	1966	B	7,399	300′ 00″	60′ 00″	23′ 00″
	Built: Todd Shipyards Corp., Houston, TX (Pittson 200 '66-'73, Pointe Levy '73-'87)							
	Norman McLeod	TK	2001	B	6,809*	379′ 02″	71′ 06″	30′ 02″
	Built: Jinling Shipyard, Nanjing, China							
	[ATB Everlast / Norman McLeod OA dimensions together]					500′ 00″	71′ 06″	30′ 02″
M-14	**McCULLOUGH CONSTRUCTION INC., PORT CLINTON, OH**							
	Manitou	TB	1934	D	19*	40′ 00″	10′ 00″	4′ 06″
M-15	**McKEIL MARINE LTD., HAMILTON, ON** *(mckeilmarine.com)*							
	Alouette Spirit	DB	1969	B	11,318*	415′ 06″	74′ 01″	29′ 05″
	Built: Gulfport Shipbuilding Co., Port Arthur, TX (KTC 135 '69-'04, Lambert's Spirit '04-'05)							
	Bonnie B. III	TB	1969	D	308*	100′ 03″	32′ 00″	17′ 00″
	(Esso Oranjestad '69-'85, Oranjestad '85-'86, San Nicolas '86-'87, San Nicolas I '87-'88)							
	Carrol C. I	TB	1969	D	291*	100′ 03″	32′ 00″	17′ 00″
	Built: Gulfport Shipbuilding Corp., Port Arthur, TX (Esso San Nicolas '69-'86, San Nicolas '86-'87, Carrol C '87-'88)							
	Condarrell	DH	1953	D	3,017	259′ 00″	43′ 06″	21′ 00″
	Built: Canadian Shipbuilding & Engineering, Kingston, ON; laid up at Port Colborne, ON (D. C. Everest '53-'81)							
	Daniele M.	TB	1984	D	251*	85′ 01″	30′ 00″	12′ 07″
	Built: Sabah Shipyard., Labaun, Malaysia (Smit Bonaire '84-'06)							
	Erie-West	DB	1951	B	1,800	290′ 00″	50′ 00″	12′ 00″
	Built: Dravo Corp., Pittsburgh, PA Dover Light)							
	Evans McKeil	TB	1936	D	284*	110′ 07″	25′ 06″	11′ 06″
	Built: Panama Canal Co., Balbo, Panama (Alhajuela '36-'70, Barbara Ann {2} '70-'89)							
	Flo-Mac	TB	1960	D	15*	40′ 00″	13′ 00″	6′ 00″
	Florence M.	TB	1961	D	236*	96′ 03″	28′ 00″	14′ 06″
	Built: P.K. Harris & Sons, Appledore, England (Foundation Vibert '61-'73, Point Vibert '73-'06)							
	General Chemical No. 37	TK	1956	D	883*	208′ 08″	42′ 08″	13′ 07″
	Built: Todd Shipyard, Houston, TX							
	James E. McGrath	TB	1963	D	90*	77′ 00″	20′ 00″	10′ 09″
	Built: Port Weller Drydock, Port Weller, ON							
	Jarrett M	TB	1945	D	96*	82′ 00″	20′ 00″	10′ 00″
	Built: Russel Brothers Ltd., Owen Sound, ON (Atomic '45-'06)							
	Jarrett McKeil	TB	1956	D	197*	91′ 08″	27′ 04″	13′ 06″
	Built: Davie Shipbuilding Co., Lauzon, QC (Robert B. No. 1 '56-'97)							
	Jean-Raymond	DB	1941	B	6,800	409′ 00″	57′ 00″	18′ 00″
	John Spence	TB	1972	D	719*	171′ 00″	38′ 00″	15′ 01″
	Built: Star Shipyard, New Westminister, BC (Mary B. VI '72-'81, Mary B. '81-'82, Mary B. VI '82-'83, Artic Tuktu '83-'94)							
	Lac Manitoba	TB	1944	D	65*	65′ 00″	16′ 10″	7′ 07″
	Built: Central Bridge Co., Trenton, ON (Tanac 75 '44-'52, Manitoba '52-'57)							
	Lambert Spirit	DB	1968	B	9,645	393′ 07″	69′ 08″	27′ 05″
	Built: Avondale Shipyards Inc., Avondale, LA (KTC 115 '68 - '06)							
	Molly M. 1	TB	1962	D	207*	98′ 05″	26′ 10″	13′ 05″
	Built: Davie Shipbuilding Co., Lauzon, QC (Foundation Vigour '62-'74, Point Vigour '74-'07)							
	Nicole M.	TB	1984	D	251*	85′ 01″	30′ 00″	12′ 07″
	Built: Sabah Shipyard., Labaun, Malaysia (Smit Aruba '84-'06)							

Fleet #	Fleet Name Vessel Name	Type of Vessel	Year Built	Type of Engine	Cargo Cap. or Gross*	Overall Length	Breadth	Depth or Draft*
	Ocean Hauler	TK	1943	B	4,540*	344′ 00″	69′ 00″	96′ 00″
	Pacific Standard	TB	1967	D	451*	127′ 08″	31′ 00″	15′ 06″
	Built: Cochrane & Sons Ltd., Selby, Yorkshire, England (Irishman '67-'76, Kwakwani '76-'78, Lorna B. '78-'81)							
	Salvor	TB	1963	D	426*	120′ 00″	32′ 09″	18′ 09″
	Built: Jakobson Shipyard, Oyster Bay, NY (Esther Moran '63-'00)							
	Sault au Cochon	DH	1969	B	9,600	337′ 10″	74′ 10″	25′ 07″
	Built: Port Weller Dry Dock, Port Weller, ON							
	Stormont	TB	1953	D	108*	80′ 00″	20′ 00″	15′ 00″
	Built: Canadian Dredge & Dock Co., Kingston, ON							
	Techno-Venture	TB	1939	D	469*	138′ 03″	30′ 06″	18′ 09″
	Built: Blyth Drydocks & Shipbuilding Co., Northumberland, England (M.I.L. Venture)							
	Tony MacKay	TB	1973	D	366*	127′ 00″	30′ 05″	14′ 05″
	Built: Richard Dunston Ltd., Hessle, England (Point Carroll '73-'01)							
	Viateur's Spirit	DB	2004	D	253*	141′ 01″	52′ 03″	5′ 01″
	Built: Port Weller Dry Dock, Port Weller, ON (Traverse René Lavasseur '04-'06)							
	Wilf Seymour	TB	1961	D	429*	120′ 00″	32′ 09″	18′ 09″
	Built: Gulfport Shipbuilding, Port Arthur, TX (M. Moran '61-'70, Port Arthur '70-'72, M. Moran '72-'00, Salvager '00-'04)							
	Willmac	TB	1959	D	16*	40′ 00″	13′ 00″	3′ 07″
	Wyatt M.	TB	1948	D	123*	86′ 00″	21′ 00″	10′ 00″
	Built: Russel Brothers Ltd., Owen Sound, ON (P. J. Murer '48-'81, Michael D. Misner '81-'93, Thomas A. Payette '93-'96, Progress '96-'06)							
	McKEIL SHIPS LTD. – A SUBSIDIARY OF McKEIL MARINE LTD., HAMILTON, ON							
	Kathryn Spirit	GC	1967	D	12,497	503′ 03″	66′ 07″	36′ 09″
	Built: Lindholmen Shipyard, Gothenburg, Sweden (Holmsund '67-'97, Menominee '97-'06)							
	MONTREAL BOATMEN LTD. – A SUBSIDIARY OF McKEIL MARINE LTD., VALLEYFIELD, QC							
	Aldo H.	PB	1979	D	37*	56′ 04″	15′ 04″	6′ 02″
	Boatman No. 3	PB	1965	D	13*	33′ 08″	11′ 00″	6′ 00″
	Boatman No. 6	PB	1979	D	39*	56′ 07″	18′ 07″	6′ 03″
M-16	**McLEOD BROTHERS MECHANICAL, SAULT STE. MARIE, ON**							
	Kam	TB	1927	D	33*	52′ 00″	13′ 00″	5′ 06″
	(North Shore Supply '27-'74)							
M-17	**McMULLEN & PITZ CONSTRUCTION CO., MANITOWOC, WI** *(mcmullenandpitz.net)*							
	Dauntless	TB	1937	D	25*	52′ 06″	15′ 06″	5′ 03″
	Erich	TB	1943	D	19*	45′ 00″	12′ 07″	5′ 09″
M-18	**McNALLY CONSTRUCTION INC., HAMILTON, ON** *(mcnallycorp.com)*							
	Bagotville	TB	1964	D	65*	65′ 00″	18′ 06″	10′ 00″
	Built: Verreault Navigation, Les Mechins, QC							
	Canadian	DR	1954	B	1,087*	173′ 08″	49′ 08″	13′ 04″
	Canadian Argosy	DR	1978	B	951*	149′ 09″	54′ 01″	10′ 08″
	Cargo Master	CS	1964	B	561*	136′ 00″	50′ 00″	9′ 00″
	Carl M.	TB	1957	D	21*	47′ 00″	14′ 06″	6′ 00″
	Greta V	TB	1951	D	14*	44′ 00″	12′ 00″	5′ 00″
	Handy Andy	DB	1925	B	313*	95′ 09″	43′ 01″	10′ 00″
	Idus Atwell	DR	1962	B	366*	100′ 00″	40′ 00″	8′ 05″
	Jerry Newberry	TB	1956	D	244*	98′ 00″	28′ 02″	14′ 04″
	Built: Davie Shipbuilding Co., Lauzon, QC (Foundation Victor '56-'73, Point Victor '73-'77, Kay Cole '77-'95)							
	John Holden	DR	1954	B	148*	89′ 08″	30′ 01″	6′ 02″
	Lac Como	TB	1944	D	63*	65′ 00″	16′ 10″	7′ 10″
	Built: Canadian Bridge Co., Walkerville, ON (Tanac 74 '44-'64)							
	Lac Vancouver	TB	1943	D	65*	65′ 00″	16′ 10″	7′ 07″
	Built: Central Bridge Co., Trenton, ON (Vancouver '43-'74)							
	Paula M.	TB	1959	D	12*	46′ 06″	16′ 01″	4′ 10″
	R. C. L. Tug II	TB	1958	D	20*	42′ 09″	14′ 03″	5′ 09″
	Sandra Mary	TB	1962	D	97*	80′ 00″	21′ 00″	10′ 09″
	Built: Russel Brothers Ltd., Owen Sound, ON (Flo Cooper '62-'00)							
	Whitby	TB	1978	D	24*	45′ 00″	14′ 00″	5′ 00″

***Burns Harbor* on the St. Marys River.** *(Roger LeLievre)*

Fleet #	Fleet Name / Vessel Name	Type of Vessel	Year Built	Type of Engine	Cargo Cap. or Gross*	Overall Length	Breadth	Depth or Draft*
	BEAVER MARINE LTD. – A SUBSIDIARY OF McNALLY CONSTRUCTION INC., HALIFAX, NS							
	Beaver Delta II	TB	1959	D	14*	35′ 08″	12′ 00″	4′ 04″
	(Halcyon Bay)							
	Beaver Gamma	TB	1960	D	17*	37′ 01″	12′ 09″	6′ 00″
	(Burlington Bertie)							
	Beaver Kay	GC	1953	B	614*	115′ 01″	60′ 00″	9′ 05″
	Dapper Dan	TB	1948	D	21*	41′ 03″	12′ 07″	5′ 09″
	Jamie L.	TB	1988	D	25*	36′ 04″	14′ 07″	5′ 09″
	(Baie Ste-Anne II '88-'05)							
	Mister Joe	TB	1964	D	70*	61′ 00″	19′ 00″	7′ 02″
	Oshawa	TB	1969	D	24*	42′ 09″	13′ 08″	5′ 04″
	William B. Dilly	DR	1957	B	473*	116′ 00″	39′ 10″	9′ 01″
M-19	**MENASHA TUGBOAT CO., SARNIA, ON**							
	Charles XX	DB	1965	B	219*	109′ 7″	31′ 09″	7′ 01″
	Menasha {2}	TB	1949	D	147*	78′ 00″	24′ 00″	9′ 08″
	Built: Bludworth, Houston, TX (W. C. Harms '49-'54, Hamilton '54-'86, Ruby Casho '86-'88, W. C. Harms '88-'97)							
M-20	**MERCURY CHICAGO'S SKYLINE CRUISELINE, CHICAGO, IL** *(mercuryskylinecruiseline.com)*							
	Chicago's First Lady	ES	1991	D	62*	96′ 00″	22′ 00″	9′ 00″
	Chicago's Little Lady	ES	1999	D	70*	69′ 02″	22′ 08″	7′ 00″
	Skyline Princess	ES	1956	D	56*	59′ 04″	16′ 00″	4′ 08″
	Skyline Queen	ES	1959	D	45*	61′ 05″	16′ 10″	6′ 00″
M-21	**MICHIGAN DEPARTMENT OF NATURAL RESOURCES, LANSING, MI** *(michigan.gov/dnr)*							
	Channel Cat	RV	1968	D	24*	46′ 00″	13′ 06″	4′ 00″
	Lake Char	RV	2006	D	26*	56′ 00″	16′ 00″	4′ 05″
	Steelhead	RV	1967	D	70*	63′ 00″	16′ 04″	6′ 06″
M-22	**MIDDLE BASS BOAT LINE, MIDDLE BASS, OH**							
	Victory	PA/CF	1960	D	14*	63′ 07″	15′ 03″	4′ 08″
M-23	**MIDLAND TOURS INC., MIDLAND, ON** *(midlandtours.com)*							
	Miss Midland	ES	1974	D	119*	68′ 07″	19′ 04″	6′ 04″
	Serendipity Princess	ES	1982	D	93*	69′ 00″	23′ 00″	4′ 03″
	(Trent Voyageur '82-'87, Serendipity Lady '87-'95)							
M-24	**MIDWEST MARITIME CORP., MILWAUKEE, WI**							
	Leona B.	TB	1972	D	99*	59′ 08″	24′ 01″	10′ 03″
	(Kings Squire '72-'89, Juanita D. '78-'89, Peggy Ann '89-'93, Mary Page Hannah {2} '93-'04)							
M-25	**MIKE OJARD, KNIFE RIVER, MN**							
	Edward H.	TB	1944	D	142*	86′ 00″	23′ 00″	10′ 04″
	Built: Equitable Equipment Co., Madisonville, LA (ST-707 '44-'60, Forney '60-'07)							
M-26	**MIKE SCHOLZ, SAULT STE. MARIE, ON**							
	Park State	TB	1938	D	16*	45′ 00″	12′ 00″	5′ 00″
	Inactive at Sault Ste. Marie, ON (Hoosier State '49-'62, Tommy B. '62-'06)							
	Seneca	TB	1939	DE	132*	94′ 20″	22′ 00″	9′ 00″
	(General {1} '39-'39, Raymond Card '39-'40, USS Keshena '40-'47, Mary L. McAllister '47-'81)							
M-27	**MILLER BOAT LINE, PUT-IN-BAY, OH** *(millerferry.com)*							
	Islander {3}	PA/CF	1983	D	92*	90′ 03″	38′ 00″	8′ 03″
	Put-In-Bay {3}	PA/CF	1997	D	95*	96′ 00″	38′ 06″	9′ 06″
	South Bass	PA/CF	1989	D	95*	96′ 00″	38′ 06″	9′ 06″
	Wm. Market	PA/CF	1993	D	95*	96′ 00″	38′ 06″	8′ 09″
M- 28	**MILWAUKEE BOAT LINE, MILWAUKEE, WI** *(mkeboat.com)*							
	Iroquois	PA	1922	D	91*	61′ 09″	21′ 00″	6′ 04″
	Voyageur	PA	1988	D	94*	67′ 02″	21′ 00″	7′ 04″
M-29	**MILWAUKEE BULK TERMINALS INC., MILWAUKEE, WI**							
	MBT 10	DH	1994	B	1,960	200′ 00″	35′ 00′	13′ 00″

Fleet #.	Fleet Name Vessel Name	Type of Vessel	Year Built	Type of Engine	Cargo Cap. or Gross*	Overall Length	Breadth	Depth or Draft*
	MBT 20	DH	1994	B	1,960	200′ 00″	35′ 00′	13′ 00″
	MBT 33	DH	1976	B	3,793	240′ 00″	52′ 06″	14′ 06″
M-30	**MUSÉE MARITIME DU QUÉBEC, L' ISLET, QC** *(mmq.qc.ca)*							
	Ernest Lapointe	MU	1941	R	1,179*	185′ 00″	36′ 00″	22′ 06″
	Built: Davie Shipbuilding Co., Lauzon, QC; former Canadian Coast Guard icebreaker; open to the public at L'Islet, QC							
M-31	**MUSEUM SHIP WILLIAM G. MATHER, CLEVELAND, OH** *(wgmather.nhlink.net)*							
	William G. Mather {2}	MU	1925	T	13,950	618′ 00″	62′ 00″	32′ 00″
	Built: Great Lakes Engineering Works, Ecorse, MI; former Cleveland-Cliffs Steamship Co. bulk carrier last operated Dec. 21, 1980; open to the public at Cleveland, OH							
M-32	**MUSEUM SHIP WILLIS B. BOYER, TOLEDO, OH** *(willisbboyer.org)*							
	Willis B. Boyer	MU	1911	T	15,000	617′ 00″	64′ 00″	33′ 01″
	Built: Great Lakes Engineering Works, Ecorse, MI; former Shenago Furance Co./Republic Steel Co./Cleveland-Cliffs Steamship Co. bulk carrier last operated in 1980; open to the public at Toledo, OH (Col. James M. Schoonmaker '11-'69)							
M-33	**MUSKOKA STEAMSHIP AND HISTORICAL SOCIETY, GRAVENHURST, ON** *(muskokasteamships.com)*							
	Segwun	PA	1887	R	168*	128′ 00″	24′ 00″	7′ 06″
	Built: Melancthon Simpson, Toronto, ON (Nipissing {2} 1887-'25)							
	Wanda III	PA	1915	R	60*	94′ 00″	12′ 00″	5′ 00″
	Built: Poulson Iron Works Ltd., Toronto, ON							
	Wenonah II	PA	2001	D	470*	127′ 00″	28′ 00″	6′ 00″
	Built: McNally Construction Inc., Belleville, ON							
N-1	**NADRO MARINE SERVICES LTD., PORT DOVER, ON** *(nadromarine.ca)*							
	Ecosse	TB	1979	D	146*	91′ 00″	26′ 01″	8′ 06″
	Built: Hike Metal Products Ltd., Wheatley, ON (R & L No. 1 '79-'96)							
	Intrepid III	TB	1976	D	39*	66′ 00″	17′ 00″	7′ 06″
	Built: Halter Marine Ltd., Chalmette, LA							
	Nadro Clipper	TB	1939	D	64*	70′ 00″	23′ 00″	6′ 06″
	Built: Port Colborne Iron Works, Port Colborne, ON (Stanley Clipper '39-'94)							
	Seahound	TB	1941	D	60*	65′ 06″	17′ 00″	7′ 00″
	Built: Equitable Equipment Co., New Orleans, LA ([Unnamed] '41-'56, Sea Hound '56-'80, Carolyn Jo '80-'00)							
	Vac	TB	1942	D	37*	65′ 00″	21′ 00″	6′ 06″
	Built: George Gamble, Port Dover, ON							
	Vigilant 1	TB	1944	D	111*	76′ 08″	20′ 09″	10′ 02″
	(HMCS Glenlivet [W-43] '44-'75, Glenlivet II '75-'77, Canadian Franko '77-'82, Glenlivet II '82-'00)							
N-2	**NAUTICA QUEEN CRUISE DINING, CLEVELAND, OH** *(nauticaqueen.com)*							
	Nautica Queen	ES	1981	D	95*	124′ 00″	31′ 02″	8′ 10″
	Built: Blount Marine Corp., Warren, RI (Bay Queen '81-'85, Arawanna Queen '85-'88, Star of Nautica '88-'92)							
N-3	**NAUTICAL ADVENTURES, TORONTO, ON** *(nauticaladventure.com)*							
	Empire Sandy	ES/3S	1943	D/W	434*	140′ 00″	32′ 08″	14′ 00″
	Built: Clellands Ltd., Wellington-Quay-on-Tyne, UK (Empire Sandy '43-'48, Ashford '48-'52, Chris M. '52-'79)							
	Wayward Princess	ES	1976	D	325*	92′ 00″	26′ 00″	10′ 00″
	Built: Marlin Yacht Co., Summerstown, ON (Cayuga II '76-'82)							
N-4	**NAVETTES MARITIMES DU SAINT-LAURENT INC., QUÉBEC, QC** *(navettesmaritimes.com)*							
	Miss Olympia	ES	1972	D	29*	62′ 08″	14′ 00″	4′ 08″
	Tandem I	PA	1991	D	108*	87′ 01″	22′ 00″	4′ 05″
	Transit	PA	1992	D	120*	68′ 00″	22′ 09″	4′ 05″
N-5	**NAVY MARINE CORPS RESERVE CENTER, BUFFALO, NY**							
	LCU 1680	TV	1943	D	170*	135′ 00″	29′ 00″	
N-6	**NEW YORK STATE MARINE HIGHWAY TRANSPORTATION CO., TROY, NY**							
	Margot	TB	1958	D	141*	90′ 00″	25′ 00″	10′ 00″
	Built: Jakobson Shipyard, Oyster Bay, NY (Jolene Rose, Margot Moran)							
N-7	**NORLAKE TRANSPORTATION CO., PORT COLBORNE, ON** *(norlaketransportation.com)*							
	Ours Polaire	TB	1997	D	9*	31′ 00″	13′ 00″	6′ 00″

COL. JAMES M. SCHOONMAKER

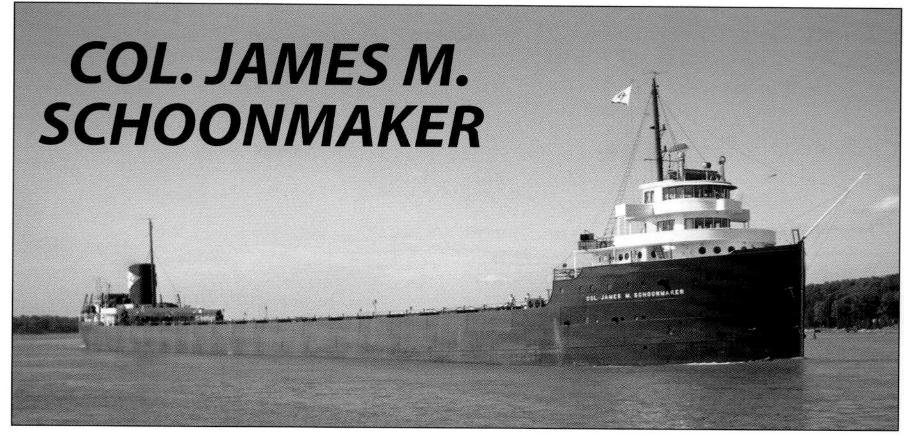

Steamer *Col. James M. Schoonmaker* in the Rock Cut in the 1960s. (*Tom Manse*)

Historic Spotlight

Labeled by newspapers as "one of the prettiest launches that ever has taken place in a local yard," the *Col. James M. Schoonmaker* was launched July 1, 1911, at the Great Lakes Engineering Works in Ecorse (Detroit), Mich. Built at a cost of $400,000 for the Shenango Furnace Co., Cleveland, Ohio, the new bulk carrier became the fourth vessel of the fleet founded in 1906 by William P. Snyder. The vessel's namesake was a recipient of the Congressional Medal of Honor and president of the Pittsburgh and Lake Erie Railroad, as well as a Civil War veteran. The *Schoonmaker*'s sister ship, *William P. Snyder Jr.*, was launched for the Shenango fleet on Jan. 27, 1912.

With her launch, the 617-foot-long *Schoonmaker* inherited the title "Queen of the Lakes" from her fleet mate, *Shenango*. With the *Schoonmaker*'s length, combined with her width of 64 feet and cargo capacity of an "amazing" 15,000 tons, the Lake Carriers' Association 1911 Annual Report proclaimed the vessel to be the "World's Largest Bulk Freighter." The *Schoonmaker* sailed on her maiden voyage Oct. 9, 1911, to Toledo for a load of 12,650 net tons of coal. As might be expected, the new steamer proceeded to set cargo records, the last in 1922.

The vessel sailed for Shenango until she was chartered to Wilson Marine Transit Co. in 1965, only to return to the fleet in 1967. On Feb. 28, 1969, the *Col. James M. Schoonmaker*, then the last vessel in the Shenango fleet, was sold to Interlake Steamship Co., which chartered the laker to Republic Steel, renaming it *Willis B. Boyer* in honor of the president of Republic Steel Corp. In August 1970, the *Willis B. Boyer* was sold to Cleveland-Cliffs Steamship Co. for $1.25 million, Cleveland-Cliffs having taken over the Republic Steel contract beginning in 1971. Though now deemed small, she was an ideal size for negotiating Cleveland's Cuyahoga River.

***Boyer,* dressed for the 1976 Bicentennial.** (*Roger LeLievre*)

By 1980, Cleveland-Cliffs had lost the Republic Steel contract and had no further use for the *Boyer*. The aging bulker was sold in 1983 to American Bulk Shipping of Los Angeles, Calif., to carry containers from Great Lakes to Canadian St. Lawrence River ports for transfer to ocean vessels. As this service could not compete with the railways, the *Boyer* never sailed, and was sold in 1986 for her scrap value of $105,000 to the city of Toledo for use as a museum.

The classic steamer was moved to Toledo's International Park and opened to the public July 4, 1987. The *Boyer* remains there today – at nearly the same location where she loaded her first cargo in 1911 – a piece of Great Lakes history saved from the scrap yard. In 2007, the Toledo Port Authority took over operation of the vessel, thus assuring her a long future on the Maumee River. – ***George Wharton***

Fleet #.	Fleet Name Vessel Name	Type of Vessel	Year Built	Type of Engine	Cargo Cap. or Gross*	Overall Length	Breadth	Depth or Draft*
	Radium Yellowknife	TB	1948	D	235*	120′ 00″	28′ 00″	6′ 06″
	Built: Yarrow's Ltd., Esquimalt, BC							
	Salvage Monarch	TB	1959	D	219*	97′ 09″	28′ 00″	14′ 06″
	Built: P.K. Harris Ltd., Appledore, England (Charlie S. '54-'75, Cathy McAllister '75-'02)							
	W. B. Indock	TB	1972	D		27′ 39″	10′ 33″	5′ 05″
	(Mokka Fjord '72-'91)							
N-8	**NORTHEASTERN MARITIME HISTORICAL FOUNDATION INC., SUPERIOR, WI**							
	(northeasternmaritime.org)							
	Islay	TB	1892	D	19*	60′ 00″	13′ 00″	5′ 00″
	Built: American Steel Barge Co., Superior, WI; laid up at Manitowoc, WI (Islay 1892-'1947, Bayfield {1} '47-'83)							
	Mount McKay	TB	1908	D	99*	80′ 00″	21′ 06″	9′ 00″
	Built: Benjamin Cowles, Buffalo, NY (Walter F. Mattick '08-' 19, Merchant '19-'24, Marinette '24-'47, Esther S. '47-'66)							
	Q.A. Gillmore	TB	1913	R	99*	80′ 00″	20′ 00″	12′ 06″
	Built: Great Lakes Towing Co., Cleveland, OH; former Reiss Steamship Co. tug last operated in 1969; at anchor in the Kalamazoo River, Saugatuck, MI (Q. A. Gillmore '13-'32, Reiss '32-'05)							
N-9	**NORTHERN MARINE TRANSPORTATION INC., SAULT STE. MARIE, MI**							
	David Allen	PB	1964	D	32*	56′ 04″	13′ 03″	6′ 00″
	Linda Jean	PB	1950	D	17*	38′ 00″	10′ 00″	5′ 00″
O-1	**OAK GROVE MARINE AND TRANSPORTATION INC., CLAYTON, NY**							
	Maple Grove	PK	1954	D	55*	73′ 07″	20′ 00″	9′ 00″
O-2	**OLSON DREDGE & DOCK CO., ALGONAC, MI**							
	John Michael	TB	1913	D	41*	55′ 04″	15′ 01″	7′ 06″
	Built: Cowles Shipyard Co., Buffalo, NY (Colonel Ward, Ross Coddington, Joseph J. Olivieri)							
O-3	**OLYMPIA CRUISE LINE INC., THORNHILL, ON**							
	Enterprise 2000	ES	1998	D	370*	121′ 06″	35′ 00″	6′ 00″
O-4	**ONTARIO MINISTRY OF NATURAL RESOURCES,UPPER GREAT LAKES MANAGEMENT UNIT, PETERBOROUGH, ON**							
	Atigamayg	RV	1954	D	82*	43′ 09″	20′ 02″	5′ 07″
	Erie Explorer	RV	1981	D	72*	53′ 05″	20′ 01″	4′ 08″
	K. H. Loftus	RV	1990	D	27*	37′ 00″	14′ 00″	4′ 04″
	Keenosay	RV	1957	D	68*	51′ 04″	20′ 07″	2′ 07″
	Namaycush	RV	1954	D	28*	65′ 03″	12′ 00″	4′ 01″
	Nipigon Osprey	RV	1990	D	33*	42′ 04″	14′ 09″	6′ 08″
	Wonda Goldie	RV	1950	D	12*	46′ 08″	12′ 00″	3′ 09″
O-5	**ONTARIO MINISTRY OF TRANSPORTATION, DOWNSVIEW, ON**							
	Frontenac II	PA/CF	1962	D	666*	181′ 00″	45′ 00″	10′ 00″
	Built: Chantier Maritime de Saint Laurent, St. Laurent, QC (Charlevoix {2} '62-'92)							
	Frontenac Howe Islander	PF/CF	2004	D	130*	100′ 00″	32′ 03″	5′ 05″
	Built: Heddle Marine Service Inc., Hamilton, ON							
	Glenora	PA/CF	1952	D	209*	127′ 00″	33′ 00″	9′ 00″
	Built: Erieau Shipbuilding & Drydock Co. Ltd., Erieau, ON (The St. Joseph Islander '52-'74)							
	Jiimaan	PA/CF	1992	D	2,830*	176′ 09″	42′ 03″	13′ 06″
	Built: Port Weller Drydock, Port Weller, ON							
	Pelee Islander	PA/CF	1960	D	334*	145′ 00″	32′ 00″	10′ 00″
	Built: Erieau Shipbuilding & Drydock Co. Ltd., Erieau, ON							
	Quinte Loyalist	PA/CF	1954	D	209*	127′ 00″	32′ 00″	8′ 00″
	Built: Erieau Shipbuilding & Drydock Co. Ltd., Erieau, ON							
	Wolfe Islander III	PA/CF	1975	D	985*	205′ 00″	68′ 00″	6′ 00″
	Built: Port Arthur Shipbuilding Co., Port Arthur, ON							
O-6	**ONTARIO POWER GENERATION INC., TORONTO, ON**							
	Niagara Queen II	IB	1992	D	57*	56′ 01″	18′ 00″	6′ 08″
O-7	**OSBORNE COMPANIES INC., GRAND RIVER, OH**							
	Emmet J. Carey	SC	1948	D	900	114′ 00″	23′ 00″	11′ 00″
	Built: Hugh E. Lee Iron Works, Saginaw, MI (Beatrice Ottinger '48-'63, James B. Lyons '63-'88)							

Fleet #	Fleet Name Vessel Name	Type of Vessel	Year Built	Type of Engine	Cargo Cap. or Gross*	Overall Length	Breadth	Depth or Draft*
	F. M. Osborne {2}	SC	1910	D	500	150′ 00″	29′ 00″	11′ 03″
	Built: J. Butman & T. Horn, Buffalo, NY (Grand Island {1} '10-'58, Lesco '58-'75)							
O-8	**OWEN SOUND TRANSPORTATION CO. LTD., OWEN SOUND, ON** *(ontarioferries.com)*							
	Chi-Cheemaun	PA/CF	1974	D	6,991*	365′ 05″	61′ 00″	21′ 00″
	Built: Canadian Shipbuilding and Engineering Ltd., Collingwood, ON							
P-1	**PAUL J. VASSALL, ORTONVILLE, MI**							
	Elizabeth	TB	1936	D	48*	61′ 05″	17′ 01″	6′ 06″
	(Chester)							
P-2	**PERE MARQUETTE SHIPPING CO., LUDINGTON, MI** *(pmship.com)*							
	Pere Marquette 41	SU	1941	B	4,545	403′ 00″	58′ 00″	23′ 06″
	Built: Manitowoc Shipbuilding Co., Manitowoc, WI; converted from powered train/car ferry to a self-unloading barge in '97 (City of Midland 41 '41-'97)							
	Undaunted	AT	1944	DE	860*	143′ 00″	33′ 01″	18′ 00″
	Built: Gulfport Boiler/Welding, Port Arthur, TX (USS Undaunted [ATR-126, ATA-199] '44-'63, USMA Kings Pointer '63-'93, Krystal K. '93-'97)							
	[ATB Undaunted / PM 41 OA dimensions together]					493′ 06″	58′ 00″	23′ 06″
P-3	**PETERSEN STEAMSHIP CO., DOUGLAS, MI** *(keewatinmaritimemuseum.com)*							
	Keewatin {2}	MU	1907	Q	3,856*	346′ 00″	43′ 08″	26′ 06″
	Built: Fairfield Shipbuilding, Govan, Scotland; former Canadian Pacific Railway Co. passenger vessel last operated Nov. 29, 1965; open to the public at Douglas, MI							
P-4	**PICTURED ROCKS CRUISES INC., MUNISING, MI** *(picturedrocks.com)*							
	Grand Island {2}	ES	1989	D	52*	68′ 00″	16′ 01″	7′ 01″
	Grand Portal	ES	2004	D	76*	64′ 08″	20′ 00″	8′ 08″
	Miners Castle	ES	1974	D	82*	68′ 00″	16′ 06″	6′ 04″
	Miss Superior	ES	1984	D	83*	68′ 00″	16′ 09″	10′ 04″
	Pictured Rocks	ES	1972	D	53*	55′ 07″	13′ 07″	4′ 04″
P-5	**PIER WISCONSIN, MILWAUKEE, WI** *(voyage.pierwisconsin.org)*							
	Denis Sullivan	TV/ES	1994	W/D	99*	138′ 00″	24′ 00″	8′ 09″
	Built: Wisconsin Lake Schooner, Milwaukee, WI							
P-6	**PLAUNT TRANSPORTATION CO. INC., CHEBOYGAN, MI**							
	Kristen D.	CF	1988	D	83*	64′ 11″	36′ 00″	6′ 05″

Canada Steamship Lines' *CSL Laurentien* in the St. Lawrence Seaway. *(Ron Walsh)*

Fleet #.	Fleet Name Vessel Name	Type of Vessel	Year Built	Type of Engine	Cargo Cap. or Gross*	Overall Length	Breadth	Depth or Draft*
P-7	**PORT CITY CRUISE LINE INC., MUSKEGON, MI** *(portcityprincesscruises.com)*							
	Port City Princess	ES	1966	D	79*	64' 09"	30' 00"	5' 06"
	Built: Blount Marine Corp., Warren, RI (Island Queen {1} '66-'87)							
P-8	**PORT HURON MUSEUM, PORT HURON, MI** *(phmuseum.org)*							
	Bramble	MU	1944	DE	1,025*	180' 00"	37' 00"	17' 04"
	Built: Zenith Dredge Co., Duluth, MN; former U.S. Coast Guard bouy tender/icebreaker was retired in 2003; open to the public at Port Huron, MI (USCGC Bramble [WLB-392] '44-'03)							
	Huron	MU	1920	D	392*	96' 05"	24' 00"	10' 00"
	Built: Charles L. Seabury Co., Morris Heights, NY; former U.S. Coast Guard lightship WLV-526 was retired Aug. 20, 1970; open to the public at Port Huron, MI (Lightship 103 – Relief [WAL-526] '20-'36)							
P-9	**PORT OF INDIANA HARBOR, BURNS HARBOR, IN** *(portsofindiana.com)*							
	Oconto	MU	1953	D	23*	45' 00"	13' 00"	7' 00"
	Retired tug is on display ashore as museum at Burns Harbor, IN (ST-2162 '53-'62)							
P-10	**PORTOFINO ON THE RIVER, WYANDOTTE, MI** *(portofinoontheriver.com)*							
	Friendship	ES	1968	D	110*	85' 00"	30' 06"	7' 03"
	Built: Hike Metal Products Ltd., Wheatley, ON (Peche Island V '68-'71, Papoose V '71-'82)							
P-11	**PROJECT H.M.S. DETROIT, AMHERSTBURG, ON** *(hmsdetroit.org)*							
	His Majesty's Ship Detroit	ES	2006	3M/D	235*	131' 02"	30' 06"	9' 10"
P-12	**PURVIS MARINE LTD., SAULT STE. MARIE, ON** *(purvismarine.com)*							
	Adanac	TB	1913	D	108*	80' 03"	19' 02"	10' 06"
	Built: Western Drydock & Shipbuilding Co., Port Arthur, ON (Edward C. Whalen '13-'66, John McLean '66-'95)							
	Anglian Lady	TB	1953	D	398*	136' 06"	30' 00"	14' 01"
	Built: John I. Thornecroft & Co., Southampton, England (Hamtun '53-'72, Nathalie Letzer '72-'88)							
	Avenger IV	TB	1962	D	293*	120' 00"	30' 05"	17' 05"
	Built: Cochrane & Sons Ltd., Selby, Yorkshire, England (Avenger '62-'85)							
	Chief Wawatam	DB	1911	B	4,500	347' 00"	62' 03"	15' 00"
	Built: Toledo Shipbuilding Co., Toledo, OH; converted from a powered train ferry to a barge in '88							
	G.L.B. No. 1	DB	1953	B	3,215	305' 00"	50' 00"	12' 00"
	Built: Nashville Bridge Co., Nashville, TN (Joe Baugh Jr. '53-'66, ORG 5503 '66-'75)							
	G.L.B. No. 2	DB	1953	B	3,215	305' 02"	50' 00"	12' 00"
	Built: Ingalls Shipbuilding Corp., Birmingham, AL (Jane Newfield '53-'66, ORG 6502 '66-'75)							
	Malden	DB	1946	B	1,075	150' 00"	41' 09"	10' 03"
	Martin E. Johnson	TB	1959	D	26*	46' 00"	16' 00"	5' 09"
	Nindawayma	PA/CF	1976	D	6,197*	333' 06"	55' 00"	36' 06"
	Last operated in 1992; laid up at Sault Ste. Marie, ON (Monte Cruceta '76-'76, Monte Castillo '76-'78, Manx Viking '78-'87, Manx '87-'88, Skudenes '88-'89, Ontario No. 1 {2} '89-'89)							
	Osprey	TB	1944	D	36*	45' 00"	13' 06"	7' 00"
	P.M.L. Alton	DB	1951	B	150	93' 00"	30' 00"	8' 00"
	P.M.L. 357	DB	1944	B	600	138' 00"	38' 00"	11' 00"
	P.M.L. 2501	TK	1980	B	1,954*	302' 00"	52' 00"	17' 00"
	Built: Cenac Shipyard, Houma, LA (CTCO 2505 '80-'96)							
	P.M.L. 9000	TK	1968	B	4,285*	400' 00"	76' 00"	20' 00"
	Built: Bethlehem Steel – Shipbuilding Division, San Francisco, CA (Palmer '68-'00)							
	Reliance	TB	1974	D	708*	148' 04"	35' 07"	21' 06"
	Built: Ulstein Hatlo A/S, Ulsteinvik, Norway (Sinni '74-'81, Irving Cedar '81-'96, Atlantic Cedar '96-'02)							
	Rocket	TB	1901	D	39*	70' 00"	15' 00"	8' 00"
	Built: Buffalo Shipbuilding Co., Buffalo, NY							
	Sheila P.	TB	1940	D	15*	40 00"	14' 00"	x' 00"
	Tecumseh II	DB	1976	B	2,500	180' 00"	54' 00"	12' 00"
	(U-727 '76-'94)							
	Wilfred M. Cohen	TB	1948	D	284*	104' 00"	28' 00"	14' 06"
	Built: Newport News Shipbuilding and Drydock Co., Newport News, VA (A. T. Lowmaster '48-'75)							
	W. I. Scott Purvis	TB	1938	D	206*	96' 06"	26' 04"	10' 04"
	Built: Marine Industries, Sorel, QC (Orient Bay '38-'75, Guy M. No. 1 '75-'90)							
	W. J. Ivan Purvis	TB	1938	D	191*	100' 06"	25' 06"	9' 00"
	Built: Marine Industries, Sorel, QC (Magpie '38-'66, Dana T. Bowen '66-'75)							

Fleet #	Fleet Name Vessel Name	Type of Vessel	Year Built	Type of Engine	Cargo Cap. or Gross*	Overall Length	Breadth	Depth or Draft*
	Waub Nav. No. 1	TB	1941	D	14*	38' 06"	10' 06"	6' 00"
	(Alona)							
	Yankcanuck {2}	CS	1963	D	4,760	324' 03"	49' 00"	26' 00"
	Built: Collingwood Shipyards, Collingwood, ON							
P-13	**PUT-IN-BAY BOAT LINE CO., PORT CLINTON, OH** *(jet-express.com)*							
	Jet Express	PF/CA	1989	D	93*	92' 08"	28' 06"	8' 04"
	Jet Express II	PF/CA	1992	D	85*	92' 06"	28' 06"	8' 04"
	Jet Express III	PF/CA	2001	D	70*	78' 02"	27' 06"	8' 02"
R-1	**RANKIN CONSTRUCTION INC., ST. CATHARINES, ON**							
	Judique Flyer	DB	1967	D	67.7*	60' 00"	29' 08"	3' 09"
	(Sweep Scow No. 4 '67-'03)							
R-2	**REBELLION TUG & BARGE INC., LOCKPORT, N.Y.** *(rebelliontug.com)*							
	Shenandoah	TB	1941	D	29*	49' 03"	14' 00"	6' 01"
	Built: Sturgeon Bay Shipbuilding Co., Sturgeon Bay, WI (Lauren E., R. H. Vaughn)							
R-3	**RIGEL SHIPPING CANADA INC., SHEDIAC, NB** *(rigelcanada.com)*							
	VESSELS CHARTERED TO PETRO-NAV INC., MONTREAL, QC							
	Diamond Star	TK	1992	D	10,511	405' 11"	58' 01"	34' 09"
	Built: MTW Shipyard, Wismar, Germany (Elbestern '92-'93)							
	Emerald Star	TK	1992	D	10,511	405' 11"	58' 01"	34' 09"
	Built: MTW Shipyard, Wismar, Germany (Emsstern '92-'92)							
	Jade Star	TK	1993	D	10,511	405' 11"	58' 01"	34' 09"
	Built: MTW Shipyard, Wismar, Germany (Jadestern '93-'94)							
R-4	**ROCKPORT BOAT LINE LTD., ROCKPORT, ON** *(rockportcruises.com)*							
	Ida M.	ES	1970	D	29*	55' 00"	14' 00"	3' 00"
	Ida M. II	ES	1973	D	116*	63' 02"	22' 02"	5' 00"
	Sea Prince II	ES	1978	D	172*	83' 00"	24' 02"	6' 08"
R-5	**ROEN SALVAGE CO., STURGEON BAY, WI** *(roensalvage.com)*							
	Chas. Asher	TB	1967	D	10*	50' 00"	18' 00"	8' 00"
	Built: Sturgeon Bay Shipbuilding Co., Sturgeon Bay, WI							
	John R. Asher	TB	1943	D	93*	70' 00"	20' 00"	8' 06"
	Built: Platzer Boat Works, Houston, TX (U. S. Army ST-71 '43-'46, Russell 8 '46-'64, Reid McAllister '64-'67, Donegal '67-'85)							
	Louie S.	TB	1956	D	43*	37' 00"	12' 00"	5' 00"
	Spuds	TB	1944	D	19*	42' 00"	12' 06"	6' 00"
	Stephan M. Asher	TB	1954	D	60*	65' 00"	19' 01"	5' 04"
	Built: Burton Shipyard Inc., Port Arthur, TX (Captain Bennie '54-'82, Dumar Scout '82-'87)							
	Timmy A.	TB	1953	D	12*	33' 06"	10' 08"	5' 02"
R-6	**ROGER CHAPMAN, MILWAUKEE, WI**							
	Mermaid	TB	1936	D	11*	41'00"	10'00"	4' 9"
	(Jake M. Kadinger)							
R-7	**ROYAL CANADIAN YACHT CLUB, TORONTO, ON**							
	Elsie D.	PA	1958	D	9*	34' 07"	10' 08"	3' 06"
	Esperanza	PA	1953	D	14*	38' 06"	11' 02"	4' 06"
	Hiawatha	PA	1895	D	46*	56' 01"	14' 04"	6' 02"
	Kwasind	PA	1912	D	47*	70' 08"	15' 09"	5' 05"
R-8	**RUSSELL ISLAND TRANSIT CO., ALGONAC, MI**							
	Islander {2}	PA/CF	1967	D	38*	41' 00"	15' 00"	3' 06"
R-9	**RYBA MARINE CONSTRUCTION CO., CHEBOYGAN, MI** *(rybamarine.com)*							
	Alcona	TB	1957	D	18*	40' 00"	12' 06"	5' 06"
	Amber Mae	TB	1922	D	67*	65' 00"	14' 01"	10' 00"
	Built: Glove Shipyard Inc. Buffalo, NY (E. W. Sutton '22-'52, Venture '52- '00)							
	Jarco 1402	CS	1981	B	473*	140' 00"	39' 00"	9' 00"
	Kathy Lynn	TB	1944	D	140*	85' 00"	24' 00"	9' 06"
	Built: Decatur Iron & Steel Co., Decatur, AL (U. S. Army ST-693 '44-'79, Sea Islander '79-'91)							

JOHN J. BOLAND

Vessel Spotlight

The name *John J. Boland* has graced the bows of four American Steamship Co. lake boats for more than a century. Considered a patriarch of the Great Lakes shipping industry, John J. Boland formed a partnership with Adam E. Cornelius, establishing the firm Boland & Cornelius in 1904, an outgrowth of which was the American Steamship Co., founded in 1907. The first *John J. Boland* was a 500-foot laker built in 1907 for York Steamship Co., a firm managed by Boland that became part of American Steamship in 1915.

John J. Boland, bow on.
(Roger LeLievre)

The modern *John J. Boland* is a 680-foot, efficient, self-unloading bulk carrier built at Bay Shipbuilding Co., Sturgeon Bay, Wis., in 1973 at a cost of almost $13.7 million. The vessel was one of the first of 10 built for American Steamship Co. under Title XI of the Merchant Marine Act of 1970, which allowed American fleets to modernize or construct new vessels with government-guaranteed funding and tax-deferred benefits. The self-unloader, launched March 10, 1973, was christened *Charles E. Wilson* later that year. With two V-20 diesel engines providing power, the vessel was capable of handling up to 34,000 tons of cargo, which could be unloaded via its stern-mounted, 250-foot discharge boom at rates up to 6,000 tons per hour.

Though smaller in size than most of her fleet mates, she could access ports that larger boats were unable to reach. Her agility was increased with the aid of bow and stern thrusters plus a controllable pitch propeller.

Following the successful completion of sea trials in September 1973, the *Wilson* sailed on her maiden voyage from Sturgeon Bay to Escanaba to load iron ore for Trenton (Detroit).

The *Charles E. Wilson* was renamed *John J. Boland* (4) in January 2000, following the sale of the third namesake to Lower Lakes Towing in late 1999 (this *Boland* now sails as *Saginaw*). The *John J. Boland* is used in the general bulk trades, carrying cargoes of iron ore pellets, coal, limestone, other stone products and grains. – ***George Wharton***

John J. Boland **upbound through spring ice above the Soo Locks.** *(Eric Treece)*

	Rochelle Kaye	TB	1963	D	52*	51′ 06″	19′ 04″	7′ 00″
	Built: St. Charles Steel Works Inc., Thibodeaux, LA (Jaye Anne '63-?, Katanni ?-'97)							
	Tenacious	TB	1960	D	149*	90′ 00″	26′ 04″	12′ 00″
	Built: Ingalls Shipbuilding Corp., Pascagoula, MS (Mobil 8 '60-'91, Tatarrax '91-'93, Nan McKay '93-'95)							
S-1	**SABLE POINT MARINE LLC, LUDINGTON, MI**							
	Snohomish	TB	1943	DE	195*	110′ 00″	26′ 06″	12′ 06″
	Built: Ira S. Bushey & Sons Inc., Brooklyn, NY (WYTM-98 Snohomish)							
S-2	**SCOTLUND STIVERS, MARINETTE, WI**							
	Arthur K. Atkinson	PA	1917	D	3,241*	384′ 00″	56′ 00″	20′ 06″
	Built: Great Lakes Engineering Works, Ecorse, MI; last operated in April 1982; laid up at DeTour, MI (Ann Arbor No. 6 '17-'59)							
	SEAWAY MARINE TRANSPORT, ST. CATHARINES, ON							
	PARTNERSHIP BETWEEN ALGOMA CENTRAL CORP. (A-7) AND UPPER LAKES GROUP (U-13) SEE RESPECTIVE FLEETS FOR VESSELS INVOLVED.							
S-3	**SELVICK MARINE TOWING CORP., STURGEON BAY, WI**							
	Carla Anne Selvick	TB	1908	D	191*	96′ 00″	23′ 00″	11′ 02″
	Built: Skinner Shipbuilding & Dry Dock Co., Baltimore, MD (S.O. Co. No. 19 '08-'16, S.T. Co. No. 19 '16-'18, Socony 19 '18-'47, Esso Tug No. 4 '47-'53, McAllister 44 '53-'55, Roderick McAllister '55-'84)							
	Cameron O.	TB	1955	D	26*	50′ 00″	15′ 00″	7′ 03″
	Built: Peterson Builders Inc., Sturgeon Bay, WI (Escort II '55-'06)							
	Jacquelyn Nicole	TB	1913	D	96*	81′ 00″	20′ 00″	12′ 06″
	Built: Great Lakes Towing Co., Cleveland, OH (Michigan {4} '13-'78, Ste. Marie II '78-'81, Dakota '81-'92, Ethel E. '92-'02)							
	Jimmy L.	TB	1939	D	148*	110′ 00″	25′ 00″	13′ 00″
	Built: Defoe Shipbuilding Co., Bay City, MI USCGC Naugatuck [WYT / WYTM-92] '39-'80, Timmy B. '80-'84)							
	Mary Page Hannah {1}	TB	1950	DE	461*	143′ 00″	33′ 01″	14′ 06″
	Built: Levingston Shipbuilding, Orange, TX (U. S. Army ATA-230 '49-'72, G. W. Codrington '72-'73, William P. Feeley {2} '73-'73, William W. Stender '73-'78)							
	Sharon M. Selvick	TB	1945	D	28*	45′ 00″	13′ 00″	7′ 00″
	Built: Kewaunee Shipbuilding & Engineering, Kewaunee, WI (USACE Judson)							
	Susan L.	TB	1944	D	163*	86′ 00″	23′ 00″	10′ 04″
	Built: Equitable Equipment Co., New Orleans LA (U. S. Army ST-709 '44-'47, USCOE Stanley '47-'99)							
	William C. Selvick	TB	1944	D	142*	85′ 00″	22′ 11″	10′ 04″
	Built: Platzer Boat Works, Houston, TX (U. S. Army ST-500 '44-'49, Sherman H. Serre '49-'77)							
S-4	**SHAMROCK CHARTERING CO., GROSSE POINTE, MI**							
	Helene	ES	1927	D	99*	96′ 09″	17′ 00″	8′ 00″
	Built: Defoe Shipbuilding Co., Bay City, MI							
S-5	**SHELL CANADA PRODUCTS LTD., MONTREAL, QC**							
	Arca	RT	1963	D	1,296	175′ 00″	36′ 00″	14′ 00″
	Built: Port Weller Dry Docks, Port Weller, ON (Imperial Lachine '63-'03, Josee M. '03-'03)							
S-6	**SHEPARD MARINE CONSTRUCTION, ST. CLAIR SHORES, MI**							
	Geraldine	TW	1988	D	26*	42 00″	19′ 00″	5′ 00″
	Robin Lynn	TB	1952	D	146*	85′ 00″	25′ 00″	11′ 00″
	Built: Alexander Shipyard Inc., New Orleans, LA (Bonita '52-'85, Susan Hoey {2} '85'-'95, Blackie B '95-'97, Susan Hoey {3 } '97-'98)							
S-7	**SHEPLER'S MACKINAC ISLAND FERRY SERVICE, MACKINAW CITY, MI** *(sheplersferry.com)*							
	Capt. Shepler	PF	1986	D	71*	84′ 00″	21′ 00″	7′ 10″
	Felicity	PF	1972	D	84*	65′ 00″	18′ 01″	8′ 03″
	Sacre Bleu	PK	1959	D	92*	94′ 10″	31′ 00″	9′ 09″
	(Put-In-Bay {2} '59-'94)							
	The Hope	PF	1975	D	87*	77′ 00″	20′ 00″	8′ 03″
	The Welcome	PF	1969	D	66*	60′ 06″	16′ 08″	8′ 02″
	Wyandot	PF	1979	D	99*	77′ 00″	20′ 00″	8′ 00″
S-8	**SHIPWRECK TOURS INC., MUNISING, MI** *(shipwrecktours.com)*							
	Miss Munising	ES	1967	D	50*	60′ 00″	14′ 00″	4′ 04″

Fleet #.	Fleet Name Vessel Name	Type of Vessel	Year Built	Type of Engine	Cargo Cap. or Gross*	Overall Length	Breadth	Depth or Draft*
S-9	**SHORELINE CHARTERS, GILLS ROCK, WI** *(shorelinecharters.net)*							
	The Shoreline	ES	1973	D	12*	33' 00"	11' 4"	3' 00"
S-10	**SHORELINE CONTRACTORS INC., CLEVELAND, OH**							
	Eagle	TB	1943	D	31*	57' 09"	14' 05"	6' 10"
S-11	**SHORELINE SIGHTSEEING CO., CHICAGO, IL** *(shorelinesightseeing.com)*							
	Cap Streeter	ES	1987	D	28*	63' 06"	24' 04"	7' 07"
	Evening Star	ES	2001	D	93*	83' 00"	23' 00"	7' 00"
	Marlyn	ES	1961	D	70*	65' 00"	25' 00"	7' 00"
	Shoreline II	ES	1987	D	89*	75' 00"	26' 00"	7' 01"
	Star of Chicago {2}	ES	1999	D	73*	64' 10"	22' 08"	7' 05"
	Voyager	CF	1960	D	98*	65' 00"	35' 00"	8' 00"
S-12	**SOCIÉTÉ DES TRAVERSIERS DU QUÉBEC, QUÉBEC, QC** *(www.traversiers.gouv.qc.ca)*							
	Alphonse Desjardins	CF	1971	D	1,741*	214' 00"	71' 06"	20' 00"
	Armand Imbeau	CF	1980	D	1,285*	203' 07"	72' 00"	18' 04"
	Camille Marcoux	CF	1974	D	6,122*	310' 09"	62' 09"	39' 00"
	Catherine Legardeur	CF	1985	D	1,348*	205' 09"	71' 10"	18' 10"
	Felix Antoine Savard	CF	1997	D	2,489*	272' 00"	70' 00"	21' 09"
	Grue des Iles	CF	1981	D	447*	155' 10"	41' 01"	12' 06"
	Jos Deschenes	CF	1980	D	1,287*	203' 07"	72' 00"	18' 04"
	Joseph Savard	CF	1985	D	1,445*	206' 00"	71' 10"	18' 10"
	Lomer Gouin	CF	1971	D	1,741*	214' 00"	71' 06"	20' 00"
	Lucien L.	CF	1967	D	867*	220' 10"	61' 06"	15' 05"
	Radisson {1}	CF	1954	D	1,043*	164' 03"	72' 00"	10' 06"
S-13	**SOO LOCKS BOAT TOURS, SAULT STE. MARIE, MI** *(soolocks.com)*							
	Bide-A-Wee {3}	ES	1955	D	99*	64' 07"	23' 00"	7' 11"
	Built: Blount Marine Corp., Warren, RI							
	Hiawatha {2}	ES	1959	D	99*	64' 07"	23' 00"	7' 11"
	Built: Blount Marine Corp., Warren, RI							
	Holiday	ES	1957	D	99*	64' 07"	23' 00"	7' 11"
	Built: Blount Marine Corp., Warren, RI							
	Le Voyageur	ES	1959	D	70*	65' 00"	25' 00"	7' 00"
	Built: Sturgeon Bay Shipbuilding and Drydock Co., Sturgeon Bay, WI							
	Nokomis	ES	1959	D	70*	65' 00"	25' 00"	7' 00"
	Built: Sturgeon Bay Shipbuilding and Drydock Co., Sturgeon Bay, WI							
S-14	**SOO RIVER MARINE LLC, WILLIAMSTON, MI**							
	Soo River Belle	PB	1961	D	25*	40' 00"	14' 00"	6' 00"
S-15	**SOUTH SHORE DREDGE AND DOCK INC., LORAIN, OH**							
	Cojak	TB	1954	D	11*	31' 07	10' 09"	6' 00"
S-16	**SPIRIT CRUISE LINE LTD., TORONTO, ON**							
	Northern Spirit I	ES	1983	D	489*	136' 00"	31' 00"	9' 00"
	Built: Blount Marine Corp., Warren, RI (New Spirit '83-'89, Pride of Toronto '89-'92)							
	Oriole	ES	1987	D	200*	75' 00"	23' 00"	9' 00"
S-17	**SPIRIT CRUISES LLC, CHICAGO, IL** *(spiritcruises.com)*							
	Spirit of Chicago	ES	1988	D	92*	156' 00"	35' 00"	7' 01"
S-18	**SPIRIT OF LASALLE CRUISE LINE, MENOMINEE, MI** *(spiritoflasalle.com)*							
	Spirit of LaSalle	ES	1978	D	99*	95' 09"	21' 05"	7' 00"
	Built: Camcraft Inc., Crown Point, LA (Melissa Briley '78-'98, Grampa Woo '98-'07)							
	Isle Royale Queen III	PA	1959	D	88*	74' 03"	18' 04"	6' 05"
	Built: T.D. Vinette Co., Escanaba, MI (Isle Royale Queen II)							
S-19	**SPIRIT OF THE SOUND SCHOONER CO., PARRY SOUND, ON** *(spiritofthesound.ca)*							
	Chippewa III	PA	1954	D	47*	65' 00"	16' 00"	6' 06"
	Built: Russel-Hipwell Engines Ltd., Owen Sound, ON (Maid of the Mist III '54-'56, Maid of the Mist '56-'92)							

Tug-barge combo *Michigan / Great Lakes* in Lake Michigan ice, seen from the U.S. Coast Guard cutter *Biscayne Bay*. *(Michael Singleton, BM1, USCG)*

Fleet #.	Fleet Name Vessel Name	Type of Vessel	Year Built	Type of Engine	Cargo Cap. or Gross*	Overall Length	Breadth	Depth or Draft*
S-20	**S.S. CITY OF MILWAUKEE-NATIONAL HISTORIC LANDMARK, MANISTEE, MI** *(carferry.com)*							
	City of Milwaukee	MU	1931	R	26 cars	360' 00"	56' 03"	21' 06"
	Built: Manitowoc Shipbuilding Co., Manitowoc,WI; train ferry sailed for the Grand Trunk Railroad '31-'78 and the Ann Arbor Railroad '78-'81; open to the public at Manistee, MI							
S-21	**S.S. METEOR WHALEBACK SHIP MUSEUM, SUPERIOR, WI** *(superiorpublicmuseums.org)*							
	Meteor {2}	MU	1896	R	40,100	380' 00"	45' 00"	26' 00"
	Built: American Steel Barge Co., Superior, WI; former ore carrier/auto carrier/tanker is the last vessel of whaleback design surviving on the Great Lakes; Cleveland Tankers vessel last operated in 1969; open to the public at Superior, WI (Frank Rockefeller 1896-'28, South Park '28-'43)							
S-22	**S.S. NORISLE HERITAGE MUSEUM, MANITOWANING, ON** *(norisle.com)*							
	Norisle	MU	1946	R	1,668*	215' 09"	36' 03"	16' 00"
	Built: Collingwood Shipyards, Collingwood, ON; former Ontario Northland Transportation Commission passenger vessel last operated in 1974; open to the public at Manitowaning, Manitoulin Island, ON							
S-23	**ST. JAMES MARINE CO., BEAVER ISLAND, MI**							
	American Girl	PK	1922	D	67*	62' 00"	14' 00"	6' 00"
	Oil Queen	TK	1949	B	50*	64' 08"	16' 00"	6' 00"
S-24	**ST. LAWRENCE CRUISE LINES INC., KINGSTON, ON** *(stlawrencecruiselines.com)*							
	Canadian Empress	PA	1981	D	463*	108' 00"	30' 00"	8' 00"
	Built: Algan Shipyards Ltd., Gananoque, ON							
S-25	**ST. LAWRENCE SEAWAY DEVELOPMENT CORP., MASSENA, NY** *(www.seaway.dot.gov)*							
	McCauley	CS	1948	B		112' 00"	52' 00"	3' 00"
	Robinson Bay	TB	1958	DE	213*	103' 00"	26' 10"	14' 06"
	Performance	TB	1997	D		50' 00"	16' 06"	7' 05"
S-26	**ST. LAWRENCE SEAWAY MANAGEMENT CORP., CORNWALL, ON** *(greatlakes-seaway.com)*							
	VM/S Hercules	GL	1962	D	2,107*	200' 00"	75' 00"	18' 08"
	Built: Marine Industries Ltd., Sorel, QC							
	VM/S Maisonneuve	TB	1974	D	56*	58' 03"	20' 03"	6' 05"
	Built: Fercraft Marine Inc., Ste. Catherine D'Alexandre, QC							
	VM/S St. Lambert	TB	1974	D	20*	30' 08"	13' 01"	6' 05"
	VM/S St. Louis III	TB	1977	D	15*	34' 02"	11' 08"	4' 00"
S-27	**ST. MARYS CEMENT INC. (CANADA), TORONTO, ON** *(stmaryscement.com)*							
	Sea Eagle II	ATB	1979	D	560*	132' 00"	35' 00"	19' 00"
	Built: Modern Marine Power Co., Houma, LA (Sea Eagle '79-'81, Canmar Sea Eagle '81-'91)							
	St. Marys Cement	CC	1986	B	9,400	360' 00"	60' 00"	23' 03"
	Built: Merce Industries East, Cleveland, OH							
	St. Marys Cement II	CC	1978	B	19,513	496' 06"	76' 00"	35' 00"
	Built: Galveston Shipbuilding Co., Galveston, TX (Velasco '78-'81, Canmar Shuttle '81-'90)							
	St. Marys Cement III	CC	1980	B	4,800	335' 00"	76' 08"	17' 09"
	Built: Robin Shipyard (Pte) Ltd., Singapore; last operated Sept. 1, '00; in use as a cement storage barge at Green Bay, WI (Bigorange XVI '80-'84, Says '84-'85, Al-Sayb-7 '85-'86, Clarkson Carrier '86-'94)							
	THE FOLLOWING THREE VESSELS MANAGED BY HMC SHIP MANAGEMENT LTD., LEMONT, IL – AN AFFILIATE OF HANNAH MARINE CORP.							
	C.T.C. No. 1	CC	1943	R	16,300	620' 06"	60' 00"	35' 00"
	Built: Great Lakes Engineering Works, River Rouge, MI; last operated Nov. 12, 1981; in use as a cement storage/transfer vessel in South Chicago, IL (Launched as McIntyre. Frank Purnell {1} '43-'64, Steelton {3} '64-'78, Hull No. 3 '78-'79, Pioneer {4} '79-'82)							
	St. Marys Challenger	CC	1906	S	10,250	552' 01"	56' 00"	31' 00"
	Built: Great Lakes Engineering Works, Ecorse, MI; repowered in '50; converted to a self-unloading cement carrier by Manitowoc Shipbuilding Co., Manitowoc, WI, in '67; celebrated its 100th season in 2006 (William P. Snyder '06-'26, Elton Hoyt II {1} '26-'52, Alex D. Chisholm '52-'66, Medusa Challenger '66-'99, Southdown Challenger '99-'04)							
	St. Marys Conquest	CC	1937	B	8,500	437' 06"	55' 00"	28' 00"
	Built: Manitowoc Shipbuilding Co., Manitowoc, WI; converted from a powered tanker to a self-unloading cement barge by Bay Shipbuilding, Sturgeon Bay, WI, in '87 (Red Crown '37-'62, Amoco Indiana '62-'87, Medusa Conquest '87-'99, Southdown Conquest '99-'04)							

Fleet #	Fleet Name / Vessel Name	Type of Vessel	Year Built	Type of Engine	Cargo Cap. or Gross*	Overall Length	Breadth	Depth or Draft*
	THE FOLLOWING VESSEL CHARTERED BY ST. MARYS CEMENT CO. FROM GREAT LAKES INTERNATIONAL TOWING & SALVAGE CO., BURLINGTON, ON							
	Petite Forte	TB	1969	D	368*	127' 00"	32' 00"	14' 06"
	Built: Cochrane and Sons Ltd., Selby, Yorkshire, England (E. Bronson Ingram '69-'72, Jarmac 42 '72-'73, Scotsman '73-'81, Al Battal '81-'86)							
S-28	**ST. MARYS RIVER MARINE CENTRE, SAULT STE. MARIE, ON** *(norgoma.org)*							
	Norgoma	MU	1950	D	1,477*	188' 00"	37' 06"	22' 06"
	Built: Collingwood Shipyards, Collingwood, ON; former Ontario Northland Transportation Commission passenger vessel last operated in 1974; open to the public at Sault Ste. Marie, ON							
S-29	**STAR LINE MACKINAC ISLAND FERRY, ST. IGNACE, MI** *(mackinacferry.com)*							
	Cadillac {5}	PF	1990	D	73*	64' 07"	20' 00"	7' 07"
	Joliet {3}	PF	1993	D	83*	64' 08"	22' 00"	8' 03"
	LaSalle {4}	PF	1983	D	55*	65' 00"	20' 00"	7' 05"
	Marquette II {2}	PF	2005	D	65*	74' 00"	23' 06"	8' 00"
	Radisson {2}	PF	1988	D	97*	80' 00"	23' 06"	7' 00"
S-30	**STATE OF NEW YORK POWER AUTHORITY, LEWISTON, NY**							
	Breaker	TB	1962	D	29*	43' 03"	14' 03"	5' 00"
	Daniel Joncaire	TB	1979	D	25*	43' 03"	15' 00"	5' 00"
S-31	**STEAMER COLUMBIA FOUNDATION, DETROIT, MI** *(boblosteamers.com)*							
	Columbia {2}	PA	1902	R	968*	216' 00"	60' 00"	13' 06"
	Built: Detroit Dry Dock Co, Detroit, MI; former Detroit to Bob-Lo Island passenger steamer last operated Sept. 2, 1991; laid up at Ecorse, MI							
T-1	**TALISMAN ENERGY INC., CALGARY, AB**							
	Vessels are engaged in oil and gas exploration on Lake Erie							
	Dr. Bob	DV	1973	B	1,022*	160' 01"	54' 01"	11' 01"
	Built: Cenac Shipyard Co. Inc., Houna, LA (Mr. Chris '73-'03)							
	J.R. Rouble	DV	1958	D	562*	123' 06"	49' 08"	16' 00"
	Built: American Marine Machinery Co., Nashville, TN (Mr. Neil)							
	Miss Libby	DV	1972	B	924*	160' 01"	54' 01"	11' 01"
	Built: Service Machine & Shipbuilding Corp., Morgan City, LA							
	Sarah No. 1	TB	1969	D	43*	72' 01"	17' 03"	6' 08"
	Built: Halter Boats Ltd., New Orleans, LA							
	Timesaver II	DB	1964	B	510*	91' 08"	70' 08"	9' 01"
T-2	**TGL MARINE HOLDINGS ULC, TORONTO, ON**							
	Jane Ann IV	ATB	1978	D	954*	137' 06"	42' 08"	21' 04"
	Built: Mitsui Engineering & Shipbuilding Co., Tokyo, Japan (Ouro Fino '78-'81, Bomare '81-'93, Tignish Sea '93-'98)							
	Sarah Spencer	SU	1959	B	23,200	611" 03"	72' 00"	40' 00"
	Built: Manitowoc Shipbuilding Co., Manitowoc, WI; engine removed, converted to a self-unloading barge by Halifax Dartmouth Industries, Halifax, NS, in '89 (Adam E. Cornelius {3} '59-'89, Capt. Edward V. Smith '89-'91, Sea Barge One '91-'96)							
	[Jane Ann IV / Sarah Spencer OA dimensions together]					729' 03"	72" 00"	40' 00"
T-3	**THOMAS A. KOWAL (APALACHEE MARINE), ROCHESTER, NY**							
	Apalachee	TB	1943	DE	224*	104' 03"	26' 04"	15' 01"
	Built: Ira S. Bushey & Sons Inc., Brooklyn, NY (Apalachee WYTM-71)							
T-4	**THOUSAND ISLANDS AND SEAWAY CRUISES, BROCKVILLE, ON** *(1000islandscruises.com)*							
	Alouette	ES	1954	D	7*	31' 00"	10' 05"	3' 02"
	General Brock III	ES	1977	D	56*	50' 05"	15' 04"	5' 02"
	(Miss Peterborough)							
	Island Heritage	ES	1929	D	21*	63' 09"	9' 08"	4' 09"
	(Miss Ivy Lea No. 1)							
	Sea Fox II	ES	1988	D	55*	39' 08"	20' 00"	2' 00"
T-5	**THUNDER BAY TUG SERVICES LTD., THUNDER BAY, ON**							
	Glenada	TB	1943	D	107*	80' 06"	25' 00"	10' 01"
	Built: Russel Brothers Ltd., Owen Sound, ON (HMCS Glenada [W-30] '43-'45)							

Fleet #.	Fleet Name Vessel Name	Type of Vessel	Year Built	Type of Engine	Cargo Cap. or Gross*	Overall Length	Breadth	Depth or Draft*
	Miseford	TB	1915	D	116*	85' 00"	20' 00"	10' 06"
	Built: M. Beatty & Sons Ltd., Welland, ON							
	Point Valour	TB	1958	D	246*	97' 08"	28' 02"	13' 10"
	Built: Davie Shipbuilding Co., Lauzon, QC (Foundation Valour '58-'83)							
	THUNDER BAY MARINE SERVICES LTD., A DIVISION OF THUNDER BAY TUG SERVICES LTD.							
	Coastal Cruiser	TB	1939	D	29*	65' 00"	18' 00"	12' 00"
	Built: George Gamble, Port Dover, ON							
	Robert W.	TB	1949	D	48*	60' 00"	16' 00"	8' 06"
	Built: Russel Brothers Ltd., Owen Sound, ON							
	Rosalee D.	TB	1943	D	22*	55' 00"	16' 00"	10' 00"
	Built: Northern Shipbuilding & Repair Co. Ltd., Bronte, ON							
T-6	**TNT DREDGING INC., GRAND RAPIDS, MI**							
	Bonnie G.	TB	1928	D	95*	86' 00"	21' 00"	12' 00"
	Built: Manitowoc Shipbuilding Co., Manitowoc, WI (E. James Fucik '28-'77, Bonnie G. Selvick '77-'04)							
	Empire State	TB	1951	D	21*	45' 00"	12' 06"	16' 08"
	Joyce Marie	TB	1960	D	36*	46' 02"	15' 02"	6' 03"
	(Kendee '60-'71, Morelli '71-?, Michelle B ?-'98, Debra Ann '98-'03)							
	Wolverine	TB	1952	D	22*	42' 05"	14' 00"	7' 00"
T-7	**TOBERMORY ADVENTURE TOURS, TOBERMORY, ON**							
	Dawn Light	TB	1891	D	64*	75' 00"	24' 00"	12' 00"
	(Le Roy Brooks 1891-'25, Henry Stokes '25-'54, Aburg '54-'81)							
T-8	**TORONTO DRYDOCK LTD., TORONTO, ON**							
	M. R. Kane	TB	1945	D	51*	60' 06"	16' 05"	6' 07"
	Built: Central Bridge Co. Ltd., Trenton, ON (Tanac V-276 '45-'47)							
	Menier Consol	FD	1962	B	2,575*	304' 05"	49' 06"	25' 06"
	Built: Davie Shipbuilding Co., Lauzon, QC; former pulpwood carrier is now a floating dry dock at Toronto, ON							
T-9	**TORONTO FIRE DEPARTMENT, TORONTO, ON**							
	Wm. Lyon Mackenzie	FB	1964	D	102*	81' 01"	20' 00"	10' 00"
	Built: Russel Brothers Ltd., Owen Sound, ON							
T-10	**TORONTO PADDLEWHEEL CRUISES LTD., NORTH YORK, ON**							
	Pioneer Princess	ES	1984	D	74*	56' 00"	17' 01"	3' 09"
	Pioneer Queen	ES	1968	D	110*	85' 00"	30' 06"	7' 03"
	(Peche Island III '68-'71, Papoose IV '71-'96)							
T-11	**TORONTO PARKS & RECREATION DEPARTMENT, TORONTO, ON**							
	Ongiara	PF	1963	D	180*	78' 00"	12' 04"	9' 09"
	Built: Russel Brothers Ltd., Owen Sound, ON							
	Sam McBride	PF	1939	D	412*	129' 00"	34' 11"	6' 00"
	Built:Toronto Dry Dock Co. Ltd., Toronto, ON							
	Thomas Rennie	PF	1950	D	419*	129' 00"	32' 11"	6' 00"
	Built: Toronto Dry Dock Co. Ltd., Toronto, ON							
	Trillium	PF	1910	R	611*	150' 00"	30' 00"	8' 04"
	Built: Poulson Iron Works, Toronto, ON							
	William Inglis	PF	1935	D	238*	99' 00"	24' 10"	6' 00"
	Built: John Inglis Co. Ltd., Toronto, ON (Shamrock {2} '35-'37)							
T-12	**TORONTO PORT AUTHORITY, TORONTO, ON** *(torontoport.com)*							
	Brutus I	TB	1992	D	10*	36' 01"	11' 09"	4' 04"
	Fred Scandrett	TB	1963	D	52*	62' 00"	17' 00"	8' 00"
	Built: Port Weller Dry Docks Ltd., St. Catharines, ON (C. E. "Ted" Smith '63-'70)							
	Maple City	PA/CF	1951	D	135*	70' 06"	36' 04"	5' 11"
	TCCA 1	PA/CF	2006	D	219*	95' 10"	37' 07"	7' 05"
	William Rest	TB	1961	D	62*	65' 00"	18' 06"	10' 06"
	Built: Erieau Shipbuilding & Drydock Co. Ltd., Erieau, ON							
	Windmill Point	PA/CF	1954	D	118*	65' 00"	36' 00"	10' 00"
T-13	**TORONTO PUBLIC WORKS DEPARTMENT, TORONTO, ON**							
	Ned Hanlan II	TB	1966	D	26*	41' 06"	14' 01"	5' 05"

***Lee A. Tregurtha* upbound below Mission Point.** *(Brian Kimball)*

Fleet #.	Fleet Name Vessel Name	Type of Vessel	Year Built	Type of Engine	Cargo Cap. or Gross*	Overall Length	Breadth	Depth or Draft*
T-14	**TORONTO TOURS LTD., TORONTO, ON** *(www.torontotours.com)*							
	Miss Kim Simpson	ES	1960	D	33*	90' 02"	13' 04"	3' 09"
	New Beginnings	ES	1961	D	28*	41' 09"	13' 01"	4' 09"
	Shipsands	ES	1972	D	23*	58' 03"	12' 01"	4' 07"
T-15	**TRANSPORT DESGAGNÉS INC., QUÉBEC, QC** *(groupedesgagnes.com)*							
	SUBSIDIARY OF GROUPE DESGAGNÉS INC., QUÉBEC CITY, QC							
	Amelia Desgagnés	GC	1976	D	7,126	355' 00"	49' 00"	30' 06"
	Built: Collingwood Shipyards, Collingwood, ON (Soodoc {2} '76-'90)							
	Anna Desgagnés	RR	1986	D	17,850	565' 00"	75' 00"	45' 00"
	Built: Kvaerner Warnow Werft GmbH, Rostock, Germany; re-registered in the Bahamas in 2006 (Truskavets '86-'96, Anna Desgagnés '96-'98, PCC Panama '98-'99)							
	Camilla Desgagnés	GC	1982	D	7,000	436' 00"	68' 05"	22' 06"
	Built: Kroeger Werft GmbH & Co. KG, Rendsburg, Germany (Camilla 1 '82-'04)							
	Catherine Desgagnés	GC	1962	D	8,350	410' 03"	56' 04"	31' 00"
	Built: Hall, Russel and Co., Aberdeen, Scotland (Gosforth '62-'72, Thorold {4} '72-'85)							
	Melissa Desgagnés	GC	1975	D	7,000	355' 00"	49' 00"	30' 06"
	Built: Collingwood Shipyards, Collingwood, ON (Ontadoc {2} '75-'90)							
	Rosaire A. Desgagnés	GC	2007	D	12,580	452' 11"	70' 01"	36' 01"
	Built: Quingshan/Jiangdong/Jiangzhou Shipyards, Jiangzhou, China (Beluga Fortification '07-'07)							
	Zelada Desgagnés	GC	2008	D	*New construction – details unavailable*			
	Built: Quingshan/Jiangdong/Jiangzhou Shipyards, Jiangzhou, China							
	THE FOLLOWING VESSELS CHARTERED TO PETRO-NAV INC., MONTREAL, QC,							
	Maria Desgagnés	TK	1999	D	14,335	393' 08"	68' 11"	40' 04"
	Built: Qiuxin Shipyard, Shanghai, China (Kilchem Asia '99-'99)							
	Petrolia Desgagnés	TK	1975	D	9,712	441' 05"	56' 06"	32' 10"
	Built: Ankerlokken Verft Glommen, Fredrikstad, Norway (Jorvan '75-'79, Lido '79-'84, Ek-Sky '84-'98)							
	Sarah Desgagnés	TK	2007	D	18,000	483'11"	73' 06"	41' 04"
	Built: Gisan Shipyard, Tuzla, Turkey (Besiktas Greenland '07 - '08)							
	Thalassa Desgagnés	TK	1976	D	9,748	441' 05"	56' 06"	32' 10"
	Built: Ankerlokken Verft Glommen, Fredrikstad, Norway (Joasla '76-'79, Orinoco '79-'82, Rio Orinoco '82-'93)							
	Vega Desgagnés	TK	1982	D	11,548	461' 11"	69' 08"	35' 01"
	Built: Kvaerner Masa-Yards, Helsinki, Finland (Shelltrans '82-'94, Acila '94-'99, Bacalan '99-'01)							
	THE FOLLOWING VESSEL CHARTERED TO RELAIS NORDIC INC., RIMOUSKI, QC							
	Nordik Express	CF	1974	D	1,697	219' 11"	44' 00"	16' 01"
	Built: Todd Pacific Shipyards Corp., Seattle, WA (Theriot Offshore IV '74-'77, Scotoil 4 '77-'79, Tartan Sea '79-'87)							
T-16	**TRANSPORT IGLOOLIK INC., MONTREAL, QC**							
	Aivik	HL	1980	D	4,860	359' 08"	63' 08"	38' 09"
	Built: ACH - Construction Navale, Le Havre, France (Mont Ventoux '80-'90, Aivik '90-'91, Unilifter '91-'92)							
T-17	**TRAVERSE TALL SHIP CO., TRAVERSE CITY, MI** *(tallshipsailing.com)*							
	Manitou {1}	ES/2S	1983	W	78*	114' 00"	21' 00"	9' 00"
T-18	**30,000 ISLANDS CRUISE LINES INC., PARRY SOUND, ON** *(island-queen.com)*							
	Island Queen V {3}	ES	1990	D	526*	130' 00"	35' 00"	6' 06"
U-1	**UNCLE SAM BOAT TOURS, ALEXANDRIA, NY** *(usboattours.com)*							
	Alexandria Belle	ES	1988	D	92*	82' 00"	32' 00"	8' 00"
	Island Duchess	ES	1988	D	73*	90' 03"	27' 08"	9' 00"
	Island Wanderer	ES	1971	D	57*	62' 05"	22' 00"	7' 02"
	Uncle Sam 7	ES	1976	D	55*	60' 04"	22' 00"	7' 01"
U-2	**U.S. ARMY CORPS OF ENGINEERS – GREAT LAKES AND OHIO RIVER DIVISION, CINCINNATI, OH** *(usace.army.mil)* **U.S. ARMY CORPS OF ENGINEERS – BUFFALO DISTRICT**							
	Cheraw	TB	1970	D	356*	109' 00"	30' 06"	16' 03"
	Built: Southern Shipbuilding Corp., Slidell, LA (USS Cheraw [YTB-802] '70-'96)							
	Simonsen	CS	1954	B		142' 00"	58' 00"	5' 00"
	U.S. ARMY CORPS OF ENGINEERS – DETROIT DISTRICT, LAKE MICHIGAN AREA OFFICE, KEWAUNEE SUB OFFICE							
	Kenosha	TB	1954	D	82*	70' 00"	20' 00"	9' 08"
	Built: Missouri Valley Bridge & Iron Works, Leavenworth, KS (U. S. Army ST-2011 '54-'65)							

Fleet #	Fleet Name Vessel Name	Type of Vessel	Year Built	Type of Engine	Cargo Cap. or Gross*	Overall Length	Breadth	Depth or Draft*
	Manitowoc	CS	1976	B		132'00"	44'00"	8'00"
	Racine	TB	1931	D	61*	66'03"	18'05"	7'08"
	U.S. ARMY CORPS OF ENGINEERS – DETROIT DISTRICT, DETROIT AREA OFFICE							
	Demolen	TB	1974	D	356*	109'00"	30'06"	16'03"
	Built: Marinette Marine Corp., Marinette, WI (USS Metacom [YTB-829] '74-'01, Metacom '01-'02)							
	Veler	CS	1991	B	613*	150'00"	46'00"	10'06"
	U.S. ARMY CORPS OF ENGINEERS – DETROIT DISTRICT, DULUTH AREA OFFICE							
	D. L. Billmaier	TB	1968	D	356*	109'00"	30'06"	16'03"
	Built: Southern Shipbuilding Corp., Slidell, LA (USS Natchitoches [YTB-799] '68-'95)							
	H. J. Schwartz	DB	1995	B		150'00"	48'00"	11'00"
	Hammond Bay	TB	1953	D	23*	45'00"	13'00"	7'00"
	U.S. ARMY CORPS OF ENGINEERS – DETROIT DISTRICT, SOO AREA OFFICE							
	Harvey	DB	1961	B		120'00"	40'00"	8'00"
	Nicolet	DB	1971	B		120'00"	40'00"	8'00"
	Owen M. Frederick	TB	1942	D	56*	65'00"	17'00"	7'06"
	Built: Sturgeon Bay Shipbuilding Co., Sturgeon Bay, WI							
	Paul Bunyan	GL	1945	B		150'00"	65'00"	12'06"
	Whitefish Bay	TB	1953	D	23*	45'00"	13'00"	7'00"
U-3	**U.S. COAST GUARD 9TH COAST GUARD DISTRICT, CLEVELAND, OH** *(uscg.mil/d9)*							
	Alder **[WLB-216]**	BT	2004	D	2,000*	225'09"	46'00"	19'08"
	Built: Marinette Marine Corp., Marinette, WI; stationed at Duluth, MN							
	Biscayne Bay **[WTGB-104]**	IB	1979	D	662*	140'00"	37'06"	12'00"
	Built: Tacoma Boatbuilding Co., Tacoma, WA; stationed at St. Ignace, MI							
	Bristol Bay **[WTGB-102]**	IB	1979	D	662*	140'00"	37'06"	12'00"
	Built: Tacoma Boatbuilding Co., Tacoma, WA; stationed at Detroit, MI							
	Buckthorn **[WLI-642]**	BT	1963	D	200*	100'00"	24'00"	4'08"
	Built: Mobile Ship Repair, Inc., Mobile, AL; stationed at Sault Ste. Marie, MI							
	CGB-12000	BT	1991	B	700*	120'00"	50'00"	6'00"
	CGB-12001	BT	1991	B	700*	120'00"	50'00"	6'00"
	Hollyhock **[WLB-214]**	BT	2003	D	2,000*	225'09"	46'00"	19'08"
	Built: Marinette Marine Corp., Marinette, WI; stationed at Port Huron, MI							
	Katmai Bay **[WTGB-101]**	IB	1978	D	662*	140'00"	37'06"	12'00"
	Built: Tacoma Boatbuilding Co., Tacoma, WA; stationed at Sault Ste. Marie, MI							
	Mackinaw **[WLBB-30]**	IB	2005	D	15'06"*	240'00"	58'00"	15'05"
	Built: Marinette Marine Corp., Marinette, WI; stationed at Cheboygan, MI							
	Mobile Bay **[WTGB-103]**	IB	1979	D	662*	140'00"	37'06"	12'00"
	Built: Tacoma Boatbuilding Co., Tacoma, WA; stationed at Sturgeon Bay, WI							
	Neah Bay **[WTGB-105]**	IB	1980	D	662*	140'00"	37'06"	12'00"
	Built: Tacoma Boatbuilding Co., Tacoma, WA; stationed at Cleveland, OH							
U-4	**U.S. ENVIRONMENTAL PROTECTION AGENCY, DULUTH, MN AND CHICAGO, IL**							
	Lake Guardian	RV	1981	D	282*	180'00"	40'00"	11'00"
	Built: Halter Marine Inc., Moss Point MS (Marsea Fourteen '81-'90)							
U-5	**U.S. FISH & WILDLIFE SERVICE, JORDAN RIVER NATIONAL FISH HATCHERY, ELMIRA, MI**							
	Spencer F. Baird	RV	2006	D	256*	95'00"	30'00"	9'05"
U-6	**U.S. NATIONAL PARK SERVICE - ISLE ROYALE NATIONAL PARK, HOUGHTON, MI**							
	Greenstone II	TK	2003	B	114*	70'01"	24'01"	8'00"
	Ranger III	PK	1958	D	648*	152'08"	34'00"	13'00"
	Built: Christy Corp, Sturgeon Bay, WI							
U-7	**U.S. NAVAL SEA CADET CORPS** *(seacadets.org)*							
	Grayfox **[TWR-825]**	TV	1985	D	213*	120'00"	25'00"	12'00"
	Built: Marinette Marine, Marinette, WI; based at Port Huron, MI (USS TWR-825 '85-'97)							
	Manatra **[YP-671]**	TV	1974	D	67*	80'05"	17'09"	5'04"
	Based at Chicago, IL; name stands for MArine NAvigation and TRaining Association (USS YP-671 '74-'89)							
	Pride of Michigan **[YP-673]**	TV	1977	D	70*	80'06"	17'08"	5'03"
	Built: Peterson Builders Inc., Sturgeon Bay, WI; based at Mount Clemens, MI (USS YP-673 '77-'89)							

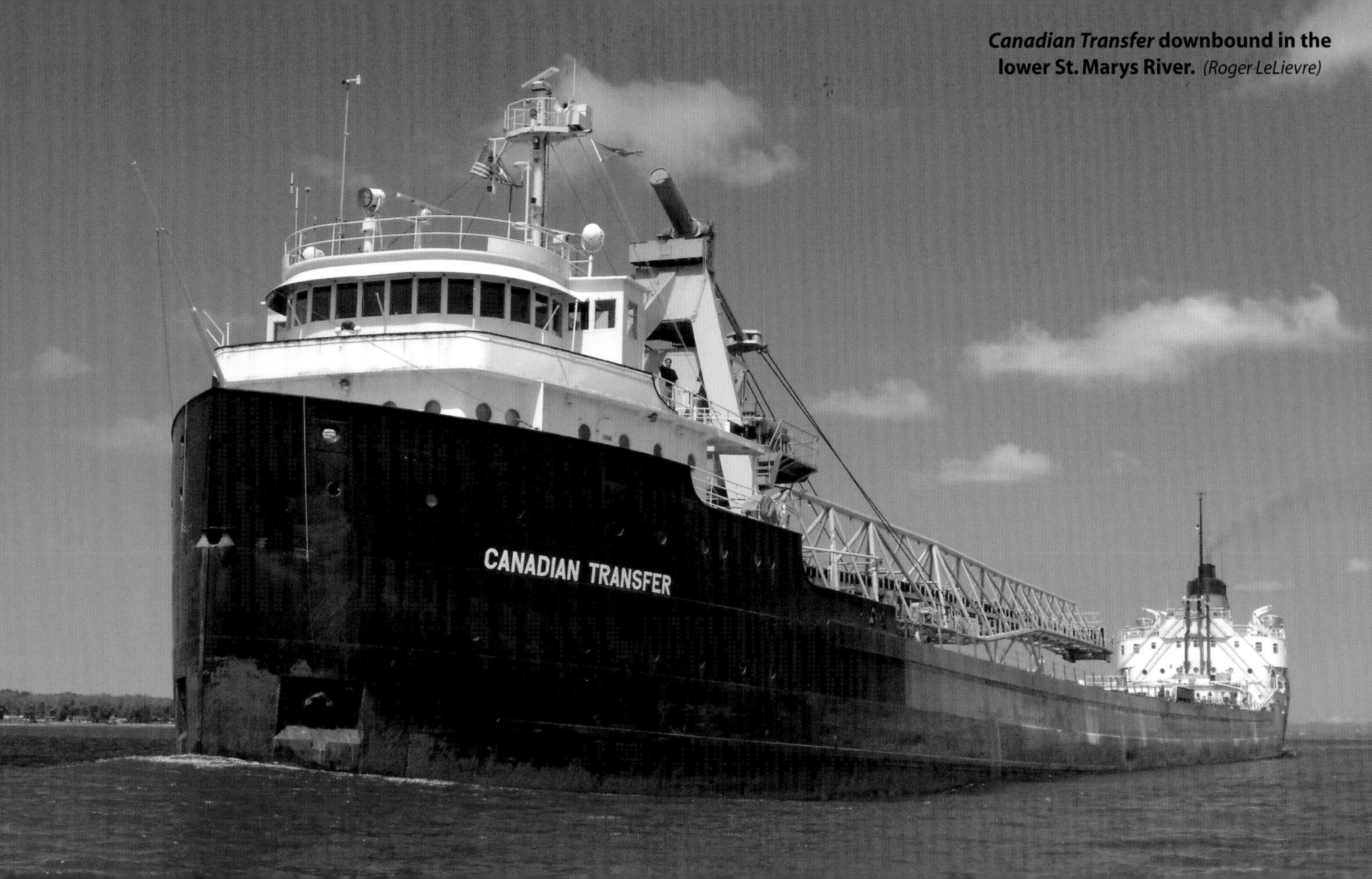

***Canadian Transfer* downbound in the lower St. Marys River.** *(Roger LeLievre)*

Fleet #	Fleet Name Vessel Name	Type of Vessel	Year Built	Type of Engine	Cargo Cap. or Gross*	Overall Length	Breadth	Depth or Draft*
U-9	**UNIVERSITÉ DU QUÉBEC À RIMOUSKI, RIMOUSKI, QC**							
	Coriolis II	RV	1990	D	836*	163'10"	36'01"	22'11"
U-10	**UNIVERSITY OF MINNESOTA-DULUTH, DULUTH, MN**							
	Blue Heron	RV	1985	D	175*	119'06"	28'00"	15'06"
	Built: Goudy and Stevens, E. Boothbay, ME (Fairtry '85-'97)							
U-11	**UNIVERSITY OF WISCONSIN, GREAT LAKES WATER INSTITUTE, MILWAUKEE, WI**							
	Neeskay	RV	1952	D	75*	71'00"	17'06"	7'06"
U-12	**UNIVERSITY OF WISCONSIN, SUPERIOR, WI**							
	L. L. Smith Jr.	RV	1950	D	38*	57'06"	16'06"	6'06"
U-13	**UPPER LAKES GROUP INC., TORONTO, ON** *(upperlakes.com)*							
	DISTRIBUTION GRANDS LACS/ST-LAURENT LTEE, TROIS RIVIERES, QC – A DIVISION OF UPPER LAKES GROUP INC.							
	Barge Laviolette	BC	1965	B	7,573	498'00"	75'00"	39'03"
	Grain storage barge built from bow/cargo sections of powered vessel Canadian Explorer by Port Weller Dry Docks, St. Catharines, ON, in '01							
	Commodore Straits	TB	1966	D	566*	130'00"	34'01"	15'07"
	Built: Dominion Steel & Coal Corp., Halifax, NS (Haida Brave '66-'79)							
	Doc Morin	TB	1954	D	225*	101'10"	26'00"	13'08"
	Built: Davie Shipbuilding Co., Lauzon, QC (Seven Sisters '54-'05)							
	PROVMAR FUELS INC., HAMILTON, ON – A DIVISION OF UPPER LAKES GROUP INC.							
	Hamilton Energy	TK	1965	D	1,282	201'05"	34'01"	14'09"
	Built: Grangemouth Dockyard Co., Grangemouth, Scotland (Partington '65-'79, Shell Scientist '79-'81, Metro Sun '81-'85)							
	Provmar Terminal	TK	1959	B	7,300	403'05"	55'06"	28'05"
	Built: Sarpsborg Mek, Verksted, Greater Norway; last operated in 1984; in use as a fuel storage barge at Hamilton, ON (Varangnes '59-'70, Tommy Wiborg '70-'74, Ungava Transport '74-'85)							
	Provmar Terminal II	TK	1948	B	6,832	408'08"	53'00"	26'00"
	Built: Collingwood Shipyards, Collingwood, ON; last operated 1986; in use as a fuel storage barge at Hamilton, ON (Imperial Sarnia {2} '48-'89)							
	UPPER LAKES SHIPPING LTD., CALGARY, AB – DIVISION OF UPPER LAKES GROUP INC. * VESSELS OPERATED AND MANAGED BY SEAWAY MARINE TRANSPORT, ST. CATHARINES, ON, A PARTNERSHIP BETWEEN ALGOMA CENTRAL CORP. AND UPPER LAKES GROUP INC.							
	Canadian Enterprise*	SU	1979	D	35,100	730'00"	75'08"	46'06"
	Built: Port Weller Dry Docks, Port Weller, ON							
	Canadian Leader*	BC	1967	T	28,300	730'00"	75'00"	39'08"
	Built: Collingwood Shipyards, Collingwood, ON; last steam-powered vessel built on lakes (Feux-Follets '67-'72)							
	Canadian Miner*	BC	1966	D	28,050	730'00"	75'00"	39'01"
	Built: Canadian Vickers, Montreal, QC (Maplecliffe Hall '66-'88, Lemoyne {2} '88-'94)							
	Canadian Navigator*	SU	1967	D	30,925	728'11"	75'10"	40'06"
	Built: J. Readhead & Sons, South Shields, England; converted from a saltwater bulk carrier in '80; converted to a self-unloader in '97; both conversions by Port Weller Dry Docks, St. Catharines, ON (Demeterton '67-'75, St. Lawrence Navigator '75-'80)							
	Canadian Olympic*	SU	1976	D	35,100	730'00"	75'00"	46'06"
	Built: Port Weller Dry Docks, Port Weller, ON							
	Canadian Progress*	SU	1968	D	32,700	730'00"	75'00"	46'06"
	Built: Port Weller Dry Docks, Port Weller, ON							
	Canadian Prospector*	BC	1964	D	30,500	730'00"	75'10"	40'06"
	Built: Short Brothers Ltd., Sunderland, England; converted from a saltwater bulk carrier by St. John Shipbuilding and Drydock, Saint John, NB, in '79 (Carlton '64-'75, St. Lawrence Prospector '75-'79)							
	Canadian Provider*	BC	1963	T	27,450	730'00"	75'00"	39'02"
	Built: Collingwood Shipyards, Collingwood, ON (Murray Bay {3} '63-'94)							
	Canadian Ranger*	SU	1943/67	D	25,900	729'10"	75'00"	39'03"
	Canadian Ranger was built by joining the stern section (pilothouse, engine room, machinery) of the former coastal package freighter Chimo with the bow and mid-body of the laker Hilda Marjanne in '84; converted to a self- unloader in '88; all work by Port Weller Dry Docks, St. Catharines, ON ***(Fore Section)*** *Built: Kaiser Inc., Portland, OR, as Grande Ronde '43-'48, Kate N. L. '48-'61, Hilda Marjanne '61-'84); converted from a saltwater bulk carrier in '61* ***(Stern Section)*** *Built: Davie Shipbuilding Co., Lauzon, QC, as Chimo '67-'83)*							

Fleet #.	Fleet Name Vessel Name	Type of Vessel	Year Built	Type of Engine	Cargo Cap. or Gross*	Overall Length	Breadth	Depth or Draft*
	Canadian Transfer*	SU	1943/65	D	22,204	650′ 06″	60′ 00″	35′ 00″
	Canadian Transfer was built by joining the stern section of Canadian Explorer (engine room, machinery) with the bow and mid-body of the World War II-era laker Hamilton Transfer in '98; all work by Port Weller Dry Docks, St. Catharines, ON ***(Fore Section)*** *Built: Great Lakes Engineering Works, Ashtabula, OH, as J. H. Hillman Jr. '43-'74, Crispin Oglebay {2} '74-'95, Hamilton Transfer '95-'98), converted to a self-unloader in '74* ***(Stern Section)*** *Built: Davie Shipbuilding Co., Lauzon, QC as Cabot {1} '65-'83, Canadian Explorer '83-'98)*							
	Canadian Transport* {2}	SU	1979	D	35,100	730′ 00″	75′ 08″	46′ 06″
	Built: Port Weller Dry Docks, Port Weller, ON							
	Gordon C. Leitch* {2}	BC	1968	D	29,700	730′ 00″	75′ 00″	42′ 00″
	Built: Canadian Vickers, Montreal, QC; converted from a self-unloader to a bulk carrier by the builders in '77 (Ralph Misener '68-'94)							
	James Norris*	SU	1952	S	18,600	663′ 06″	67′ 00″	35′ 00″
	Built: Midland Shipyards, Midland, ON; converted to a self-unloader by Port Weller Dry Docks, St. Catharines, ON, in '81							
	John D. Leitch*	SU	1967	D	31,600	730′ 00″	78′ 00″	45′ 00″
	Built: Port Weller Dry Docks, Port Weller, ON; rebuilt with new mid-body, widened 3' by the builders in '02 (Canadian Century '67-'02)							
	Montrealais*	BC	1962	T	27,800	730′ 00″	75′ 00″	39′ 00″
	Built: Canadian Vickers, Montreal, QC (Launched as Montrealer)							
	Quebecois*	BC	1963	T	27,800	730′ 00″	75′ 00″	39′ 00″
	Built: Canadian Vickers, Montreal, QC							
U-14	**UPPER LAKES TOWING CO., ESCANABA, MI**							
	Joseph H. Thompson	SU	1944	B	21,200	706′ 06″	71′ 06″	38′ 06″
	Built: Sun Shipbuilding & Drydock Co., Chester, PA; converted from a saltwater vessel to a Great Lakes bulk carrier by Maryland Dry Dock, Baltimore, MD, and American Shipbuilding, South Chicago, IL, in '52; converted to a self-unloading barge by the owners in '91 (USNS Marine Robin '44-'52)							
	Joseph H. Thompson Jr.	ATB	1990	D	841*	146′ 06″	38′ 00″	35′ 00″
	Built: At Marinette, WI, from steel left over from the conversion of Joseph H. Thompson (see above)							
U-15	**USLHS MAPLE LLC, WAUWATOSA, WI**							
	Maple	MU	1939	D	350*	122′ 03″	27′ 00″	7′ 06″
	Built: Marine Ironworks and Shipbuilding Corp., Duluth, MN; former U.S. Coast Guard lighthouse tender EPA vessel (USCGC Maple [WLI / WAGL-234] '39-'73, Roger R. Simons '73-'94)							

Canadian Coast Guard research vessel *Limnos*. *Alain Gindroz)*

Fleet #	Fleet Name Vessel Name	Type of Vessel	Year Built	Type of Engine	Cargo Cap. or Gross*	Overall Length	Breadth	Depth or Draft*
U-16	**USS COD SUBMARINE MEMORIAL, CLEVELAND, OH** *(usscod.org)*							
	Cod	MU	1943	D/V	1,525*	311′08″	27′02″	33′09″
	Built: Electric Boat Co., Groton, CT; former U.S. Navy Albacore (Gato) class submarine IXSS-224 open to the public at Cleveland, OH							
V-1	**VANENKEVORT TUG & BARGE INC., BARK RIVER, MI**							
	Great Lakes Trader	SU	2000	B	39,600	740′00″	78′00″	45′00″
	Built: Halter Marine, Pearlington, MS							
	Joyce L. VanEnkevort	AT	1998	D	1,179*	135′04″	50′00″	26′00″
	Built: Bay Shipbuilding Co., Sturgeon Bay, WI							
	[ATB VanEnkevort / GL Trader OA dimensions together]					844′10″	78′00″	45′00″
V-2	**VIC POWELL, DUNNVILLE, ON**							
	Beaver D.	TB	1955	D	15*	36′02″	14′09″	4′04″
	Lac Erie	TB	1944	D	65*	65′00″	16′10″	7′07″
	Built: Central Bridge Co., Trenton, ON (Tanmac '44-'74)							
	Toni D	TB	1959	D	15*	46′00″	15′07″	4′01″
V-3	**VICTORIAN PRINCESS CRUISE LINES INC., ERIE, PA**							
	Victorian Princess	ES	1985	D	46*	67′00″	24′00″	4′05″
	(Rosie 1, Rosie O'Shea)							
V-4	**VINCENT KLAMERUS, DRUMMOND ISLAND, MI**							
	Lime Island	PA	1953	D	24*	42′08″	12′00″	6′00″
V-5	**VISTA FLEET, DULUTH, MN** *(vistafleet.com)*							
	Vista King	ES	1978	D	60*	78′00″	23′00″	5′02″
	Vista Queen	ES	1987	D	97*	64′00″	16′00″	6′02″
	Vista Star	ES	1987	D	95*	91′00″	24′09″	5′02″
	(Island Empress '87-'88)							
V-6	**VOIGHT'S MARINE SERVICES LTD., ELLISON BAY AND GILLS ROCK, WI**							
	Island Clipper {2}	ES	1987	D	71*	65′00″	20′00″	8′00″
	Yankee Clipper	ES	1971	D	41*	46′06″	17′00″	6′00″
V-7	**VOYAGEUR MARINE TRANSPORT LTD., RIDGEVILLE, ON** *(voyageurtransport.com)*							
	VOYAGEUR MARITIME TRADING INC., OWNER							
	Maritime Trader	BC	1967	D	19,093	607′10″	62′00″	36′00″
	Built: Collingwood Shipyards, Collingwood, ON; commercially operated under contract of affreightment to Lower Lakes Towing Ltd. (Mantadoc '67-'02, Teakglen '02-'05)							
W-1	**WASHINGTON ISLAND FERRY LINE INC., WASHINGTON ISLAND, WI** *(wisferry.com)*							
	Arni J. Richter	PA/CF	2003	D	92*	104′00″	38′06″	10′11″
	C. G. Richter	PA/CF	1950	D	82*	70′06″	25′00″	9′05″
	Eyrarbakki	PA/CF	1970	D	95*	87′00″	36′00″	7′06″
	Robert Noble	PA/CF	1979	D	97*	90′04″	36′00″	8′03″
	Washington {2}	PA/CF	1989	D	93*	100′00″	37′00″	9′00″
W-2	**WENDELLA BOAT TOURS, CHICAGO, IL** *(wendellaboats.com)*							
	Sunliner	ES	1959	D	41*	67′00″	20′00″	4′00″
	Wendella	ES	1961	D	35*	68′00″	17′00″	6′05″
	Wendella LTD	ES	1992	D	66*	68′00″	20′00″	4′09″
W-3	**WINDY OF CHICAGO LTD., CHICAGO, IL** *(tallshipwindy.com)*							
	Windy	ES/4S	1996	W	75*	148′00″	25′00″	8′00″
	Built: Detyens Shipyards Inc., Charleston, SC							
	Windy II	ES/4S	2000	W	99*	150′00″	25′00″	8′05″
	Built: Detyens Shipyards Inc., Charleston, SC							
W-4	**WISCONSIN DEPARTMENT OF NATURAL RESOURCES, BAYFIELD AND STURGEON BAY, WI**							
	Barney Devine	RV	1937	D	42*	50′00″	14′05″	6′00″
	Hack Noyes	RV	1947	D	50*	56′00″		4′00″

Fleet #.	Fleet Name Vessel Name	Type of Vessel	Year Built	Type of Engine	Cargo Cap. or Gross*	Overall Length	Breadth	Depth or Draft*
W-5	**WISCONSIN MARITIME MUSEUM, MANITOWOC, WI** *(wisconsinmaritime.org)*							
	Cobia	MU	1944	D/V	1,500*	311′ 09″	27′ 03″	33′ 09″
	Built: Manitowoc Shipbuilding Co., Manitowoc, WI; former U. S. Navy Gato class submarine AGSS-245 is open to the public at Manitowoc, WI							
Y-1	**YALMER MATTILA CONTRACTING INC., HANCOCK, MI**							
	J. E. Colombe	TB	1954	D	23*	45′ 00″	13′ 00″	7′ 00″
	(ST-2174)							
	Oshkosh # 15	DB	1944	B	238*	137′ 00″	21′ 06″	9′ 00″
Z-1	**ZENITH TUGBOAT CO., DULUTH, MN**							
	Anna Marie Altman	TB	1950	D	146*	88′ 06″	25′ 06″	11′ 00″
	Built: Alexander Shipyard Inc., New Orleans, LA (Navajo {1} '50-'52, Seaval '52-'63, Mary T. Tracy '63-'69, Yankee '69-'70, Minn '70-'74, William S. Bell '74-'83, Newcastle '83-'93, Laura Lynn '93-'99, Susan Hoey {3} '99-'06)							
	Franz A. Von Riedel	TB	1957	D	167*	96′ 00″	25′ 00″	10′ 06″
	Gesine Von Riedel	TB	1940	D	195*	101′ 00″	26′ 09″	11′ 10″
	Lacey Von Riedel	TB	1942	D	178*	96′ 00″	10′ 06″	11′ 10″
	Sioux	TB	1921	D	96*	81′ 00″	20′ 00″	12′ 06″
	Built: Great Lakes Towing Co., Cleveland, OH (Oregon {1} '21-'78, Ste. Marie I '78-'81, Sioux {2} '81-'91, Susan E. '91-'05)							
	Victor J. Altman	TB	1965	D	195*	108′ 00″	27′ 10″	12′ 00″
	Built: Walter M. Edwards, New Iberia, LA (Trans World '65-'69, Rosemary McAllister '69-'07)							
	Yankton	TB	1943	D	195*	110′ 00″	26′ 10″	13′ 08″
	Built: Ira S. Bushey & Sons Inc., Brooklyn, NY (Yankton - WYTM-72)							

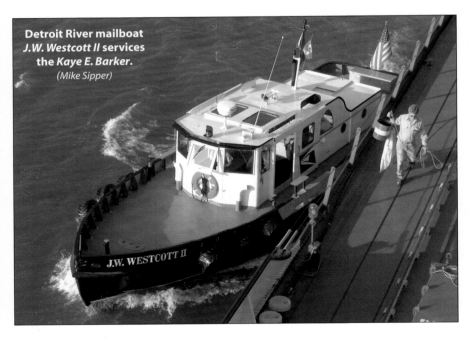

Detroit River mailboat *J.W. Westcott II* services the *Kaye E. Barker.*
(Mike Sipper)

The information in this book, current as of Feb. 15, 2008, was obtained from the United States Coast Guard, the Lake Carriers' Association, Lloyd's Register of Shipping, Transport Canada, the U.S. Army Corps of Engineers, the St. Lawrence Seaway Authority, "Shipfax," The Tugboat Enthusiasts Society of the Americas, vessel owners and operators, BoatNerd.com and publications of the Toronto Marine Historical Society, the Marine Historical Society of Detroit and the Welland Canal Ship Society.

LAKER LONGEVITY

*(re = major rebuild; * inactive)*

1898: E.M. Ford *(re: '56)**

1902: Columbia*; **1904**: J.B. Ford *(re: '59)**; **1906**: St. Marys Challenger *(re: '67)*; **1910**: Ste. Claire*; **1927**: S.T. Crapo*; **1929**: Maumee *(re: '61)*

1936: J.A.W. Iglehart *(re: '65)**; **1937**: St. Marys Conquest *(re: '87)*

1940s

1941: Pere Marquette 41 *(re: '97)*; **1942**: Alpena *(re: '91)*, American Victory *(re: '61, '82)*, Lee A. Tregurtha *(re: '61)*; **1943**: Canadian Transfer *(re: '98)*, C.T.C. #1*, Cuyahoga *(re: '74)*, Manistee *(re: '64)*, Mississagi *(re: '67)*; **1944**: Joseph H. Thompson *(re '52 and '91)*, McKee Sons *(re: '53, '91)*; **1945**: Paul H. Townsend *(re: '52)**; **1949**: Wilfred Sykes

1950s

1952: Arthur M. Anderson *(re: '75, '82)*, Kaye E. Barker *(re: '76 '81)*, Cason J. Callaway *(re: '74, '82)*, Philip R. Clarke *(re: '74, '82)*, Lewis J. Kuber *(re: '06)*, Michipicoten *(re: '57, '80)*, Ojibway, John G. Munson, James Norris *(re: '81)*; **1953**: American Valor *(re: '74, '82)*, American Fortitude *(re: '81)*, Badger, James L. Kuber *(re: '07)*, Pathfinder *(re: '98)*, Saginaw, Spartan*; **1958**: John Sherwin*; **1959**: Cedarglen *(re: '77)*, Charles M. Beeghly *(re: '72, '81)*, Herbert C. Jackson *(re: '75)*, Sarah Spencer *(re: '89)*

1960s

1960: Algontario *(re: '76)*, Edward L. Ryerson; **1961**: Canadian Ranger *(re: '84)*, English River *(re: 74)*; **1962**: Catherine Desgagnés, Montrealais; **1963**: Algoisle, Canadian Provider, Halifax, *(re: '80)*, Quebecois, Yankcanuck; **1964:** Canadian Prospector *(re: '79)*; **1965**: Stephen B. Roman *(re: '83)*; **1966**: Algosteel *(re: '89)*, Canadian Miner; **1967**: Algocape, Algoville *(re: '96)*, Canadian Leader, Canadian Navigator *(re: '80, '97)*, John D. Leitch *(re: '02)*, Maritime Trader; **1968**: Algomarine *(re: '89)*, Algorail, Canadian Progress, Frontenac *(re: '73)*, Gordon C. Leitch; **1969**: CSL Tadoussac *(re: '01)*

1970s

1970: Agawa Canyon, Sauniere *(re: '76)*; **1971**: Algonorth; **1972**: Algoway, Roger Blough, CSL Niagara *(re: '99)*, Stewart J. Cort; **1973**: Adam E. Cornelius, Manitowoc, Calumet (2), John J. Boland, Rt. Hon. Paul J. Martin *(re: '00)*, Presque Isle; **1974**: Algosoo, Chi-Cheemaun, H. Lee White, Robert S. Pierson; **1975**: Melissa Desgagnés, Petrolia Desgagnés, Sam Laud; **1976**: James R. Barker, Joseph L. Block, Canadian Olympic, Amelia Desgagnés, Thalassa Desgagnés, St. Clair; **1977**: Algoeast, Algolake, CSL Assiniboine *(re: '05)*, Laurentien *(re: '01)*, Walter J. McCarthy Jr., Mesabi Miner; **1978**: Algobay*, Algosar, American Integrity, American Spirit, Buffalo; **1979**: Algoport, American Courage, Canadian Enterprise, Canadian Transport, Edwin H. Gott, Indiana Harbor

1980s

1980: American Mariner, Burns Harbor, Nanticoke, Edgar B. Speer; **1981**: Algowood *(re: '00)*, American Century, American Republic, Capt. Henry Jackman *(re: '96)*, Paul R. Tregurtha; **1982**: Algowest, Atlantic Superior, Camilla Desgagnes, Peter R. Cresswell *(re: '98)*, Michigan, Vega Desgagnés; **1983**: John B. Aird, Birchglen, Spruceglen, Kaministiqua; **1984**: Atlantic Huron *(re: '89, '03)*; **1985**: Atlantic Erie, Pineglen; **1986**: Anna Desgagnes

1990s

1992: Diamond Star, Emerald Star; **1993**: Jade Star; **1996**: Integrity; **1998**: Algosea; **1999**: Maria Desgagnés

2000s

2000: Great Lakes Trader; **2004**: Algoscotia, Lake Express; **2006**: Innovation; **2007:** Rosaire A. Desgagnés, Sara Desgagnés; **2008:** Algocanada, Algonova

VESSEL ENGINE DATA

bhp: brake horsepower, a measure of diesel engine output measured at the crankshaft before entering gearbox or any other power take-out device

ihp: indicated horsepower, based on an internal measurement of mean cylinder pressure, piston area, piston stroke and engine speed; used for reciprocating engines

shp: shaft horsepower, a measure of engine output at the propeller shaft at the output of the reduction gearbox; used for steam and diesel-electric engines

cpp: controllable pitch propeller

Vessel Name	Engine Manufacturer & Model #	Engine Type	Total Engines	Total Cylinders	Rated HP	Total Props	Speed MPH
Adam E. Cornelius	GM - Electro-Motive Div. - 20-645-E7B	Diesel	2	20	7,200 bhp	1 cpp	16.1
Agawa Canyon	Fairbanks Morse - 10-38D8-1/8	Diesel	4	10	6,662 bhp	1 cpp	13.8
Algobay	Pielstick - 10PC2-3V-400	Diesel	2	10	10,700 bhp	1 cpp	13.8
Algocanada	MaK - 9M32C	Diesel	1	9	6,118 bhp	1 cpp	16.1
Algocape	Sulzer - 6RND76	Diesel	1	6	9,600 bhp	1 cpp	17.3
Algoeast	B&W - 6K45GF	Diesel	1	6	5,300 bhp	1 cpp	15.8
Algoisle	M.A.N. - K6Z78/155	Diesel	1	6	9,000 bhp	1 cpp	19.3
Algolake	Pielstick - 10PC2-2V-400	Diesel	2	10	9,000 bhp	1 cpp	17.3
Algomarine	Sulzer - 6RND76	Diesel	1	6	9,600 bhp	1 cpp	17.0
Algonorth	Werkspoor - 9TM410	Diesel	2	9	12,000 bhp	1 cpp	16.1
Algonova	MaK - 9M32C	Diesel	1	9	6,118 bhp	1 cpp	16.1
Algontario	B&W - 7-74VTBF-160	Diesel	1	7	8,750 bhp	1 cpp	14.4
Algoport	Pielstick - 10PC2-3V-400	Diesel	2	10	10,700 bhp	1 cpp	13.8
Algorail	Fairbanks Morse - 10-38D8-1/8	Diesel	4	10	6,662 bhp	1 cpp	13.8
Algosar	Alco - 16V251E	Diesel	2	16	5,150 bhp	2	14.4
Algoscotia	Wartsila - 6L46C	Diesel	1	6	8,445 bhp	1 cpp	16.0
Algosoo	Pielstick - 10PC2-V-400	Diesel	2	10	9,000 bhp	1 cpp	15.0
Algosea	Wartsila - 6L46A	Diesel	1	6	6,434 bhp	1 cpp	15.0
Algosteel	Sulzer - 6RND76	Diesel	1	6	9,599 bhp	1	17.0
Algoville	MaK model 8M43C	Diesel	1	8	10,750 bhp	1 cpp	
Algoway	Fairbanks Morse - 10-38D8-1/8	Diesel	4	10	6,662 bhp	1 cpp	13.8
Algowood	MaK - 6M552AK	Diesel	2	6	10,200 bhp	1 cpp	13.8
Alpena	De Laval Steam Turbine Co.	Turbine	1	**	4,400 shp	1	14.1
Amelia Desgagnés	Allen - 12PVBCS12-F	Diesel	2	12	4,000 bhp	1 cpp	16.1
American Century	GM - Electro-Motive Div. - 20-645-E7B	Diesel	4	20	14,400 bhp	2 cpp	17.3
American Courage	GM - Electro-Motive Div. - 20-645-E7	Diesel	2	20	7,200 bhp	1 cpp	16.1
American Fortitude	General Electric Co.	Turbine	1	**	7,700 shp	1	16.7
American Integrity	GM - Electro-Motive Div. - 20-645-E7	Diesel	4	20	14,400 bhp	2 cpp	18.4
American Mariner	GM - Electro-Motive Div. - 20-645-E7	Diesel	2	20	7,200 bhp	1 cpp	15.0
American Republic	GM - Electro-Motive Div. - 20-645-E7	Diesel	2	20	7,200 bhp	2 cpp	15.0
American Spirit	Pielstick - 16PC2-2V-400	Diesel	2	16	16,000 bhp	2 cpp	17.3
American Valor	Westinghouse Elec. Corp.	Turbine	1	**	7,700 shp	1	16.1
American Victory	Bethlehem Steel Corp.	Turbine	1	**	7,700 shp	1	19.0
Anglian Lady	***(Tug / Barge, usually paired with PML2501)***						
	Deutz	Diesel	2	12	3,480 bhp	2 cpp	15.5
Anna Desgagnés	M.A.N. - K5SZ70/125B	Diesel	1	5	10,332 bhp	1	17.8
Arctic	M.A.N. 14V52/55A	Diesel	1	14	14,770 bhp	1 cpp	17.8
Arthur M. Anderson	Westinghouse Elec. Corp.	Turbine	1	**	7,700 shp	1	16.1
Atlantic Erie	Sulzer - 6RLB66	Diesel	1	6	11,100 bhp	1 cpp	16.1
Atlantic Huron	Sulzer - 6RLB66	Diesel	1	6	11,094 bhp	1 cpp	17.3
Atlantic Superior	Sulzer - 6RLA66	Diesel	1	6	11,095 bhp	1 cpp	17.3
Avenger IV	***(Tug / Barge, usually paired with Chief Wawatam or PML 9000)***						
	British Polar	Diesel	1	9	2,700 bhp	1 cpp	12.0
Badger	Skinner Engine Co.	Steeple Compound Uniflow	2	4	8,000 ihp	2	18.4
Barbara Andrie	***(Tug / Barge, usually paired with A-390)***						
	GM Electro-Motive Div. 16-645-EF	Diesel	1	16	2,000 bhp	1	
Birchglen	Sulzer 4RLB76	Diesel	1	4	10,880 bhp	1cpp	13.8
Buffalo	GM - Electro-Motive Div. - 20-645-E7	Diesel	2	20	7,200 bhp	1 cpp	16.1
Burns Harbor	GM - Electro-Motive Div. - 20-645-E7	Diesel	4	20	14,400 bhp	2 cpp	18.4
Calumet (2)	Alco - 16V251E	Diesel	2	16	5,600 bhp	1	16.1
Canadian Enterprise	M.A.N. - 7L40/45	Diesel	2	7	8,804 bhp	1 cpp	13.8
Canadian Leader	Canadian General Electric Co. Ltd.	Turbine	1	**	9,900 shp	1	19.0
Canadian Miner	Fairbanks Morse - 12-38D8-1/8	Diesel	4	12	8,000 bhp	1 cpp	15.0
Canadian Navigator	Doxford Engines Ltd. - 76J4	Diesel	1	4	9,680 bhp	1	16.7

Vessel Name	Engine Manufacturer & Model #	Engine Type	Total Engines	Total Cylinders	Rated HP	Total Props	Speed MPH
Canadian Olympic	M.A.N. - 8L40/54A	Diesel	2	8	10,000 bhp	1 cpp	15.0
Canadian Progress	Caterpillar - 3612-TA	Diesel	2	12	9,000 bhp	1 cpp	15.5
Canadian Prospector	Gotaverken - 760/1500VGS6U	Diesel	1	6	7,500 bhp	1	16.1
Canadian Provider	John Inglis Co. Ltd.	Turbine	1	**	10,000 shp	1	17.3
Canadian Ranger	Sulzer - 5RND68	Diesel	1	5	6,100 shp	1 cpp	19.6
Canadian Transfer	Sulzer - 5RND68	Diesel	1	5	6,100 bhp	1 cpp	18.4
Canadian Transport	M.A.N. - 8L40/45	Diesel	2	8	10,000 bhp	1 cpp	13.8
Capt. Henry Jackman	MaK - 6M552AK	Diesel	2	6	9,465 bhp	1 cpp	17.3
Cason J. Callaway	Westinghouse Elec. Corp.	Turbine	1	**	7,700 shp	1	16.1
Catherine Desgagnés	Sulzer - 6SAD60	Diesel	1	6	3,841 bhp	1	15.5
Cedarglen	B&W - 7-74VTBF-160	Diesel	1	7	8,750 bhp	1 cpp	15.5
Charles M. Beeghly	General Electric Co.	Turbine	1	**	9,350 shp	1	17.8
Chi-Cheemaun	Caterpillar C280-6	Diesel	4	6	9,280 bhp	2	
Cleveland	***(Tug / Barge, paired with Cleveland Rocks)***						
	Caterpillar 3516-B	Diesel	2	16	5,000 bhp	2	
CSL Assiniboine	Pielstick - 10PC2-2V-400	Diesel	2	10	9,000 bhp	1 cpp	15.0
CSL Laurentien	Pielstick - 10PC2-2V-400	Diesel	2	10	9,000 bhp	1 cpp	16.1
CSL Niagara	Pielstick - 10PC2-2V-400	Diesel	2	10	9,000 bhp	1 cpp	15.0
CSL Tadoussac	Sulzer - 6RND76	Diesel	1	6	9,600 bhp	1	17.0
Cuyahoga	Caterpillar - 3608	Diesel	1	8	3,000 bhp	1 cpp	12.6
Diamond Star	B&W - 6L35MC	Diesel	1	6	5,030 bhp	1 cpp	14.4
Dorothy Ann	***(Articulated Tug / Barge, paired with Pathfinder)***					2 Ulstein	
	GM - Electro-Motive Div. - 20-645-E7B	Diesel	2	20	7,200 bhp	Z-Drive	16.1
E. M. Ford	Cleveland Shipbuilding Co.	Quad. Exp	1	4	1,500 ihp	1	11.5
Edgar B. Speer	Pielstick - 18PC2-3V-400	Diesel	2	18	19,260 bhp	2 cpp	17.0
Edward L. Ryerson	General Electric Co.	Turbine	1	**	9,900 shp	1	19.0
Edwin H. Gott	Enterprise - DMRV-16-4	Diesel	2	16	19,500 bhp	2 cpp	16.7
Emerald Star	B&W - 6L35MC	Diesel	1	6	5,030 bhp	1 cpp	14.4
English River	Werkspoor - TMAB-390	Diesel	1	8	1,850 bhp	1 cpp	13.8
Everlast	***(Articulated Tug / Barge, paired with Norman McLeod)***						
	Daihatsu - 8DSM-32	Diesel	2	8	6,000 bhp	2	16.5
Frontenac	Sulzer - 6RND76	Diesel	1	6	9,600 bhp	1 cpp	17.0
G.L. Ostrander	***(Articulated Tug / Barge, paired with Integrity)***						
	Caterpillar - 3608-DITA	Diesel	2	8	6,008 bhp	2	17.3
Gordon C. Leitch	Sulzer - 6RND76	Diesel	1	6	9,600 bhp	1 cpp	17.3
Grayfox	Caterpillar - 3512 TAC	Diesel	2	12	2,350 bhp.	2	20.7
H. Lee White	GM - Electro-Motive Div. - 20-645-E7B	Diesel	2	20	7,200 bhp	1 cpp	15.0
Halifax	John Inglis Co. Ltd.	Turbine	1	**	10,000 shp	1	19.6
Herbert C. Jackson	General Electric Co.	Turbine	1	**	6,600 shp	1	16.0
Indiana Harbor	GM - Electro-Motive Div. - 20-645-E7	Diesel	4	20	14,400 bhp	2 cpp	16.1
Invincible	***(Articulated Tug / Barge, paired with McKee Sons)***						
	GM - Electro-Motive Div. - 16-645-E7B	Diesel	2	16	5,750 bhp	2	13.8
J. A. W. Iglehart	De Laval Steam Turbine Co.	Turbine	1	**	4,400 shp	1	15.0
J. B. Ford	American Shipbuilding Co.	Triple Exp.	1	3	1,500 ihp	1	
J. S. St. John	GM - Electro-Motive Div. - 8-567	Diesel	1	8	850 bhp	1	11.5
Jade Star	B&W - 6L35MC	Diesel	1	6	5,030 bhp	1 cpp	14.4
James Norris	Canadian Vickers Ltd.	Uniflow	1	5	4,000 ihp	1	16.1
James R. Barker	Pielstick - 16PC2-2V-400	Diesel	2	16	16,000 bhp	2 cpp	15.5
Jane Ann IV	***(Articulated Tug / Barge, paired with Sarah Spencer)***						
	Pielstick - 8PC2-2L-400	Diesel	2	8	8,000 bhp	2	15.8
Jiimaan	Ruston Paxman Diesels Ltd. - 6RK215	Diesel	2	6	2,839 bhp	2 cpp	15.0
John B. Aird	MaK - 6M552AK	Diesel	2	6	9,460 bhp	1 cpp	13.8
John D. Leitch	B&W - 5-74VT2BF-160	Diesel	1	5	7,500 bhp	1 cpp	16.1
John G. Munson	General Electric Co.	Turbine	1	**	7,700 shp	1	17.3
John J. Boland	GM - Electro-Motive Div. - 20-645-E7B	Diesel	2	20	7,200 bhp	1 cpp	15.0
John Sherwin	De Laval Steam Turbine Co.	Turbine	1	**	9,350 shp	1	16.7
John Spence	***(Tug / Barge, usually paired with McAsphalt 401)***						
	GM Electro-Motive Div. 16-567-C	Diesel	2	16	3,280 bhp	2	13.8
Joseph H. Thompson Jr.	***(Articulated Tug / Barge, paired with Joseph H. Thompson)***						
	Caterpillar	Diesel	2			1	
Joseph L. Block	GM - Electro-Motive Div. - 20-645-E7	Diesel	2	20	7,200 bhp	1 cpp	17.3
Joyce L. VanEnkevort	***(Articulated Tug / Barge, paired with Great Lakes Trader)***						
	Caterpillar - 3612	Diesel	2	12	10,200 bhp	2 cpp	
Kaministiqua	Sulzer 4RLB76	Diesel	4	4	10,880 bhp	1cpp	15.5
Karen Andrie	***(Tug / Barge, usually paired with A-397)***						
	GM Electro-Motive Div. 16-567-BC	Diesel	2	16	3,600 bhp	2	19
Kathryn Spirit	Pielstick 10PC2-V-400	Diesel	2		8,000 bhp	1 ccp	19
Kaye E. Barker	De Laval Steam Turbine Co.	Turbine	1	**	7,700 shp	1	17.3

Vessel Name	Engine Manufacturer & Model #	Engine Type	Total Engines	Total Cylinders	Rated HP	Total Props	Speed MPH
Lee A. Tregurtha	Rolls-Royce Bergen B32:40L6P	Diesel	2	6	8,160 shp	1 ccp	17.0
Mackinaw (USCG)	Caterpillar - 3612	Diesel	3	12	9,119 bhp	2 Azipod	17.3
Manistee	GM - Electro-Motive Div. - 20-645-E6	Diesel	1	20	2,950 bhp	1	
Manitowoc	Alco - 16V251E	Diesel	2	16	5,600 bhp	1	16.1
Maria Desgagnés	B&W - 6S42MC	Diesel	1	6	8,361 bhp	1 cpp	16.1
Maritime Trader	Fairbanks Morse -8-38D8-1/8	Diesel	4	8	5,332 bhp	1 cpp	16.1
Maumee	Nordberg - FS-1312-H5C	Diesel	1	12	3,240 bhp	1	11.5
Melissa Desgagnés	Allen - 12PVBCS12-F	Diesel	2	12	4,000 bhp	1 cpp	13.8
Mesabi Miner	Pielstick - 16PC2-2V-400	Diesel	2	16	16,000 bhp	2 cpp	15.5
Michigan	***(Articulated Tug / Barge, paired with Michigan)***						
	GM - Electro-Motive Div. - 20-645-E6	Diesel	2	16	3,900 bhp	2	13.2
Michipicoten	Bethlehem Steel Co.	Turbine	1	**	7,700 shp	1	17.3
Mississagi	Caterpillar - 3612-TA	Diesel	1	12	4,500 bhp	1 cpp	13.8
Montrealais	Canadian General Electric Co. Ltd.	Turbine	1	**	9,900 shp	1	19.0
Nanticoke	Pielstick - 10PC2-2V-400	Diesel	2	10	10,700 bhp	1 cpp	13.8
Nordik Express	GM Electro-Motive Div. 20-645-E7	Diesel	2	20	7,200 bhp	2 ccp	16.0
Ojibway	2005 GE 7FDM EFI	Diesel	1	16	4,100 bhp	1 cpp	
Olive L. Moore	***(Tug / Barge, usually paired with Lewis J. Kuber)***						
	Alco 16V251	Diesel	2	16	5,830 bhp	1	
Paul H. Townsend	Nordberg TSM-216	Diesel	1	6	2,150 bhp	1	12.1
Paul R. Tregurtha	Pielstick - 16PC2-3V-400	Diesel	2	16	17,120 bhp	2 cpp	15.5
Peter R. Cresswell	MaK - 6M552AK	Diesel	2	6	9,460 bhp	1 cpp	13.8
Petite Forte	***(Tug / Barge, usually paired with St. Marys Cement)***						
	Ruston 8ATC	Diesel	2	8	4,200 bhp	2	15.5
Petrolia Desgagnés	B&W - 8K42EF	Diesel	1	8	5,000 bhp	1 cpp	16.4
Philip R. Clarke	Westinghouse Elec. Corp.	Turbine	1	**	7,700 shp	1	16.1
Pineglen	MaK - 6M601AK	Diesel	1	6	8,158 bhp	1 cpp	15.5
Presque Isle	***(Integrated Tug / Barge paired with Presque Isle)***						
	Mirrlees Blackstone Ltd. - KVMR-16	Diesel	2	16	14,840 bhp	2 cpp	
Quebecois	Canadian General Electric Co. Ltd.	Turbine	1	**	9,900 shp	1	19.0
Rebecca Lynn	***Tug / Barge, usually paired with A-410)***						
	GM Electro-Motive Div. 16-567-BC	Diesel	2	16	3,600 bhp	2	
Reliance	***(Tug / Barge, usually paired with PML9000)***						
	A.B. Nohab SVI 16VS-F	Diesel	2	16	5,600 bhp	1 cpp	17.6
Robert S. Pierson	Alco - 16V251E	Diesel	2	16	5,600 bhp	1	17.8
Roger Blough	Pielstick - 16PC2V-400	Diesel	2	16	14,200 bhp	1 cpp	16.7
Rosaire A. Desgagnés	MaK - 6M43	Diesel	1	6	7,341 bhp	1 cpp	17.8
Rt. Hon. Paul J. Martin	Pielstick - 10PC2-V-400	Diesel	2	10	9,000 bhp	1 cpp	15.0
Saginaw	(Conversion from steam to diesel power underway at press time; engine details unavailable)						
Sam Laud	GM - Electro-Motive Div. - 20-645-E7	Diesel	2	20	7,200 bhp	1 cpp	16.1
Samuel de Champlain	***(Articulated Tug / Barge, paired with Innovation)***						
	GM - Electro-Motive Div. - 20-645-E5	Diesel	2	20	7,200 bhp	2 cpp	17.3
Samuel Risley (CCG)	Wartsila - VASA 16V22HF	Diesel	2	16	7,590 bhp	2 cpp	17.3
Sauniere	MaK - 6M552AK	Diesel	2	6	8,799 bhp	1 cpp	15.0
Sea Eagle II	***(Tug / Barge, usually paired with St. Marys Cement II)***						
	GM Electro-Motive Div. 20-645-E7	Diesel	2	20	7,200 bhp	2	13.8
Spruceglen	Sulzer 4RLB76	Diesel	1	4	10,880 bhp	1cpp	13.8
St. Clair	GM - Electro-Motive Div. - 20-645-E7	Diesel	3	20	10,800 bhp	1 cpp	16.7
St. Marys Challenger	Skinner Engine Co.	Uniflow	1	4	3,500 ihp	1	12.0
Ste. Claire	Toledo Ship Building Co.	Triple Exp.	1	3	1,083 ihp	1	
Stephen B. Roman (Total)		Diesel			5,996 bhp	1 cpp	18.4
Stephen B. Roman (Center)	Fairbanks Morse - 10-38D8-1/8	Diesel	2	10	3,331 bhp		
Stephen B. Roman (Wing)	Fairbanks Morse - 8-38D8-1/8	Diesel	2	8	2,665 bhp		
Stewart J. Cort	GM - Electro-Motive Div. - 20-645-E7	Diesel	4	20	14,400 bhp	2 cpp	18.4
Susan W. Hannah	***(Articulated Tug / Barge, paired with St. Marys Conquest)***						
	GM - Electro-Motive Div. - 12-645-E5	Diesel	2	12	4,320 bhp	2	11.5
Thalassa Desgagnés	B&W - 8K42EF	Diesel	1	8	5,000 bhp	1 cpp	16.4
Undaunted	***(Articulated Tug / Barge, paired with Pere Marquette 41)***						
	GM - Cleveland Diesel Div. - 12-278A	Diesel	1	12	2,400 bhp	1	11.5
Vega Desgagnés	Wartsila - 9R32	Diesel	2	9	7,560bhp	1 cpp	16.1
Victory	***(Articulated Tug / barge, usually paired with James L. Kuber)***						
	MaK - 6MU551AK	Diesel	2	6	7,880 bhp	2	16.1
Walter J. McCarthy Jr.	GM - Electro-Motive Div. - 20-645-E7B	Diesel	4	20	14,400 bhp	2 cpp	16.1
Wilfred Sykes	Westinghouse Elec. Corp.	Turbine	1	16	7,700 shp	1	16.1
William J. Moore	***(Tug / Barge, usually paired with McLeary's Spirit)***						
	GM Electro-Motive Div. 16-645-E	Diesel	2	16	4,000 bhp	2 cpp	15.5
Wolf River	Fairbanks Morse - 10-38D8-1/8	Diesel	1	10	1,880 bhp	1	10.4
Yankcanuck	Cooper-Bessemer Corp.	Diesel	1	8	1,860 bhp	1	11.5

Saltwater Fleets

Magdalena Green **enters the MacArthur Lock at Sault Ste. Marie.** *(Roger LeLievre)*

Listed after each vessel in order are: Type of Vessel, Year Built, Type of Engine, Maximum Cargo Capacity (at midsummer draft in long tons) or Gross Tonnage*, Overall Length, Breadth and Depth (from the top of the keel to the top of the upper deck beam). This list reflects vessels whose primary trade routes are on saltwater but which also regularly visit Great Lakes and St. Lawrence Seaway ports. It is not meant to be a complete listing of every saltwater vessel that could potentially visit the Great Lakes and St. Lawrence Seaway. To attempt to do so, given the sheer number of world merchant vessels, would be space prohibitive. Fleets listed may operate other vessels worldwide than those included herein; additional vessels may be found on fleet Web sites, which have been listed where available. Former names listed in boldface type indicate the vessel visited the system under that name.

Fleet #.	Fleet Name Vessel Name	Type of Vessel	Year Built	Type of Engine	Cargo Cap. or gross*	Overall Length	Breadth	Depth or Draft*
IA-1	**ALLROUNDER MARITIME CO. INC., MANILA, PHILIPPINES**							
	Sir Walter	BC	1996	D	18,315	486' 03"	74' 10"	40' 00"
	*(**Rubin Stork** '96-'03)*							
IA-2	**ALVARGONZALEZ NAVIGATION, GIJON, SPAIN**							
	Covadonga	TK	2005	D	6,967	390' 09"	55' 05"	27' 07"
IA-3	**AMALTHIA MARINE INC., ATHENS, GREECE**							
	Antikeri	BC	1984	D	28,788	606' 11"	75' 09"	48' 02"
	*(**LT Argosy** '84-'98, **Millenium Hawk** '98-'02, **Cashin** '02-'05)*							
	Seneca	BC	1983	D	28,788	606' 11"	75' 09"	48' 02"
	*(**Mangal Desai** '83-'98, **Millenium Eagle** '98-'02, **Stokmarnes** '02-'05)*							
	Tuscarora	BC	1983	D	28,031	639' 09"	75' 09"	46' 11"
	*(Manila Spirit '83-'86, **Rixta Oldendorff** '86-'06)*							
IA-4	**AMERICAN CANADIAN CARIBBEAN LINE INC., WARREN, RI, USA** *(accl-smallships.com)*							
	Grande Caribe	PA	1997	D	97*	182' 07"	39' 01"	9' 10"
	Grande Mariner	PA	1998	D	97*	182' 07"	39' 01"	9' 10"
	Niagara Prince	PA	1994	D	99*	174' 00"	40' 00"	9' 00"
IA-5	**ANBROS MARITIMA S.A, PIRAEUS, GREECE** *(anbros.gr)*							
	Platytera	BC	1987	D	28,358	590' 07"	75' 10"	48' 07"
	*(Green Laker '87-'94, **Great Laker** '94-'02, **Kolguev** '02-'07)*							
	Ypermachos	BC	1983	D	9,653	584' 08"	75' 09"	48' 07"
	*(**Socrates** '88-'92, **Union** '92-'97, **Mecta Sea** '97-'05)*							
IA-6	**ANDERS UTKILENS REDERI AS, BERGEN,NORWAY** *(utkilen.no)*							
	Sundstraum	TK	1993	D	4,737	316' 01"	50' 04"	26' 05"
IA-7	**ATHENA MARINE CO. LTD., LIMASSOL, CYPRUS**							
	FOLLOWING VESSELS UNDER CHARTER TO FEDNAV LTD.							
	Federal Danube	BC	2003	D	37,372	652' 11"	78' 05"	50' 02"
	Federal Elbe	BC	2003	D	37,372	652' 11"	78' 05"	50' 02"
	Federal Ems	BC	2002	D	37,372	652' 11"	78' 05"	50' 02"
	Federal Leda	BC	2003	D	37,372	652' 11"	78' 05"	50' 02"
	Federal Patroller	BC	1999	D	17,451	469' 02"	74' 10"	43' 08"
	*(Atlantic Pride '99-'01, Seaboard Rover '01-'02, **Atlantic Patroller** '02-'05, African Patroller '05-'06)*							
	Federal Pioneer	BC	1999	D	17,451	469' 02"	74' 10"	43' 08"
	(Atlantic Pioneer '99-'01, Seaboard Pioneer '01-'07)							
	Federal Power	BC	2000	D	17,451	469' 02"	74' 10"	43' 08"
	(Atlantic Power '00-'01, Seaboard Power '01-'07)							
	Federal Pride	BC	2000	D	17,451	469' 02"	74' 10"	43' 08"
	*(Atlantic Pride '00-'01, Seaboard Rover '01-'02, **Atlantic Pride** '02-'05, Seabord Chile II '05-'06)*							
	Federal Weser	BC	2002	D	37,372	652' 11"	78' 05"	50' 02"
IA-8	**ATLANTSKA PLOVIDBA D.D., DUBROVNIK, REPUBLIC OF CROATIA** *(atlant.hr)*							
	Mljet	BC	1982	D	29,643	622' 01"	74' 11"	49' 10"
	FOLLOWING VESSEL CURRENTLY UNDER CHARTER TO FEDNAV LTD.							
	Orsula	BC	1996	D	34,372	656' 02"	77' 01"	48' 10"
	*(**Federal Calumet** {2} '96-'97)*							

Fleet #	Fleet Name Vessel Name	Type of Vessel	Year Built	Type of Engine	Cargo Cap. or Gross*	Overall Length	Breadth	Depth or Draft*
IB-1	**B & N MOORMAN BV, RIDDERKERK, NETHERLANDS**							
	Andromeda	GC	1999	D	6,663	388' 09"	49' 10"	27' 06"
	Capricorn	GC	2000	D	6,715	388' 09"	49' 08"	27' 02"
IB-2	**BARU DELTA MARITIME INC., PIRAEUS, GREECE**							
	Doxa D	BC	1984	D	30,820	617' 05"	76' 01"	47' 06"
	*(**Alberta** '84-'93, **Nea Doxa** '93-'02)*							
IB-3	**BELUGA SHIPPING GMBH, BREMEN, GERMANY** *(beluga-group.com)*							
	BBC India	BC	1998	D	17,538	465' 10"	70' 06"	43' 08"
	(Maria Green '98-'04)							
	Beluga Constitution	BC	2006	D	12,477	514' 04"	70' 06"	36' 06"
	Beluga Efficiency	BC	2004	D	12,806	452' 09"	68' 11"	36' 01"
	(Beluga Efficiency '04-'06, BBC Carolina '06-'07)							
	Beluga Elegance	BC	2004	D	12,828	452' 09"	68' 11"	36' 01"
	Beluga Emotion	BC	2004	D	12,828	452' 09"	68' 11"	36' 01"
	Beluga Endurance	BC	2005	D	12,782	452' 09"	68' 11"	36' 01"
	Beluga Energy	BC	2005	D	12,828	452' 09"	68' 11"	36' 01"
	Beluga Eternity	BC	2004	D	12,782	452' 09"	68' 11"	36' 01"
	Beluga Expectation	BC	2005	D	12,744	452' 11"	70' 01"	36' 01"
	Beluga Federation	BC	2006	D	11,380	452' 11"	70' 01"	36' 01"
	Beluga Formation	BC	2007	D	11,526	453' 00"	68' 11"	36' 01"
	Beluga Fusion	BC	2000	D	11,380	452' 11"	70' 01"	36' 01"
	Beluga Indication	BC	2005	D	11,380	452' 11"	70' 01"	36' 01"
	Beluga Legislation	BC	2007	D	12,000	469' 00"	62' 02"	35' 11"
	*(**Morgenstond II** '07-'07)*							
	Beluga Recognition	BC	2005	D	11,380	452' 11"	70' 01"	36' 01"
	Beluga Recommendation	BC	2005	D	10,536	439' 04"	70' 06"	30' 06"
	Beluga Resolution	BC	2005	D	10,536	439' 04"	70' 06"	30' 06"
	Beluga Revolution	BC	2005	D	10,536	439' 04"	70' 06"	30' 06"
	Magdalena Green	BC	2001	D	17,538	465' 10"	70' 06"	43' 10"
	Makiri Green	BC	1999	D	17,538	465' 10"	70' 06"	43' 08"
	Margaretha Green	BC	2000	D	17,538	465' 10"	70' 06"	43' 08"
	*(**Margaretha Green** '00-'00, Coral Green '00-'01, Nirint Voyager '01-'02, **Margaretha Green** '02-'04, Newpac Cumulus '04-'05)*							
	Marinus Green	BC	2000	D	17,538	465' 10"	70' 06"	43' 08"
	Marion Green	BC	1999	D	17,538	465' 10"	70' 06"	43' 08"
	Marlene Green	BC	2001	D	17,538	465' 10"	70' 06"	43' 08"
IB-4	**BERNHARD SCHULTE GROUP OF COMPANIES, HAMBURG, GERMANY** *(beschulte.de)*							
	Kristina Theresa	TK	2006	D	12,972	417' 04"	66' 11"	37' 09"
	(Songa Emerald '06-'06)							
IB-5	**BIGLIFT SHIPPING BV, ROOSENDAAL, NETHERLANDS** *(www.bigliftshipping.com)*							
	Happy Ranger	HL	1998	D	15,065	454' 01"	74' 10"	42' 04"
	Tracer	HL	2000	D	8,874	329' 09"	73' 06"	26' 11"
	Tramper	HL	2000	D	8,874	329' 09"	73' 06"	26' 11"
	Transporter	HL	1999	D	8,469	329' 09"	80' 01"	36' 05"
	Traveller	HL	2000	D	8,874	329' 09"	73' 06"	26' 11"
IB-6	**BLYSTAD TANKERS INC., OSLO, NORWAY** *(blystad.com)*							
	FOLLOWING VESSEL CURRENTLY UNDER CHARTER TO SONGA OFFSHORE							
	Songa Crystal	TK	2006	D	12,800	417' 04"	66' 11"	37' 09"
	(Samho Crystal '06-'06)							
IB-7	**BOOMSMA SHIPPING BV, SNEEK, NETHERLANDS** *(boomsmashipping.nl)*							
	Frisian Spring	GC	2006	D	5,023	390' 01"	44' 00"	29' 10"
	Built: Port Weller Dry Docks, Port Weller, ON							
IB-8	**BRIESE SCHIFFAHRTS GMBH & CO. KG, LEER, GERMANY** *(briese.de)*							
	Bavaria	GC	1996	D	3,500	288' 09"	42' 00"	23' 04"

Fednav's *Federal* *Maas.* *(Eric Treece)*

Fleet #	Fleet Name Vessel Name	Type of Vessel	Year Built	Type of Engine	Cargo Cap. or Gross*	Overall Length	Breadth	Depth or Draft*
	BBC Asia	GC	2003	D	7,530	393′ 00″	66′ 03″	32′ 02″
	(Embse '03-'03)							
	BBC Atlantic	GC	2005	D	6,192	378′ 11″	54′ 02″	26′ 01″
	(Westerriede '05-'05)							
	BBC Australia	GC	2005	D	7,530	393′ 00″	66′ 03″	32′ 02″
	BBC Elbe	GC	2006	D	17,348	469′ 07″	75′ 11″	42′ 08″
	(Horumersiel '06-'06)							
	BBC Ems	GC	2006	D	17,348	469′ 07″	75′ 11″	42′ 08″
	BBC Finland	GC	2000	D	7,650	353′ 06″	59′ 09″	33′ 02″
	(Norderney '00-'00)							
	BBC France	GC	2005	D	4,309	324′ 06″	45′ 03″	24′ 03″
	BBC Iceland	GC	1999	D	4,806	330′ 01″	54′ 06″	26′ 07″
	(Industrial Accord '99-'02)							
	BBC Mexico	GC	2001	D	5,018	330′ 08″	53′ 10″	26′ 11″
	(Deborah '01-'01)							
	BBC Mississippi	GC	2006	D	17,348	469′ 07″	75′ 11″	42′ 08″
	(Greetsiel '06-'07)							
	BBC Scandinavia	GC	2007	D	7,530	393′ 00″	66′ 03″	32′ 02″
	(Rysum '07-'07)							
	BBC Scotland	GC	2002	D	4,713	330′ 01″	54′ 06″	26′ 07″
	BBC Shanghai	GC	2001	D	4,900	330′ 01″	54′ 06″	26′ 07″
	(Baltic Sea '01-'01, BBC Shanghai '01-'03, TLI Aquila '03-'03)							
	BBC Singapore	GC	1990	D	4,900	328′ 01″	54′ 06″	26′ 07″
	(Randzel '90-'97, Bremer Timber '97-'04)							
	BBC Venezuela	GC	1999	D	5,240	324′ 10″	51′ 11″	26′ 07″
	(Fockeburg '99-'00, Global Africa '00-'01)							
	Borkum	GC	1994	D	18,355	486′ 07″	74′ 10″	40′ 00″
	*(**Erna Oldendorff** '94-'05)*							
	Leda	GC	2002	D	7,530	393′ 00″	66′ 03″	32′ 02″
	*(**BBC Germany** '03-'03)*							
	Santiago	GC	1997	D	3,525	280′ 10″	42′ 00″	23′ 04″
	Skaftafell	GC	1997	D	4,900	328′ 01″	54′ 06″	26′ 07″
	*(Launched as Torum, Industrial Harmony '97-'00, **BBC Brazil** '00-'03, Brake '03-'03, BBC Brazil '04-'04)*							
IC-1	**CANADA FEEDER LINES BV, GRONIGEN, NETHERLANDS** *(canadafeederlines.com)*							
	CFL Prospect	GC	2007	D	6,500	387′ 07″	43′ 10″	29′ 10″
	Vessel is scheduled to enter service under the Canadian flag in April 2008							
IC-2	**CANADIAN FOREST NAVIGATION (CANFORNAV) CO. LTD., MONTREAL, QUEBEC, CANADA** *(www.canfornav.com)*							
	At press time, Canadian Forest Navigation Co. Ltd. had the following vessels under long-or short-term charter. Please consult their respective fleets for details: Apollon, Bluebill, Bluewing, Cinnamon, Eider, Gadwall, Garganey, Goldeneye, Greenwing, Mandarin, Milo, Miltiades, Orna, Pochard, Puffin, Redhead, Whistler, Woody							
IC-3	**CANSHIP LTD., ST. JOHN'S, NEWFOUNDLAND, CANADA** *(canship.com)*							
	Astron	RR	1971	D	1,910	278′ 08″	45′ 03″	21′ 03″
	(Atlantic Bermudian '71-'75, Londis '75-'76, Merzario Sardinia '76-'78)							
IC-4	**CARISBROOKE SHIPPING LTD, COWES, ENGLAND** *(carisbrookeshipping.net)*							
	Catharina-C	BC	1999	D	5,057	311′ 04″	43′ 04″	23′ 05″
	Johanna-C	BC	1998	D	4,570	292′ 00″	43′ 02″	23′ 05″
	Vanessa-C	BC	2003	D	10,500	477′ 09″	60′ 03″	33′ 10″
IC-5	**CANDLER SCHIFFAHRT GMBH, BREMEN, GERMANY**							
	Glory	BC	2005	D	7,378	381′ 04″	59′ 01″	34′ 01″
	(FCC Glory '05-'06)							
IC-6	**CHARTWORLD SHIPPING CORP., ATHENS, GREECE** *(chartworld.gr)*							
	Chem Bothnia	TK	1985	D	6,730	351′ 01″	55′ 10″	27′ 11″
	(Ace '85-'85, Ace Chemi '85-'91, Kilchem Bothnia '91-'99)							

Fleet #.	Fleet Name Vessel Name	Type of Vessel	Year Built	Type of Engine	Cargo Cap. or gross*	Overall Length	Breadth	Depth or Draft*
IC-7	**CHINA OCEAN SHIPPING CO., BEIJING, PEOPLE'S REPUBLIC OF CHINA** *(www.cosco.com/en)*							
	Yick Hua	BC	1984	D	28,086	584' 08"	75' 09"	48' 07"
	(Santa Lucia '84-'84, Pacific Defender '84-'85, Lori '85-'91)							
IC-8	**CLIPPER ELITE CARRIERS AS, COPENHAGEN, DENMARK** *(clipper-elite.com)*							
	CEC Fantasy	GC	1994	D	7,121	331' 08"	61' 08"	30' 06"
	(Arktis Fantasy '94-'00)							
	CEC Fighter	GC	1994	D	7,121	331' 08"	61' 08"	30' 06"
	(Arktis Fighter '94-'94, Ville de Rodae '94-'96, Arktis Fighter '96-'02)							
	CEC Spring	GC	1993	D	4,110	290' 00"	49' 03"	24' 07"
	(Arktis Spring '93-'94, Mekong Spring '94-'95, Arktis Spring '95-'01, CEC Spring '01-'01, Anking '01-'02 CEC Spring '02-'03, Sofrana Bligh '03-'04)							
	Thor Sofia	BC	1984	D	4,281	288' 09"	50' 09"	27' 03"
IC-9	**CLIPPER WONSILD TANKERS AS, COPENHAGEN, DENMARK** *(crescentplc.com)*							
	Clipper Golfito	TK	2006	D	14,227	440' 02"	67' 03"	38' 01"
	Clipper Karen	TK	2006	D	11,259	382' 03"	65' 07"	38' 05"
	Clipper Kira	TK	2007	D	11,259	382' 03"	65' 07"	38' 05"
	Clipper Kristin	TK	2006	D	11,259	382' 03"	65' 07"	38' 05"
	Clipper Krystal	TK	2006	D	11,259	382' 03"	65' 07"	38' 05"
	Clipper Kylie	TK	2007	D	11,259	382' 03"	65' 07"	38' 05"
	Clipper Lancer	TK	2006	D	10,098	388' 04"	62' 04"	33' 02"
	Clipper Leader	TK	2004	D	10,098	388' 04"	62' 04"	33' 02"
	*(**Panam Trinity** '04-'06)*							
	Clipper Leaner	TK	2006	D	10,098	388' 04"	62' 04"	33' 02"
	Clipper Legacy	TK	2005	D	10,098	388' 04"	62' 04"	33' 02"
	Clipper Legend	TK	2004	D	10,098	388' 04"	62' 04"	33' 02"
	Clipper Loyalty	TK	2007	D	10,098	388' 04"	62' 04"	33' 02"
	Clipper Tasmania	TK	2007	D	12,800	417' 04"	67' 00"	37' 09"
	Clipper Tobago	TK	1999	D	8,834	367' 05"	61' 08"	31' 08"
	(Botany Treasure '99-'06)							
	Clipper Trinidad	TK	1998	D	5,483	370' 09"	61' 08"	31' 08"
	*(**Botany Trust** '98-'06)*							
	Clipper Trojan	TK	1996	D	9,553	452' 09"	71' 06"	39' 08"
	*(Botany Trojan '96-'98, Stolt Trojan '98-'04, **Botany Trojan** '04-'06)*							
IC-10	**COASTAL SHIPPING LTD., GOOSE BAY, NEWFOUNDLAND, CANADA**							
	Tuvaq	TK	1977	D	15,955	539' 08"	72' 10"	39' 04"
	(Tiira '02)							
IC-11	**COMMERCIAL FLEET OF DONBASS LLC, DONETSK, UKRAINE** *(cfd.com.ua/en)*							
	Avdeevka	BC	1977	D	26,398	570' 11"	75' 03"	47' 07"
	(Goldensari '77-'80, Bogasari Tiga '80-'86)							
	Berdyansk	BC	1977	D	27,559	584' 04"	75' 02"	48' 03"
	(Baltic Skou '77-'85)							
	Dobrush	BC	1982	D	28,136	644' 08"	75' 09"	46' 11"
	*(**World Goodwill** '82-'85)*							
	General Blazhevich	BC	1981	D	7,805	399' 09"	67' 00"	27' 03"
	*(Traun '81-'85, **General Blazhevich** '85-'00, **Regina** '00-'03)*							
	Makeevka	BC	1982	D	28,136	644' 08"	75' 09"	46' 11"
	*(**World Shanghai** '82-'85)*							
	Mariupol	BC	1977	D	27,559	584' 04"	75' 02"	48' 03"
	*(**Arctic Skou** '77-'85, Zdhanov '85-'89)*							
IC-12	**COMMERCIAL TRADING & DISCOUNT CO. LTD., ATHENS, GREECE**							
	Ira	BC	1979	D	26,697	591' 02"	75' 10"	45' 08"
	Ivi	BC	1979	D	26,697	591' 04"	75' 10"	45' 08"
IC-13	**COMMON PROGRESS COMPANIA NAVIERA SA, PIRAEUS, GREECE**							
	Kastor P	BC	1983	D	22,713	528' 03"	75' 07"	45' 07"
	(Sea Augusta '83-'85, Jovian Lily '85-'91)							

Fleet #	Fleet Name / Vessel Name	Type of Vessel	Year Built	Type of Engine	Cargo Cap. or Gross*	Overall Length	Breadth	Depth or Draft*
	Polydefkis P	BC	1982	D	22,713	528′ 03″	75′ 07″	45′ 07″
	(Sea Astrea '82-'85, Jovian Luzon '85-'91)							
IC-14	**COPENHAGEN TANKERS AS, GENTOFTE, DENMARK** *(clipper-group.com)*							
	Panam Sol	TK	1998	D	12,756	406′ 10″	66′ 03″	36′ 09″
	(Opal Sun '98-'02)							
IC-15	**CRESCENT MARINE SERVICES, COPENHAGEN, DENMARK** *(crescentplc.com)*							
	Panam Atlantico	TK	2001	D	14,003	439′ 08″	67′ 03″	38′ 01″
	Panam Felice	TK	1999	D	11,616	384′ 10″	65′ 07″	36′ 09″
	Panam Flota	TK	1999	D	11,642	384′ 06″	65′ 07″	36′ 09″
	Panam Oceanica	TK	2005	D	12,000	406′ 10″	65′ 07″	36′ 09″
	Panam Trinity	TK	2004	D	10,048	388′ 04″	62′ 04″	33′ 02″
IC-16	**CRYSTAL POOL GROUP, HELSINKI, FINLAND** *(crystal.fi)*							
	Crystal Diamond	TK	2006	D	11,340	414′ 00″	62′ 04″	35′ 01″
	Crystal Topaz	TK	2006	D	11,340	414′ 00″	62′ 04″	35′ 01″
	At press time, Crystal Pool Group also had the following vessel under charter. Please consult its respective fleet for details: Acquamarina							
IC-17	**CSL GROUP INC., MONTREAL, QUEBEC, CANADA** *(csl.ca)*							
	MARBULK SHIPPING INC. – MANAGED BY CSL INTERNATIONAL INC.							
	PARTNERSHIP BETWEEN CSL INTERNATIONAL INC. AND ALGOMA CENTRAL CORP.							
	Ambassador	SU	1983	D	37,448	730′ 00″	75′ 10″	50′ 00″
	*Built: Port Weller Dry Docks, Port Weller, ON (**Canadian Ambassador** '83-'85, **Ambassador** '85-'00, **Algosea** {2} '00-'00)*							
	Pioneer	SU	1981	D	37,448	730′ 00″	75′ 10″	50′ 00″
	*Built: Port Weller Dry Docks, Port Weller, ON (**Canadian Pioneer** '81-'86)*							
IC-18	**CYPRUS MARITIME CO. LTD., ATHENS, GREECE**							
	Lake Superior	BC	1982	D	30,670	617′ 04″	76′ 00″	47′ 07″
	*(**Broompark** '82-'99, **Millenium Raptor** '99-'02, Cardinal '02-'02)*							
ID-1	**DOUN KISEN CO. LTD., OCHI EHIME PREFECTURE, JAPAN**							
	Bright Laker	BC	2001	D	30,778	606′ 11″	77′ 05″	48″ 11″
	FOLLOWING VESSEL UNDER CHARTER TO FEDNAV LTD.							
	Federal Kushiro	BC	2003	D	32,787	624′ 08″	77′ 05″	49′ 10″
IE-1	**EASTWIND SHIP MANAGEMENT PTE. LTD., SINGAPORE, SINGAPORE** *(eastwindgroup.com)*							
	Arabian Wind	TK	1987	D	17,484	496′ 05″	73′ 06″	39′ 10″
	*(Akademik Vekua '87-'94, **Vekua** '94-'00, **Gali** '00-'05)*							
	Seram Wind	TK	1987	D	16,970	497′ 01″	73′ 07″	39′ 10″
	*(**Ilya Erenburg** '87-'07)*							
	Silver Wind	TK	1988	D	17,485	496′ 01″	73′ 06″	39′ 08″
	*(Kapitan Rudynev '88-'94, **Kapitan Rudnev** '94-'03, **Lake Maya** '03-'06, Songa Maya '06-'06, **Sichem Maya** '06-'07)*							
	Sulu Wind	TK	1989	D	16,970	497′ 01″	73′ 07″	39′ 10″
	*(**Leonid Utesov** '89-'07)*							
	FOLLOWING VESSELS CURRENTLY UNDER CHARTER TO FEDNAV LTD.							
	Yamaska	BC	1984	D	28,303	580′ 08″	75′ 09″	47′ 07″
	*(**Vamand Wave** '84-'07)*							
	Yarmouth	BC	1985	D	29,462	600′ 04″	76′ 01″	48′ 10″
	*(**Paolo Pittaluga** '85-'91, **Federal Oslo** '91-'00)*							
	Yellowknife	BC	1984	D	29,651	622′ 00″	74′ 08″	49′ 08″
	*(**Bihac** '84-'93, **La Boheme** '93-'95, Lindsey M. '98-'99, Med Pride '99-'01)*							
	Yosemite	BC	1985	D	28,019	584′ 08″	75′ 11″	48′ 05″
	*(**Astral Mariner** '85-'90, **Lake Challenge** '90-'97, **Manila Angus** '97-'98, **Darya Devi** '98-'06)*							
	Yucatan	BC	1996	D	30,838	606′ 11″	77′ 05″	48′ 11″
	(Golden Laker '96-'04)							
IE-2	**EGYPTIAN NAVIGATION CO., ALEXANDRIA, EGYPT** *(www.enc.com.eg)*							
	Ebn El Waleed	GC	1988	D	12,800	433′ 01″	67′ 04″	40′ 01″

Fleet #.	Fleet Name / Vessel Name	Type of Vessel	Year Built	Type of Engine	Cargo Cap. or gross*	Overall Length	Breadth	Depth or Draft*
IE-3	**EITZEN CHEMICAL ASA, OSLO, NORWAY** *(eitzen-chemical.com)*							
	Fen	TK	2006	D	12,956	417' 04"	66' 11"	37' 09"
	(Launched as Songa Onyx, ***Brovig Ocean*** *'06-'07,* ***Liquid Blue*** *'07-'07)*							
	Glen	TK	2005	D	12,956	417' 04"	66' 11"	37' 09"
	(Launched as Songa Pearl, ***Brovig Fjord*** *'06-'07)*							
	Moor	TK	2006	D	12,956	417' 04"	66' 11"	37' 09"
	(Brovig Sea '06-'06, Songa Saphire '06-'07, ***Liquid Elegance*** *'07-'07)*							
	North Fighter	TK	2006	D	19,932	474' 05"	77' 09"	42' 08"
	Sichem Aneline	TK	1998	D	8,941	378' 03"	61' 00"	33' 08"
	(Alexander '98-'04, Garonne '04-'04, Gironde '04-'05, ***Songa Aneline*** *'04-'05)*							
	Sichem Beijing	TK	2007	D	13,141	421' 11"	67' 11"	37' 09"
	Sichem Challenge	TK	1998	D	17,485	382' 06"	62' 04"	33' 02"
	(Queen of Montreaux '98-'99, ***North Challenge*** *'99-'06, Songa Challenge'06-'07)*							
	Sichem Defiance	TK	2001	D	17,369	442' 11"	74' 10"	41' 00"
	*(****North Defiance*** *'01-'06,* ***Songa Defiance*** *'06-'07)*							
	Sichem Manila	TK	2007	D	13,141	421' 11"	66' 11"	37' 09"
	Sichem Mumbai	TK	2006	D	13,141	421' 11"	66' 11"	37' 09"
	Sichem New York	TK	2007	D	12,956	417' 04"	66' 11"	37' 09"
	Sichem Padua	TK	1993	D	9,214	382' 06"	62' 04"	33' 02"
	(Anne Sif '93-'01, Sichem Anne '01-'02)							
	Sichem Palace	TK	2004	D	8,807	367' 05"	62' 04"	32' 10"
	Sichem Peace	TK	2005	D	8,807	367' 05"	62' 04"	32' 10"
	Sichem Princess Marie-Chantal	TK	2003	D	7,930	370' 09"	60' 00"	31' 06"
	Sichem Singapore	TK	2006	D	13,141	421' 11"	66' 11"	37' 09"
IE-4	**ELDER SHIPPING LTD., LONDON, ENGLAND**							
	Balticland	BC	1977	D	17,161	511' 10"	73' 10"	45' 11"
	(Pollux '77-'88, Baltikum '88-'89, ***Pollux*** *'89-'90,* ***Nomadic Pollux*** *'90-'04)*							
IE-5	**EMIRATES TRADING AGENCY LLC, DUBAI, UNITED ARAB EMIRATES**							
	Siam Star	BC	1984	D	29,617	587' 03"	75' 11"	47' 07"
	*(****Trident Mariner*** *'84-'01,* ***Taxideftis*** *'01-'06)*							
IE-6	**EMPROS LINES SHIPPING CO., ATHENS, GREECE**							
	Adamastos	BC	1986	D	17,792	479' 00"	74' 10"	40' 01"
	*(****Clipper Bueno*** *'86-'93, Clipper Atria '93-'95)*							
IE-7	**ENZIAN SHIP MANAGEMENT AG, BERNE, SWITZERLAND** *(www.enzian-shipping.com)*							
	Celine	BC	2001	D	8,600	423' 03"	52' 00"	32' 00"
	Claudia	BC	1999	D	5,647	311' 06"	42' 09"	23' 02"
	Kathrin	BC	1999	D	5,647	311' 04"	42' 11"	23' 03"
	Marie-Jeanne	BC	1999	D	5,049	311' 11"	43' 04"	23' 05"
	Sabina	BC	2000	D	9,231	419' 06"	52' 05"	32' 00"
	SCL Bern	BC	2005	D	12,680	459' 03"	70' 06"	38' 03"
	(SCL Bern '05-'05, SITC Bern '05-'06)							
IE-8	**EURONAV NV, ANTWERP, BELGUIM** *(euronav.com)*							
	Cap Charles	TK	2006	D	159,049	899' 07"	157' 07"	76' 01"
	Cap Diamant	TK	2001	D	149,996	898' 11"	173' 11"	76' 09"
	Cap Georges	TK	1998	D	147,444	898' 11"	156' 10"	74' 10"
	Cap Guillaume	TK	2006	D	159,049	899' 07"	157' 07"	76' 01"
	Cap Lara	TK	2007	D	159,049	899' 07"	157' 07"	76' 01"
	Cap Laurent	TK	1998	D	147,444	898' 11"	156' 10"	74' 10"
	Cap Leon	TK	2003	D	159,049	899' 07"	157' 07"	76' 01"
	Cap Philippe	TK	2006	D	159,049	899' 07"	157' 07"	76' 01"
	Cap Pierre	TK	2004	D	159,049	899' 07"	157' 07"	76' 01"
IE-10	**EXECUTIVE SHIP MANAGEMENT PTE. LTD., SINGAPORE, SINGAPORE** *(executiveship.com)*							
	Chemical Trader	TK	2005	D	8,801	367' 05"	61' 04"	32' 10"

Fleet #	Fleet Name Vessel Name	Type of Vessel	Year Built	Type of Engine	Cargo Cap. or Gross*	Overall Length	Breadth	Depth or Draft*
IF-1	**FAIRPLAY TOWAGE, HAMBURG, GERMANY** *(fairplay-towage.com)*							
	Fairplay XIV	TB	1971	D	814	162′ 04″	37′ 02″	23′ 04″
	(Rega 1 '71-'78, Hanseatic '78-'79)							
IF-2	**FAR EASTERN SHIPPING CO. (FESCO), VLADIVOSTOK, RUSSIA** *(fesco.ru/en)*							
	Grigoriy Aleksandrov	BC	1986	D	24,105	605′ 08″	75′ 02″	46′ 07″
	Khudozhnik Kraynev	BC	1986	D	24,105	605′ 08″	75′ 02″	46′ 07″
IF-3	**FEDNAV LTD., MONTREAL, QUEBEC, CANADA** *(fednav.com)*							
	FEDNAV INTERNATIONAL LTD. - DIVISION OF FEDNAV LTD.							
	Federal Agno	BC	1985	D	29,643	599′ 09″	76′ 00″	48′ 07″
	*(**Federal Asahi** {1} '85-'89)*							
	Federal Asahi {2}	BC	2000	D	36,563	656′ 02″	77′ 11″	48′ 09″
	Federal Hudson {3}	BC	2000	D	36,563	656′ 02″	77′ 11″	48′ 09″
	Federal Hunter {2}	BC	2001	D	36,563	656′ 02″	77′ 11″	48′ 09″
	Federal Katsura	BC	2005	D	32,787	624′ 08″	77′ 05″	49′ 10″
	Federal Kivalina	BC	2000	D	36,563	656′ 02″	77′ 11″	48′ 09″
	Federal Maas {2}	BC	1997	D	34,372	656′ 02″	77′ 01″	48′ 10″
	Federal Mackinac	BC	2004	D	27,000	606′ 11″	77′ 09″	46′ 25″
	Federal Margaree	BC	2005	D	27,000	606′ 11″	77′ 09″	46′ 25″
	Federal Nakagawa	BC	2005	D	36,563	656′ 02″	77′ 11″	48′ 09″
	Federal Oshima	BC	1999	D	36,563	656′ 02″	77′ 11″	48′ 09″
	Federal Progress	BC	1989	D	38,130	580′ 07″	86′ 07″	48′ 08″
	(Northern Progress '89-'02)							
	Federal Rhine {2}	BC	1997	D	34,372	656′ 02″	77′ 01″	48′ 10″
	Federal Rideau	BC	2000	D	36,563	656′ 02″	77′ 11″	48′ 09″
	Federal Saguenay {2}	BC	1996	D	34,372	656′ 02″	77′ 01″	48′ 10″
	Federal Sakura	BC	2005	D	32,787	624′ 08″	77′ 05″	49′ 10″
	Federal Schelde {3}	BC	1997	D	34,372	656′ 02″	77′ 01″	48′ 10″
	Federal Seto	BC	2004	D	36,563	656′ 02″	77′ 11″	48′ 09″
	Federal St. Laurent {3}	BC	1996	D	34,372	656′ 02″	77′ 01″	48′ 10″
	Federal Venture	BC	1989	D	38,130	580′ 07″	86′ 07″	48′ 08″
	(Northern Venture '89-'02)							
	Federal Welland	BC	2000	D	36,563	656′ 02″	77′ 11″	48′ 09″
	Federal Yukon	BC	2000	D	36,563	656′ 02″	77′ 11″	48′ 09″
	Lake Erie	BC	1980	D	38,294	730′ 00″	76′ 01″	47′ 03″
	*(**Federal Ottawa** '80-'95)*							
	Lake Michigan	BC	1981	D	38,294	730′ 00″	76′ 01″	47′ 03″
	*(**Federal Maas** {1} '81-'95)*							
	Lake Ontario	BC	1980	D	38,294	730′ 00″	76′ 01″	47′ 03″
	*(**Federal Danube** '80-'95)*							
	Lake Superior	BC	1981	D	38,294	730′ 00″	76′ 01″	47′ 03″
	*(**Federal Thames** '81-'95)*							

At press time, FedNav Ltd. also had the following vessels under charter. Please consult their respective fleets for details: Daviken, Federal Asahi, Federal Danube, Federal Elbe, Federal Ems, Federal Fuji, Federal Kumano, Federal Kushiro, Federal Leda, Federal Manitou, Federal Matane, Federal Mattawa, Federal Miramichi, Federal Patroller, Federal Pioneer, Federal Power, Federal Pride, Federal Polaris, Federal Pride, Federal Seto, Federal Shimanto, Federal Weser, Federal Yoshino, Goviken, Inviken, Orsula, Sandviken, Spar Garnet, Spar Jade, Spar Opal, Spar Ruby, Utviken, Yamaska, Yarmouth, Yellowknife, Yosemite, Yucatan

Fleet #	Fleet Name Vessel Name	Type of Vessel	Year Built	Type of Engine	Cargo Cap. or Gross*	Overall Length	Breadth	Depth or Draft*
IF-4	**FINBETA, SAVONA, ITALY** *(finbeta.com)*							
	Ocean Pride	TK	1997	D	14,015	465′ 10″	72′ 02″	36′ 01″
	(Sapphire '97-'04)							
	Turchese	TK	1999	D	12,004	447′ 10″	66′ 11″	33′ 10″
	FOLLOWING VESSEL UNDER CHARTER TO CRYSTAL POOL GROUP							
	Acquamarina	TK	2004	D	12,004	447′ 10″	66′ 11″	33′ 10″
IF-5	**FISSER & V. DOORNUM KG GMBH & CO., HAMBURG, GERMANY** *(fissership.com)*							
	Okapi	GC	1972	D	6,364	332′ 10″	52′ 07″	30′ 03″
	(Imela Fisser '72-'75, Boca Tabla '75-'82, Tabla '82-'86)							

Heavy-lift vessel *Global Carrier*, seen at Port Huron. *(Roger LeLieve)*

***Spar Garnet* at the Soo.** *(Matt Miner)*

Chemical tanker *Fen*, registered in Singapore, on the Welland Canal. *(John C. Knecht)*

Fleet #	Fleet Name Vessel Name	Type of Vessel	Year Built	Type of Engine	Cargo Cap. or Gross*	Overall Length	Breadth	Depth or Draft*
	Pyrgos	GC	1972	D	6,364	332′ 10″	52′ 07″	30′ 03″
	(Elisabeth Fisser '72-'79, Villiers '79-'86)							
IF-6	**FLINTER GRONINGEN BV (ANCORA AFS MGRS.), GRONINGEN, THE NETHERLANDS** *(flinter.nl)*							
	Flinterdam	GC	1996	D	4,506	325′ 07″	44′ 06″	23′ 06″
	Flinterdijk	GC	2000	D	6,250	366′ 07″	48′ 08″	26′ 09″
	Flinterduin	GC	2000	D	6,359	364′ 01″	49′ 02″	26′ 09″
	Flintereems	GC	2000	D	6,200	366′ 07″	48′ 08″	26′ 09″
	Flintermaas	GC	2000	D	6,200	366′ 05″	48′ 10″	26′ 10″
	Flinterspirit	GC	2001	D	6,358	366′ 07″	48′ 08″	26′ 09″
IF-7	**FORTUM OIL AND GAS OY, FORTUM, FINLAND** *(fortum.com)*							
	Purha	TK	2003	D	25,000	556′ 01″	78′ 00″	48′ 11″
IF-8	**FRANCO COMPANIA NAVIERA SA, ATHENS, GREECE** *(franco.gr)*							
	Barbro	BC	1984	D	29,692	599′ 09″	75′ 09″	48′ 07″
	*(**Olympic Dignity** '84-'92, **Alam Sejahtera** '92-'07)*							
	Stefania I	BC	1985	D	28,269	584′ 08″	75′ 11″	48′ 05″
	*(**Astral Ocean** '85-'95, Sea Crystal '95-'97, **Stefania** '97-'98)*							
IF-9	**FRANK DAHL SHIPPING, CUXHAVEN, GERMANY** *(dahl-shipping.com)*							
	FOLLOWING VESSELS UNDER CHARTER TO WAGENBORG SHIPPING							
	Finex	GC	2001	D	9,857	433′ 10″	52′ 01″	31′ 08″
	*(**Volmeborg** '01-'06)*							
	Veerseborg	GC	1998	D	8,664	433′ 10″	52′ 01″	31′ 08″
	*(**Veerseborg** '98-'04, **Matfen** '04-'07)*							
	Vossborg	GC	2000	D	8,737	433′ 10″	52′ 01″	31′ 08″
	*(Vossborg '01-'04, **Morpeth** '04-'07)*							
IF-10	**FUKUJIN KISEN CO. LTD., OCHI EHIME PREFECTURE, JAPAN**							
	FOLLOWING VESSELS UNDER CHARTER TO FEDNAV LTD.							
	Federal Kumano	BC	2001	D	32,787	624′ 08″	77′ 05″	49′ 10″
	Federal Shimanto	BC	2001	D	32,787	624′ 08″	77′ 05″	49′ 10″
	Federal Yoshino	BC	2001	D	32,787	624′ 08″	77′ 05″	49′ 10″
IG-1	**GALATIA SHIPPING CO. SA, PIRAEUS, GREECE**							
	Panos G.	BC	1996	D	10,100	370′ 09″	63′ 08″	34′ 01″
	(Ayutthaya Ruby '96-'06)							
IG-2	**GULMAR DENIZCILIK NAKLIYAT TICARET LTD., ISTANBUL, TURKEY**							
	Gulmar	BC	1981	D	27,048	627′ 07″	75′ 07″	44′ 03″
	*(Oakstar '81-'82, **Soren Toubro** '82-'98, **Millenium Falcon** '98-'02, Giant '02-'04, Atlas Sun '04-'04)*							
IH-1	**HDS AS, BILLINGSTAD, NORWAY** *(www.vee-marine.com)*							
	Viscaya	TK	1982	D	26,328	569′ 00″	75′ 00″	46′ 07″
	*(**Lake Anina** '82-'90, Jo Breid '90-'99)*							
IH-2	**HAPAG-LLOYD GMBH, HAMBURG, GERMANY** *(hapag-lloyd.com/en/)*							
	Endurance	CO	1983	D	32,424	727′ 02″	105′ 08″	49′ 03″
	(Tokyo Maru '83-'90, Alligator Joy '90-'95, CanMar Endeavour '96-'98, Contship Endeavour '98-'99, Cast Performance '99-'03, CanMar Endurance '03-'05, CP Endurance '05-'06)							
	Glory	CO	1979	D	18,643	580′ 10″	88′ 09″	44′ 03″
	(Seatrain Saratoga '79-'80, TFL Jefferson '80-'86, Jefferson '86-'88, Asian Senator '88-'90, CMB Monarch '90-'91, Sea Falcon '91-'94, CanMar Glory '94-'05, CP Glory '05-'06)							
	Lisbon Express	CO	1995	D	34,330	709′ 01″	105′ 10″	62′ 04″
	(CanMar Fortune '95-'03, Cast Prospect '03-'05, CP Prospector '05-'06)							
	Mississauga Express	CO	1998	D	40,879	803′ 10″	105′ 08″	62′ 05″
	(CanMar Pride '98-'05, CP Pride '05-'06)							
	Montreal Express	CO	2003	D	47,840	964′ 11″	106′ 00″	60′ 00″
	(CanMar Spirit '03-'05, CP Spirit '05-'06)							
	Ottawa Express	CO	1998	D	40,879	803′ 10″	105′ 11″	62′ 05″
	(CanMar Honour '98-'05, CP Honour '05-'06)							

Fleet #.	Fleet Name Vessel Name	Type of Vessel	Year Built	Type of Engine	Cargo Cap. or gross*	Overall Length	Breadth	Depth or Draft*
	Power	CO	1982	D	32,207	730'00"	105'10"	61'08"
	(America Maru '82-'90, Alligator Excellence '90-'95, CanMar Success '98-98, Contship Success '98-'99, Cast Power '99-'03, Montreal Senator '03-'05, CP Power '05-'06)							
	Toronto Express	CO	2003	D	47,840	964'11"	106'00"	60'00"
	(CanMar Venture '03-'05, CP Venture '05-'06)							
	Triumph	CO	1978	D	18,643	580'10"	88'10"	44'04"
	(Seatrain Independence '78-'81, Dart Americana '81-'87, American Senator '87-'89, CMB Marque '89-'90, CanMar Triumph '90-'05, CP Triumph '05-'06)							
	Valencia Express	CO	1996	D	34,330	709'01"	105'10"	62'04"
	(CanMar Courage '96-'03, Cast Prominence '96-'05, CP Performer '05-'06)							
	Victory	CO	1979	D	18,643	580'10"	88'10"	44'04"
	(Seatrain Chesapeake '79-'81, Dart Atlantica '81-'87, Singapore Senator '87-'89, American Senator '89-'90, CanMar Victory '79-'05, CP Victory '05-'06)							
IH-3	**HARBOR SHIPPING & TRADING CO. SA., CHIOS, GREECE**							
	Agios Minas	BC	1981	D	29,002	589'11"	76'01"	47'07"
	*(**Violetta** '81-'86, **Capetan Yiannis** '86-'88, **Federal Nord** '88-'96, **Nordic Moor** '96-'98, **Chios Charity** '98-'07)*							
IH-4	**HARREN & PARTNER SCHIFFAHRTS GMBH, BREMEN, GERMANY** *(harren-partner.de)*							
	Palawan	RR	1996	D	5,085	331'00"	61'00"	31'10"
	*(Palawan '96-'96, **Scan Partner** '97-'01, Palawan '01-'01, **Fret Meuse** '02-'03)*							
	Palessa	HL	2000	D	7,069	387'02"	64'08"	31'00"
	(Pantaleon '00-'00, Fret Moselle '00-'04)							
	Pancaldo	HL	2000	D	7,069	387'02"	64'08"	31'00"
	FOLLOWING VESSELS UNDER CHARTER TO CANADIAN FOREST NAVIGATION LTD.							
	Pochard	BC	2003	D	35,200	631'04"	77'09"	50'02"
	Puffin	BC	2003	D	35,200	629'09"	77'05"	50'00"
IH-5	**HARTMANN REEDEREI, LEER, GERMANY** *(hartmann-reederei.de)*							
	OSC Vlistdiep	GC	2007	D	7,800	388'11"	49'10"	27'09"
	(Launched as Vlistdiep)							
IH-6	**HELIKON SHIPPING ENTERPRISES LTD., LONDON, ENGLAND**							
	Elikon	BC	1980	D	16,106	582'00"	75'02"	44'04"
	(Bailey '80-'89)							
IH-7	**HERMANN BUSS GMBH, LEER, GERMANY** *(bussgruppe.de)*							
	Bornholm	BC	2006	D	7,869	388'11"	49'10"	27'11"
IH-8	**HERNING SHIPPING AS, HERNING, DENMARK** *(herning-shipping.dk)*							
	Ditte Theresa	TK	1977	D	4,501	301'10"	47'07"	29'10"
	(Bravado '77-'96)							
II-1	**ILVA SERVIZI MARITIME., MILAN, ITALY**							
	Sagittarius	BC	1987	D	29,365	613'06"	75'11"	46'11"
II-2	**INTERSEE SCHIFFAHRTS GMBH & CO., HAREN-EMS, GERMANY** *(intersee.de)*							
	Aachen	GC	2004	D	5,726	348'02"	47'03"	26'07"
	(Lea '04-'04)							
	Amalia	GC	2006	D	5,726	348'02"	47'03"	26'07"
	Amanda	GC	2005	D	5,726	348'02"	47'03"	26'07"
	Anja	GC	1999	D	9,200	419'06"	52'00"	32'00"
	(Anja '99-'01, TMC Brazil '01-'02)							
	Annalisa	GC	2000	D	8,737	433'10"	52'01"	31'08"
	(Malte Rainbow '00-'03)							
	Carola	GC	2000	D	9,000	424'08"	52'00"	33'04"
	(Beatrice '00-'00)							
	Jana	GC	2001	D	8,994	433'09"	52'01"	31'08'
	(Chandra Kirana '01-'01)							
	Julia	GC	2006	D	5,726	348'02"	47'03"	26'07"
	Julietta	GC	2002	D	10,500	468'02"	59'10"	33'04"
	Katja	GC	2000	D	9,000	424'08"	52'00"	33'04"
	(Katja '00-'01, MSC Apapa '01-'02)							

***Beluga Formation* on the Detroit River with a load of wind turbine parts.** *(Alain Gindroz)*

Fleet #.	Fleet Name Vessel Name	Type of Vessel	Year Built	Type of Engine	Cargo Cap. or gross*	Overall Length	Breadth	Depth or Draft*
	Lara	GC	1998	D	5,500	330′ 10″	49′ 01″	27′ 07″
	Nicola	GC	2000	D	5,050	312′ 02″	43′ 02″	23′ 05′
	Nina	GC	1998	D	5,726	329′ 09″	49′ 03″	27′ 07″
	(Nina '98-'98, Melody '98-'02)							
	Rebecca	GC	2002	D	10,500	468′ 02″	59′ 10″	33′ 04″
	Serena	GC	2004	D	10,500	468′ 02″	59′ 10″	33′ 04″
	Sofia	GC	2005	D	5,726	348′ 02″	47′ 03″	26′ 07″
	Tatjana	GC	2000	D	9,000	424′ 08″	52′ 00″	33′ 04″
	(Tatjana '00-'02, TMC Brazil '02-'02)							
	Thekla	GC	2003	D	8,994	433′ 09″	52′ 01″	31′ 08′
	(Suryawati '03-'03)							
	Uta	GC	2007	D	11,211	477′ 09″	59′ 10″	33′ 10″
	Victoria	GC	2004	D	10,500	468′ 02″	59′ 10″	33′ 04″
	Winona	GC	2003	D	10,000	433′ 09″	52′ 06″	32′ 10″
	(Vermontborg '03-'03)							
	Xenia	GC	2003	D	10,500	468′ 02″	59′ 10″	33′ 04″
II-3	**INTERSHIP NAVIGATION CO. LTD., LIMASSOL, CYPRUS** *(intership-cyprus.com)*							
	BBC Korea	BC	2003	D	17,477	469′ 02″	74′ 10″	43′ 08″
	*(**Atlantic Pendant** '03-'05)*							
	BBC Russia	BC	2002	D	17,477	469′ 02″	74′ 10″	43′ 08″
	(Atlantic Progress '02-'03)							
II-4	**IONIA MANAGEMENT SA, PIRAEUS, GREECE**							
	Alkyon	BC	1981	D	18,277	487′ 05″	73′ 06″	38′ 05″
	(Rich Arrow '81-'89, Pisagua '89-'95)							
II-5	**ISKO MARINE SHIPPING CO., ISTANBUL, TURKEY** *(iskomarine.com)*							
	Global Carrier	HL	1982	D	9,864	403′ 06″	67′ 08″	33′ 10″
	*(**Titan Scan** '82-'02, Scan Trader '02-'03, Global Traveller '03-'04, Taipan Scan '04-'05)*							
IJ-1	**JO TANKERS BV, SPIJKENISSE, NETHERLANDS** *(jotankers.com)*							
	Jo Spirit	TK	1998	D	6,248	352′ 02″	52′ 02″	30′ 02″
IJ-2	**JSM SHIPPING GMBH & CO., JORK, GERMANY**							
	BBC England	GC	2003	D	10,300	465′ 10″	59′ 10″	33′ 04″
	(Frida '03-'04)							
	S Pacific	GC	2004	D	10,385	468′ 02″	59′ 10″	24′ 02″
IJ-3	**JUMBO SHIPPING CO. SA, ROTTERDAM, NETHERLANDS** *(jumboshipping.nl)*							
	Daniella	HL	1989	D	7,600	322′ 09″	60′ 03″	37′ 02″
	(Stellaprima '89-'90)							
	Fairlane	HL	2000	D	7,123	361′ 03″	68′ 05″	44′ 03″
	Fairlift	HL	1990	D	7,780	330′ 08″	68′ 10″	43′ 08″
	Fairload	HL	1995	D	5,198	314′ 00″	60′ 03″	37′ 02″
	Fairmast	HL	1983	D	6,375	360′ 11″	67′ 09″	34′ 05″
	Fairpartner	HL	2004	D	10,975	469′ 06″	86′ 11″	44′ 03″
	Fairplayer	HL	2007	D	10,975	469′ 06″	86′ 11″	44′ 03″
	Jumbo Challenger	HL	1983	D	6,375	360′ 11″	63′ 10″	34′ 05″
	Jumbo Javelin	HL	2004	D	10,975	469′ 06″	86′ 11″	44′ 03″
	Jumbo Jubilee	HL	2008	D	10,975	469′ 06″	86′ 11″	44′ 03″
	Jumbo Spirit	HL	1995	D	5,198	314′ 00″	60′ 03″	37′ 02″
	Jumbo Vision	HL	2000	D	7,123	361′ 03″	68′ 05″	44′ 03″
	Stellanova	HL	1996	D	5,198	314′ 00″	60′ 03″	37′ 02″
	Stellaprima	HL	1991	D	7,780	330′ 08″	68′ 10″	43′ 08″
IK-1	**KNUTSEN O.A.S. SHIPPING AS, HAUGESUND, NORWAY** *(knutsenoas.com)*							
	Ellen Knutsen	TK	1992	D	17,071	464′ 03″	75′ 07″	38′ 09″
	Sidsel Knutsen	TK	1993	D	22,625	533′ 03″	75′ 06″	48′ 07″
	Synnove Knutsen	TK	1992	D	17,071	464′ 03″	75′ 07″	38′ 09″
	Torill Knutsen	TK	1990	D	14,910	464′ 08″	75′ 07″	38′ 09″
	Turid Knutsen	TK	1993	D	22,625	533′ 03″	75′ 06″	48′ 07″

Fleet #	Fleet Name Vessel Name	Type of Vessel	Year Built	Type of Engine	Cargo Cap. or Gross*	Overall Length	Breadth	Depth or Draft*
IK-2	**KREY SCHIFFAHRTS GMBH, SIMONSWOLDE, GERMANY** *(krey-schiffahrt.de)*							
	BBC Ontario	GC	2004	D	12,711	452' 10"	68' 11"	36' 01"
IL-1	**LATVIAN SHIPPING CO. (LSC SHIPMANAGEMENT LTD.) RIGA, LATVIA** *(www.lscsm.lv)*							
	Dzintari	TK	1985	D	17,585	497' 00"	73' 06"	39' 10"
	(Moris Bishop '85 -'91)							
	Zanis Griva	TK	1985	D	17,585	497' 00"	73' 06"	39' 10"
	(Zhan Griva '85 -'91)							
IL-2	**LAURANNE SHIPPING BV, GHENT, NETHERLANDS** *(lauranne-shipping.com)*							
	LS Jacoba	TK	2006	D	15,602	485' 07"	70' 10"	37' 01"
IL-3	**LAURIN MARITIME (AMERICA) INC., HOUSTON, TEXAS, USA** *(laurinmar.com)*							
	Mountain Blossom	TK	1986	D	19,993	527' 07"	74' 11"	39' 04"
	Swan Lake	TK	1982	D	10,579	445' 04"	62' 04"	33' 02"
IL-4	**LIETUVOS JURU LAIVININKYSTE (LITHUANIAN SHIPPING CO.), KLAIPEDA, LITHUANIA** *(ljl.lt)*							
	Deltuva	BC	1994	D	16,906	490' 02"	75' 04"	39' 08"
	*(**Clipper Eagle** '82-'97)*							
	Clipper Falcon	BC	1994	D	16,906	490' 02"	75' 04"	39' 08"
	Kapitonas Serafinas	BC	1980	D	14,550	479' 08"	67' 11"	42' 04"
	*(Kapitan Stulov '80-'91, **Kapitonas Stulov** '91-'97)*							
	Kapitonas Stulpinas	BC	1981	D	14,550	479' 08"	67' 11"	42' 04"
	(Yustas Paleckis '81-'92)							
	Staris	BC	1985	D	9,650	403' 06"	65' 08"	50' 09"
	*(Abitibi Concord '85-'92, Concord '92-'94, Abitibi Concord '94-'96, **Concord** '96-'02)*							
IL-5	**LYDIA MAR SHIPPING CO. SA, ATHENS, GREECE** *(lydiamar.gr)*							
	Dorothea	BC	1984	D	22,025	508' 05"	74' 08"	44' 06"
	(Garnet Star '84-'94)							
IM-1	**MARLOW SHIP MANAGEMENT DEUTSCHLAND GMBH, HAMBURG, GERMANY**							
	Emsmoon	GC	2000	D	6,359	366' 08"	49' 01"	32' 02"
	(Morgenstond III '00-'05)							
IM-2	**MEDITERRANEA DI NAVIGAZIONE, RAVENNA, ITALY** *(mediterraneanav.it)*							
	Longobarda	TK	1992	D	10,006	452' 09"	62' 04"	30' 00"
IM-3	**MURMANSK SHIPPING CO., MURMANSK, RUSSIA** *(msco.ru)*							
	Aleksandr Suvorov	BC	1979	D	19,885	531' 06"	75' 02"	44' 05"
	Mikhail Strekalovskiy	BC	1981	D	19,252	531' 06"	75' 02"	44' 05"
	Pavel Vavilov	BC	1981	D	19,252	531' 06"	75' 02"	44' 05"
IN-1	**NAVARONE SA MARINE ENTERPRISES, LIMASSOL, CYPRUS**							
	FOLLOWING VESSELS UNDER CHARTER TO CANADIAN FOREST NAVIGATION LTD.							
	Bluebill	BC	2004	D	37,200	632' 10"	77' 09"	50' 10"
	Bluewing	BC	2002	D	26,747	611' 00"	77' 09"	46' 07"
	Cinnamon	BC	2002	D	26,747	611' 00"	77' 09"	46' 07"
	Greenwing	BC	2002	D	26,747	611' 00"	77' 09"	46' 07"
	Mandarin	BC	2003	D	26,747	611' 00"	77' 09"	46' 07"
IN-2	**NAVIGATION MARITIME BULGARE LTD., VARNA, BULGARIA** *(navbul.com)*							
	Bogdan	BC	1997	D	14,011	466' 02"	72' 08"	36' 04"
	Kamenitza	BC	1980	D	24,150	605' 08"	75' 00"	46' 05"
	Kapitan Georgi Georgiev	BC	1980	D	24,150	605' 08"	75' 00"	46' 05"
	Kom	BC	1997	D	13,971	466' 02"	72' 10"	36' 05"
	Koznitsa	BC	1984	D	24,100	605' 08"	75' 02"	46' 07"
	Malyovitza	BC	1982	D	24,456	605' 08"	75' 02"	46' 07"
	Milin Kamak	BC	1979	D	25,857	607' 07"	75' 02"	46' 07"
	Okoltchitza	BC	1982	D	24,148	605' 08"	75' 05"	46' 06"
	Perelik	BC	1998	D	13,887	466' 02"	72' 10"	36' 05"
	Persenk	BC	1998	D	13,900	466' 02"	72' 08"	36' 04"
	Shipka	BC	1978	D	24,385	607' 07"	75' 02"	46' 07"

Fleet #.	Fleet Name Vessel Name	Type of Vessel	Year Built	Type of Engine	Cargo Cap. or gross*	Overall Length	Breadth	Depth or Draft*
IN-3	**NOVOROSSIYSK SHIPPING CO. (NOVOSHIP), NOVOROSSIYSK, RUSSIA** *(novoship.co.uk)*							
	Vladimir Vysotskiy	TK	1988	D	16,970	497' 01"	73' 07"	39' 10"
IO-1	**OCEAN FREIGHTERS LTD., PIRAEUS, GREECE**							
	Pontokratis	BC	1981	D	28,738	590' 02"	75' 11"	47' 07"
	Pontoporos	BC	1984	D	29,155	590' 02"	75' 11"	47' 07"
IO-2	**OCEANEX INC., MONTREAL, QUEBEC, CANADA** *(oceanex.com)*							
	ASL Sanderling	RR	1977	D	15,195	364' 01"	88' 05"	57' 07"
	(Rauenfels '77-'80, Essen '80-'81, Kongsfjord '81-'83, Onno '83-'87)							
	Cabot {2}	RR	1979	D	7,132	564' 09"	73' 11"	45' 09"
	Oceanex Avalon	CO	2005	D	14,747	481' 11"	85' 00"	45' 11"
IO-3	**OLDENDORFF CARRIERS GMBH & CO., LUBECK, GERMANY** *(oldendorff.com)*							
	Elise Oldendorff	BC	1998	D	20,142	488' 10"	75' 09"	44' 03"
	FOLLOWING VESSELS CURRENTLY UNDER CHARTER TO KENT LINE							
	Kent Pioneer	BC	1999	D	20,427	688' 10"	75' 09"	47' 07"
	*(**Mathilde Oldendorff** '99-'05)*							
	Kent Timber	BC	1999	D	20,427	688' 10"	75' 09"	47' 07"
	(Antonie Oldendorff '99-'05)							
IO-4	**OLYMPIC SHIPPING AND MANAGEMENT SA, MONTE CARLO, MONACO** *(olyship.com)*							
	Calliroe Patronicola	BC	1985	D	29,640	599' 09"	75' 11"	48' 07"
	Olympic Melody	BC	1984	D	29,640	599' 09"	75' 11"	48' 07"
	Olympic Mentor	BC	1984	D	29,640	599' 09"	75' 11"	48' 07"
	*(Calliroe Patronicola '84-'84, **Patricia-R.** '84-'88)*							
	Olympic Merit	BC	1985	D	29,640	599' 09"	75' 11"	48' 07"
	Olympic Miracle	BC	1984	D	29,640	599' 09"	75' 11"	48' 07"
IO-5	**OMICRON SHIP MANAGEMENT INC., MOSCHATO, GREECE**							
	Starlight	BC	1984	D	28,354	644' 06"	75' 06"	46' 11"
	*(**Noble River** '84-'86, **Helena Oldendorff** '86-'06)*							
IO-6	**ONEGO SHIPPING & CHARTERING, RHOON, NETHERLANDS** *(onegoshipping.com)*							
	Onego Merchant	BC	2004	D	7,800	393' 08"	49' 10"	27' 09"
	Onego Trader	BC	2003	D	7,800	393' 08"	49' 10"	27' 09"
	Onego Traveller	BC	2004	D	7,800	393' 08"	49' 10"	27' 09"
IO-7	**ORION SCHIFFAHRTS, HAMBURG, GERMANY**							
	Meta	BC	1987	D	18,612	477' 04"	75' 09"	40' 08"
IP-1	**PACIFIC CARRIERS LTD., SINGAPORE, SINGAPORE** *(www.pclsg.com)*							
	Alam Sempurna	BC	1984	D	28,094	584' 08"	75' 11"	48' 05"
	(Saint Laurent '84-'91)							
IP-2	**PARAKOU SHIPPING LTD., HONG KONG, PEOPLE'S REPUBLIC OF CHINA** *(parakougroup.com)*							
	FOLLOWING VESSELS UNDER CHARTER TO CANADIAN FOREST NAVIGATION LTD.							
	Eider	BC	2004	D	37,272	655' 10"	77' 09"	50' 02"
	Gadwall	BC	2007	D	37,272	655' 10"	77' 09"	50' 02"
	Garganey	BC	2007	D	37,272	655' 10"	77' 09"	50' 02"
	Redhead	BC	2005	D	37,272	655' 10"	77' 09"	50' 02"
	Whistler	BC	2007	D	37,272	655' 10"	77' 09"	50' 02"
IP-3	**POT SCHEEPVAART BV, DELFZIJL, NETHERLANDS**							
	FOLLOWING VESSELS UNDER CHARTER TO WAGENBORG SHIPPING							
	Doggersbank	GC	1996	D	4,149	294' 07"	44' 11"	23' 07"
	Kwintebank	GC	2002	D	8,664	433' 10"	52' 01"	31' 08"
	Varnebank	GC	2000	D	8,664	433' 10"	52' 01"	31' 08"
IP-4	**POLISH STEAMSHIP CO., SZCZECIN, POLAND** *(polsteam.com)*							
	Irma	BC	2000	D	34,946	655' 10"	77' 05"	50' 02"
	Iryda	BC	1999	D	34,946	655' 10"	77' 05"	50' 02"
	Isa	BC	1999	D	34,946	655' 10"	77' 05"	50' 02"
	Isadora	BC	1999	D	34,946	655' 10"	77' 05"	50' 02"

Fleet #	Fleet Name Vessel Name	Type of Vessel	Year Built	Type of Engine	Cargo Cap. or Gross*	Overall Length	Breadth	Depth or Draft*
	Isolda	BC	1999	D	34,946	655′ 10″	77′ 05″	50′ 02″
	Kopalnia Borynia	BC	1989	D	11,898	471′ 07″	63′ 06″	36′ 04″
	Nida	BC	1993	D	13,756	469′ 02″	68′ 08″	37′ 02″
	Nogat	BC	1999	D	17,064	488′ 10″	75′ 06″	39′ 08″
	Odra	BC	1992	D	13,756	469′ 02″	68′ 08″	37′ 02″
	*(**Odranes** '92-'99)*							
	Orla	BC	1999	D	17,064	488′ 10″	75′ 06″	39′ 08″
	Pilica	BC	1999	D	17,064	488′ 10″	75′ 06″	39′ 08″
	Pomorze Zachodnie	BC	1985	D	26,696	591′ 06″	75′ 10″	45′ 07″
	(Launched as Ziemia Tarnowska)							
	Rega	BC	1995	D	17,064	488′ 10″	75′ 06″	39′ 08″
	*(**Fossnes** '95-'02)*							
	Warta	BC	1992	D	13,756	469′ 02″	68′ 08″	37′ 02″
	*(**Wartanes** '92-'99)*							
	Ziemia Chelminska	BC	1984	D	26,696	591′ 06″	75′ 10″	45′ 07″
	Ziemia Cieszynska	BC	1993	D	26,264	591′ 02″	75′ 09″	45′ 07″
	*(**Ziemia Cieszynska** '93-'93, **Lake Carling** '93-'03)*							
	Ziemia Gnieznienska	BC	1985	D	26,696	591′ 06″	75′ 10″	45′ 07″
	Ziemia Gornoslaska	BC	1990	D	26,264	591′ 02″	75′ 09″	45′ 07″
	*(**Ziemia Gornoslaska** '90-'91, **Lake Charles** '91-'03)*							
	Ziemia Lodzka	BC	1992	D	26,264	591′ 02″	75′ 09″	45′ 07″
	*(**Ziemia Lodzka** '92-'92, **Lake Champlain** '92-'03)*							
	Ziemia Suwalska	BC	1984	D	26,696	591′ 06″	75′ 10″	45′ 07″
	Ziemia Tarnowska	BC	1985	D	26,696	591′ 06″	75′ 10″	45′ 07″
	Ziemia Zamojska	BC	1984	D	26,696	591′ 06″	75′ 10″	45′ 07″
IP-5	**PRECIOUS SHIPPING PUBLIC CO. LTD., BANGKOK, THAILAND** *(preciousshipping.com)*							
	Manora Naree	BC	1980	D	29,159	590′ 10″	75′ 09″	47′ 06″
	(High Peak '84 -'90, Federal Bergen '90 -'92, Thunder Bay '92-'93, Federal Bergen '93-'04							
IR-1	**REDERIJ WESSELS B.V., ROTTERDAM, NETHERLANDS**							
	Dutch Runner	BC	1988	D	2,279*	251′ 09″	51′ 03″	20′ 01″
	Vessel is scheduled to enter service under the Canadian flag in April 2008, owned by Great Lakers Feeder Lines Inc., Burlington, ON (North King '88-'00, Dutch Runner '00-'01, P&O Nedlloyd Douala '01-'02)							
IR-2	**REEDEREI KARL SCHLUTER GMBH & CO., RENDSBURG, GERMANY**							
	FOLLOWING VESSEL UNDER CHARTER TO FEDNAV LTD.							
	Federal Mattawa	GC	2005	D	18,825	606′ 11″	77′ 09″	46′ 03″
IR-3	**RIGEL SCHIFFAHRTS GMBH & CO. KG, BREMEN, GERMANY** *(rigel-hb.com)*							
	Isarstern	TK	1995	D	17,078	528′ 03″	75′ 06″	38′ 05″
	Weserstern	TK	1992	D	10,932	417′ 04″	58′ 01″	34′ 09″
IR-4	**ROHDEN BEREEDERUNG GMBH & CO. KG, HAMBURG, GERMANY** *(rohden.de)*							
	Agena	GC	2001	D	3,380	283′ 06″	42′ 00″	23′ 04″
IS-1	**SEALINK MARINE INC., PIRAEUS, GREECE**							
	Halandriani	BC	1980	D	27,125	627′ 07″	75′ 02″	44′ 03″
	*(**Regent Palm** '80-'86, **World Palm** '86-'87, **Pontoporos III** '87-'88, **Crystal B** '88-'95, **Ocean Leader** '95-'97, **Chios Pride** '97-'07)*							
IS-2	**SEA OBSERVER SHIPPING SERVICES SA, PIRAEUS, GREECE**							
	Krios	BC	1983	D	12,319	423′ 04″	65′ 07″	36′ 09″
	*(**Fjordnes** '83-'87, Elpis '87-'90, **Kamtin** '90-'96, **Falknes** '96-'00, **Demi Green** '00-'01, **Lia** '01-'03)*							
IS-3	**SEASTAR NAVIGATION CO. LTD., ATHENS, GREECE**							
	FOLLWING VESSELS UNDER CHARTER TO CANADIAN FOREST NAVIGATION LTD.							
	Apollon	BC	1996	D	30,855	606′ 11″	77′ 05″	48′ 11″
	*(**Spring Laker** '96-'06)*							
	Goldeneye	BC	1986	D	26,706	591′ 06″	75′ 09″	48′ 07″
	*(**Sun Ocean** '86-'93, **Luna Verde** '93-'00)*							
	Milo	BC	1984	D	27,915	584′ 00″	75′ 10″	48′ 05″
	*(**Silver Leader** '84-'95, **Alam United** '95-'98, **United** '98-'00)*							

Fleet #.	Fleet Name Vessel Name	Type of Vessel	Year Built	Type of Engine	Cargo Cap. or gross*	Overall Length	Breadth	Depth or Draft*
	Miltiades	BC	1983	D	28,126	584' 06"	75' 07"	46' 09"
	(***La Liberte*** *'83-'87, Liberte '87-'88,* ***Astart*** *'88-'93,* ***Ulloa*** *'93-'00,* ***Toro*** *'00-'07)*							
	Orna	BC	1984	D	27,915	584' 00"	75' 10"	48' 05"
	(***St. Catheriness*** *'84-'90,* ***Asian Erie*** *'90-'92,* ***Handy Laker*** *'92-'98,* ***Moor Laker*** *'98-'03)*							
	Woody	BC	1984	D	25,166	593' 02"	75' 09"	47' 07"
	(***High Light*** *'84-'90,* ***Scan Trader*** *'90-'95,* ***Asia Trader*** *'95-'96,* ***NST Challenge*** *'96-'03)*							
IS-4	**SERROMAH SHIPPING BV, ROTTERDAM, NETHERLANDS** *(serromahshipping.com)*							
	Oriental Kerria	TK	2004	D	14,298	440' 02"	67' 04"	38' 01"
IS-5	**SHIH WEI NAVIGATION CO. LTD., TAIPEI, TAIWAN** *(www.swnav.com.tw)*							
	Fodas Pescadores	BC	2001	D	11,600	387' 02"	64' 04"	36' 01"
	Royal Pescadores	BC	1997	D	18,369	486' 01"	74' 10"	40' 00"
IS-6	**SICILNAVI S.R.L., PALERMO, ITALY**							
	Vindemia	TK	1979	D	3,603	295' 11"	44' 07"	21' 04"
	(Zaccar '79-'02)							
IS-7	**SIOMAR ENTERPRISES LTD., PIRAEUS, GREECE**							
	Island Skipper	BC	1984	D	28,031	584' 08"	76' 02"	48' 05"
	Island Triangle	BC	1984	D	28,031	584' 08"	76' 02"	48' 05"
	(***Island Gem*** *'84-'07)*							
IS-8	**SPAR SHIPPING AS, BERGEN, NORWAY**							
	FOLLOWING VESSELS UNDER CHARTER TO FEDNAV LTD.							
	Spar Garnet	BC	1984	D	30,674	589' 11"	75' 09"	50' 10"
	(***Mary Anne*** *'84-'93,* ***Federal Vigra*** *'93-'97)*							
	Spar Jade	BC	1984	D	30,674	589' 11"	75' 10"	50' 11"
	(***Fiona Mary*** *'84-93,* ***Federal Aalesund*** *'93-'97)*							
	Spar Opal	BC	1984	D	28,214	585' 00"	75' 10"	48' 05"
	(***Lake Shidaka*** *'84-'91,* ***Consensus Atlantic*** *'91-'92,* ***Federal Matane*** *'92-'97,* ***Matane*** *'97-'97)*							

Netherlands-flagged *Fairlift* plays tag with a sailboat. *(Roger LeLievre)*

Fleet #	Fleet Name Vessel Name	Type of Vessel	Year Built	Type of Engine	Cargo Cap. or Gross*	Overall Length	Breadth	Depth or Draft*
	Spar Ruby	BC	1985	D	28,259	584' 08"	75' 11"	48' 05"
	*(**Astral Neptune** '85-'92, **Liberty Sky** '92-'98, **Manila Bellona** '98-'98, **Solveig** '98-'00)*							
IS-9	**STARMARINE MANAGEMENT INC., ATHENS, GREECE**							
	Elpida	GC	1984	D	30,850	617' 04"	75' 11"	47' 07
	*(**Radnik** '84-'96, **Grant Carrier** '96-'01, **Chios Sailor** '01-'07)*							
IS-10	**STOLT PARCEL TANKERS INC., GREENWICH, CT, USA** *(stolt-nielsen.com)*							
	Stolt Aspiration	TK	1987	D	12,219	422' 11"	66' 03"	36' 01
	(Golden Angel '87-'87)							
	Stolt Kite	TK	1992	D	4,735	314' 11"	49' 06"	26' 05
	(Randi Terkol '92-'96)							
IS-11	**STX PAN OCEAN SHIPPING CO. LTD., SEOUL, SOUTH KOREA** *(stxpanocean.co.kr)*							
	Pan Voyager	BC	1984	D	29,433	589' 11"	78' 01"	47' 07"
IS-12	**SUNSHIP & MLB M. LAUTERJUNG., EMDEN, GERMANY** *(sunship.de)*							
	FOLLOWING VESSELS UNDER CHARTER TO FEDNAV LTD.							
	Federal Manitou	BC	2004	D	27,000	606' 11"	77' 09"	46' 03"
	Federal Matane	BC	2004	D	27,000	606' 11"	77' 09"	46' 03"
	Federal Miramichi	BC	2004	D	27,000	606' 11"	77' 09"	46' 03"
IT-1	**TEO SHIPPING CORP., PIRAEUS, GREECE**							
	Antalina	BC	1984	D	28,082	584' 08"	75' 10"	48' 05"
	*(**Union Pioneer** '84-'88, **Manila Prosperity** '88-'89, **Consensus Sea** '89-'92, **Wiltrader** '92-'94)*							
IT-2	**THALKAT SHIPPING SA, PIRAEUS, GREECE**							
	Dora	BC	1981	D	21,951	508' 06"	75' 00"	44' 07"
	*(**Verdant** '81-'87, Luntian '87-'93, Verdin '93-'94, **Oak** '94-'02)*							
IT-3	**THENAMARIS (SHIPS MANAGEMENT) INC., ATHENS, GREECE** *(thenamaris.gr)*							
	Seaguardian II	BC	1984	D	28,251	639' 09"	75' 10"	46' 11"
	*(**Seamonarch** '84-'86, Sea Master II '86-'88, Sea Monarch '88- '97, **Sealuck V** '97- '00, **Seaharmony II** '00-'01, **Seamonarch II** '01-'02)*							
	Sealink	BC	1983	D	28,234	639' 09"	75' 10"	46' 11"
	(Seaglory '83-'86, Sea Star II '86-'97)							
IT-4	**THOME SHIP MANAGEMENT, SINGAPORE, SINGAPORE**							
	Mount Ace	TK	1986	D	27,350	557' 09"	75' 11"	50' 04"
	(Rita Maersk '86-'96, Magdalena '96-'97, Maersk Baltic '97-'01, Cielo del Baltico '01-'06)							
IT-5	**TORVALD KLAVENESS GROUP, OSLO, NORWAY** *(www.klaveness.com)*							
	KCL Barracuda	CC	1984	D	17,722	482' 11"	74' 11"	40' 01"
	(Kiwi Star '84-'03, Thai Ho '03-'04)							
IT-6	**TRADEWIND TANKERS SL, BARCELONA, SPAIN** *(www.tradewindtankers.com)*							
	Tradewind Union	TK	1997	D	10,600	387' 02"	63' 08"	34' 01"
	(Southern Lion '97-'03)							
IT-7	**TRANSADRIATIC, UMAG, REPUBLIC OF CROATIA**							
	Orfea	GC	1977	D	9,008	416' 08"	61' 03"	32' 06"
	(Washigton '77-'99, Orlec '99-'06)							
IU-1	**UNION MARINE ENTERPRISES SA OF PANAMA, PIRAEUS, GREECE**							
	Capetan Michalis	BC	1981	D	28,600	593' 02"	75' 09"	47' 07"
	(Vasiliki '81-'85)							
IV-1	**VENUS ENTERPRISE SA, VOULA, GREECE**							
	Sea Veteran	BC	1981	D	30,900	617' 05"	76' 01"	47' 07"
	*(**Nosira Sharon** '81-'89, **Berta Dan** '89-'93, **Gunay-A** '93-'06)*							
IV-2	**VIKEN SHIPPING AS, BERGEN, NORWAY** *(vikenshipping.com)*							
	FOLLOWING VESSELS UNDER CHARTER TO FEDNAV LTD.							
	Daviken	BC	1987	D	35,532	729' 00"	75' 09"	48' 05"
	*(**Malinska** '87-'97)*							
	Federal Fuji	BC	1986	D	29,643	599' 09"	76' 00"	48' 07"
	Federal Polaris	BC	1985	D	29,643	599' 09"	76' 00"	48' 07"

Fleet #.	Fleet Name Vessel Name	Type of Vessel	Year Built	Type of Engine	Cargo Cap. or gross*	Overall Length	Breadth	Depth or Draft*
	Goviken	BC	1987	D	35,532	729' 00"	75' 09"	48' 05"
	*(**Omisalj** '87-'97)*							
	Inviken	BC	1986	D	30,052	621' 05"	75' 10"	47' 11"
	*(**Bar** '86-'97)*							
	Sandviken	BC	1986	D	35,532	729' 00"	75' 09"	48' 05"
	*(**Petka** '86-'00)*							
	Utviken	BC	1987	D	30,052	621' 05"	75' 10"	47' 11"
	*(**Bijelo Polje** '87-'92, C. Blanco '92-'95)*							
IW-1	**W. BOCKSTIEGEL REEDEREI KG, EMDEN, GERMANY** *(reederei-bockstiegel.de)*							
	BBC Campana	GC	2003	D	12,837	452' 09"	68' 11"	36' 01"
	(Asian Cruiser '03-'03)							
	BBC Italy	GC	2001	D	7,820	353' 00"	59' 09"	33' 02"
	(BBC Italy '99-'01, Buccaneer '01-'03)							
	BBC Peru	GC	2001	D	7,598	351' 01"	59' 09"	33' 02"
	BBC Plata	GC	2005	D	12,837	452' 09"	68' 11"	36' 01"
	BBC Spain	GC	2001	D	7,598	351' 01"	59' 09"	33' 02"
	Nils B.	GC	1998	D	3,440	283' 06"	42' 00"	23' 04"
IW-2	**WAGENBORG SHIPPING BV, DELFZIJL, NETHERLANDS** *(wagenborg.com)*							
	Americaborg	GC	2007	D	17,356	469' 02"	70' 06"	43' 08"
	Dagna	GC	2005	D	6,000	363' 05"	45' 11"	26' 08"
	Diezeborg	GC	2000	D	8,867	437' 08"	52' 00"	32' 02"
	Dongeborg	GC	1999	D	8,867	437' 08"	52' 00"	32' 02"
	Drechtborg	GC	2000	D	8,865	437' 08"	52' 02"	32' 02"
	(Drechtborg '00-'00, MSC Skaw '00-'02, Drechtborg '02-'03, Normed Rotterdam '03-'05)							
	Egbert Wagenborg	GC	1998	D	9,141	441' 05"	54' 02"	32' 02"
	*(Maasborg '98-'98, **Egbert Wagenborg** '98-'02, MSC Bothnia '02-'03)*							
	Kasteelborg	GC	1998	D	9,150	427' 01"	52' 01"	33' 06"
	Keizersborg	GC	1996	D	9,150	427' 01"	52' 01"	33' 06"
	Koningsborg	GC	1999	D	9,150	427' 01"	52' 01"	33' 06"
	Kroonborg	GC	1995	D	9,085	428' 10"	52' 02"	33' 06"
	Maineborg	GC	2001	D	9,141	441' 05"	54' 02"	32' 02"
	Medemborg	GC	1997	D	9,141	441' 05"	54' 02"	32' 02"
	*(**Arion** '97-'03)*							
	Michiganborg	GC	1999	D	9,141	441' 05"	54' 02"	32' 02"
	Moezelborg	GC	1999	D	9,141	441' 05"	54' 02"	32' 02"
	Nassauborg	GC	2006	D	16,615	467' 06"	72' 02"	39' 04"
	Prinsenborg	GC	2003	D	16,615	467' 06"	72' 02"	39' 04"
	Vaasaborg	GC	1999	D	8,664	433' 10"	52' 01"	31' 08"
	Vancouverborg	GC	2001	D	9,857	433' 10"	52' 01"	31' 08"
	Vechtborg	GC	1998	D	8,664	433' 10"	52' 01"	31' 08"
	Victoriaborg	GC	2001	D	9,857	433' 10"	52' 01"	31' 08"
	(Volgaborg '01-'01)							
	Virginiaborg	GC	2001	D	9,857	433' 10"	52' 01"	31' 08"
	Vlistborg	GC	1999	D	8,664	433' 10"	52' 01"	31' 08"
	Voorneborg	GC	1999	D	8,664	433' 10"	52' 01"	31' 08"
	At press time, Wagenborg Shipping also had the following vessels under charter. Please consult their respective fleets for details: Doggersbank, Finex, Kwintebank, Varnebank, Veerseborg, Vossborg, Zeus							
IY-1	**WAKER SHIPPING BV, DELFZIJL, NETHERLANDS**							
	FOLLOWING VESSEL UNDER CHARTER TO WAGENBORG SHIPPING							
	Zeus	GC	2000	D	9,150	427' 01"	52' 01"	33' 06"
IY-2	**YAHATA KISEN CO. LTD., OCHI EHIME PREFECTURE, JAPAN**							
	Lodestar Grace	TK	2002	D	14,298	439' 08"	67' 03"	38' 01"
IY-3	**YILMAR SHIPPING & TRADING LTD., ISTANBUL, TURKEY** *(yilmar.com)*							
	YM Jupiter	TK	2007	D	15,995	393' 08"	57' 09"	27' 11"

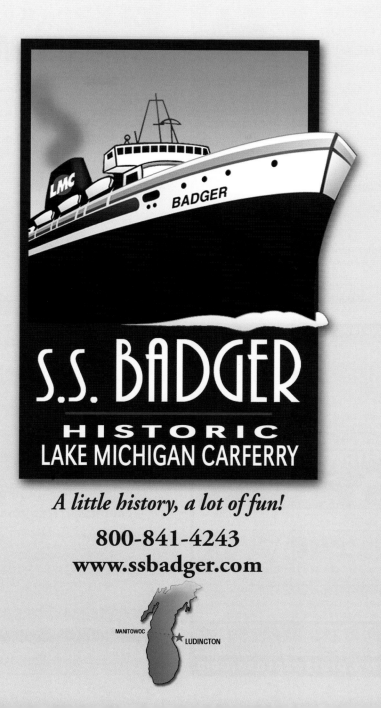

Models
& More
at Your
Great Lakes
Superstore
www.GreatLakesFreighters.com
We Specialize in Kits
& Custom Models
of Great Lakes Freighters
Videos
Clothing
Gifts
(440) 298-1243
5305 Emerson Rd.
Madison, OH 44057
www.greatlakesfreighters.com
www.bearcomarine.com

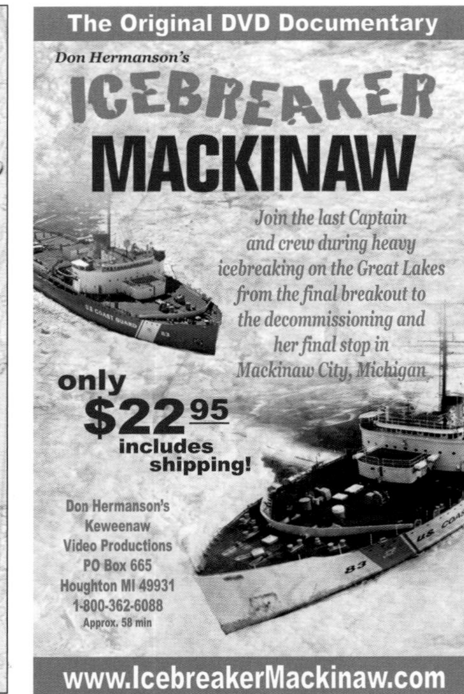
The Original DVD Documentary
Don Hermanson's
ICEBREAKER
MACKINAW
Join the last Captain
and crew during heavy
icebreaking on the Great Lakes
from the final breakout to
the decommissioning and
her final stop in
Mackinaw City, Michigan
only
$22.95
includes
shipping!
Don Hermanson's
Keweenaw
Video Productions
PO Box 665
Houghton MI 49931
1-800-362-6088
Approx. 58 min
www.IcebreakerMackinaw.com

SHIPS IN ACTION ON THE GREAT LAKES!
GREAT LAKES SHIPS
THE DVD / VIDEO SERIES
Each video features 15 ships in action as seen on various Great Lakes, ports, river and locks. The U.S. & Canadian flagged boats include: ★ Classic Lakers ★ Steamers ★ Self-Unloaders ★ Tankers ★ 1000 Foot Super Lakers. Plus ship info & history.
— VOLUMES 1-10 • DVD & Limited VHS —
65 MIN. EACH • COLOR • LIVE AUDIO • NARRATION
☐DVD -OR- ☐LIMITED VHS
Only $24.95 EACH
Buy 2 or More Titles
Only $22.95 EACH
Plus S&H: One $6 • Two $7 • Three FREE
Wisconsin Residents add 5.5% sales tax
Coming Soon!
★ Lake Superior Sight Seeing Travel Guide Vol. 1-2
★ Lake Superior Lighthouses ★ Waterfalls
PLETS EXPRESS
P.O. Box 217 • Altoona, WI 54720 • 715-833-8899
www.pletsexpress.com

THE
BOOK
BLUES
Freighter & ship
watch right from
our store on the
beautiful blue
water of the
St. Clair River!

Extra Tonnage

Edward L. Ryerson **enters the St. Lambert Lock.** *(Eric Treece)*

Stewart J. Cort **loading ore at the BNSF dock in Superior.** *(Sam Lapinski)*

MAJOR GREAT LAKES LOADING PORTS

Iron Ore
Duluth, Minn.
Superior, Wis.
Two Harbors, Minn.
Marquette, Mich.
Escanaba, Mich.

Petroleum
Sarnia, Ont.
E. Chicago, Ind.

Limestone
Port Inland, Mich.
Cedarville, Mich.
Drummond Island, Mich.
Calcite, Mich.
Rogers City, Mich.
Stoneport, Mich.
Marblehead, Ohio

Coal
Superior, Wis.
S. Chicago, Ill.
Toledo, Ohio
Sandusky, Ohio
Ashtabula, Ohio
Conneaut, Ohio

Grain
Thunder Bay, Ont.
Duluth, Minn.
Milwaukee, Wis.
Superior, Wis.
Sarnia, Ont.
Toledo, Ohio
Port Stanley, Ont.
Owen Sound, Ont.

Cement
Charlevoix, Mich.
Alpena, Mich.

Salt
Goderich, Ont.
Windsor, Ont.
Cleveland, Ont.
Fairport, Ohio

MAJOR UNLOADING PORTS

The primary U.S. iron ore and limestone receiving ports are Cleveland, Chicago, Gary, Burns Harbor, Indiana Harbor, Detroit, Toledo, Ashtabula and Conneaut. Nanticoke, Hamilton and Sault Ste. Marie, Ont. , are major ore-receiving ports in Canada. Coal is carried by self-unloaders to power plants in the U.S. and Canada. Most grain loaded on the lakes is destined for export via the St. Lawrence Seaway. Cement is delivered to terminals from Lake Superior to Lake Ontario. Tankers bring petroleum products to cities as diverse in size as Cleveland, Detroit, Escanaba and Muskegon. Self-unloaders carry limestone, road salt and sand to cities throughout the region.

MEANINGS OF BOAT WHISTLES

1 SHORT: I intend to leave you on my port side (answered by same if agreed upon).
2 SHORT: I intend to leave you on my starboard side (answered by same if agreed upon). (Passing arrangements may be agreed upon by radio. If so, no whistle signal is required.)
5 OR MORE SHORT BLASTS SOUNDED RAPIDLY: Danger.

1 PROLONGED: Vessel leaving dock.
3 SHORT: Operating astern propulsion.
1 PROLONGED, SOUNDED AT INTERVALS OF NOT MORE THAN 2 MINUTES: Vessel moving in restricted visibility.
1 SHORT, 1 PROLONGED, 1 SHORT: Vessel at anchor in restricted visibility (optional). May be accompanied by the ringing of a bell on the forward part of the ship and a gong on the aft end.
3 PROLONGED and 2 SHORT: Salute (formal).
1 PROLONGED and 2 SHORT: Salute (commonly used).
3 PROLONGED and 1 SHORT: Internationl Shipmasters' Association member salute.

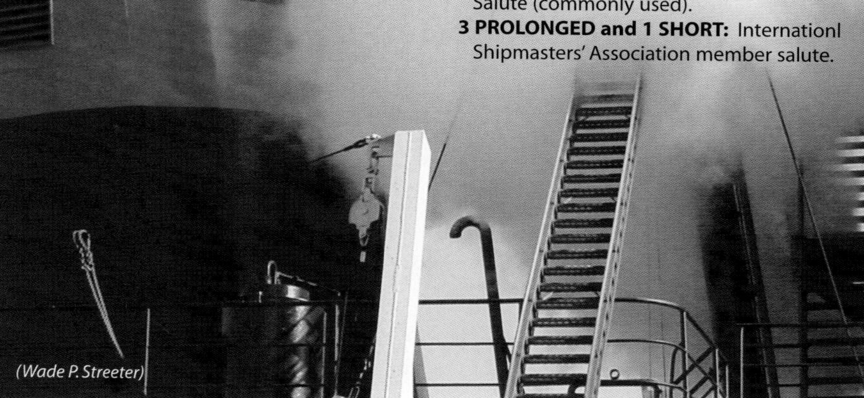
(Wade P. Streeter)

***Voyageur Independent* takes on a cargo of grain at Thunder Bay.** *(Gene Onchulenko)*

LOCKS & CANALS

MacArthur Lock

Named after World War II Gen. Douglas MacArthur, the MacArthur Lock is 800 feet long (243.8 meters) between inner gates, 80 feet wide (24.4 meters) and 31 feet deep (9.4 meters) over the sills. The lock was built in 1942-43 and opened to traffic on July 11, 1943. The largest vessel that can transit the MacArthur Lock is 730 feet long (222.5 meters) by 76 feet wide (23 meters).

Poe Lock

The Poe Lock is 1,200 feet long (365.8 meters), 110 feet wide (33.5 meters) and has a depth over the sills of 32 feet (9.8 meters). Named after Col. Orlando M. Poe, it was built by the United States in the years 1961-68. The lock's vessel size limit is 1,100 feet long (335.3 meters) by 105 feet wide (32 meters).

Davis Lock

Named after Col. Charles E.L.B. Davis, the Davis Lock measures 1,350 feet long (411.5 meters) between inner gates, 80 feet wide (24.4 meters) and 23 feet deep (7 meters) over the sills. Built in 1908-14, it sees limited use due to its shallow depth.

Sabin Lock

The same size as the Davis Lock, the Sabin Lock was built from 1913-19. The lock is currently inactive.

As part of its mission of building and maintaining the country's ports and waterways, the U.S. Army Corps of Engineers operates and maintains the Soo Locks, as well as all of the Great Lakes' connecting channels.

The Soo Locks

The Soo Locks, which celebrated their 150th anniversary in 2005, operate on gravity, as do all locks in the St. Lawrence Seaway system. No pumps are used to empty or fill the lock chambers; valves are opened, and water is allowed to seek its own level. All traffic passes through the locks toll-free.

Vessels in the St. Marys River system, of which the Soo Locks are a part, are under control of the U.S. Coast Guard at Sault Ste. Marie, Mich. In the vicinity of the locks, they fall under jurisdiction of the lockmaster, who must be contacted on VHF Ch. 14 (156.700 MHz) for lock assignments.

Traffic is dispatched to the appropriate lock according to size, other vessels in the locks area and by the time the captain first calls in to the lockmaster. All vessels longer than 730 feet and/or wider than 76 feet are restricted by size to the Poe, or second, lock. A vessel is under engine and thruster control at all times, with crews ready to drop mooring lines over bollards on the lock wall to stop its movement.

As soon as the vessel is in position, engines are stopped and mooring lines made fast. If the vessel is being lowered, valves at the lower end of the lock chamber are opened to allow the water inside to flow out. If the vessel is being raised, valves at the upper end of the lock chamber are opened to allow water to enter. When the water reaches the desired level, the valves are closed, the protective boom is raised, the gates are opened, and the vessel proceeds on her way.

Vessels passing through the locks spend an average of 65 minutes from the time they enter the canal at one end until they pass the outer piers at the other end. Of this time, an average of 30 minutes is consumed in entering, raising or lowering, and leaving the lock chamber.

The first lock was built on the Canadian side of the river by the Northwest Fur Co. in 1797-98. The first ship canal on the American side, known as the State Lock, was built from 1853-55 by Charles T. Harvey. There were two tandem locks on masonry, each 35 feet (106.7 meters) long by 70 feet (21.3 meters) wide, with a lift of about 9 feet (2.7 meters). That canal was destroyed in 1888 by workers making way for newer and bigger locks.

Discussion continues about building a new lock in the space occupied by the Davis and Sabin locks. Cost of such a lock was estimated at $342 million in 2007. Funding has been allocated but not approved.

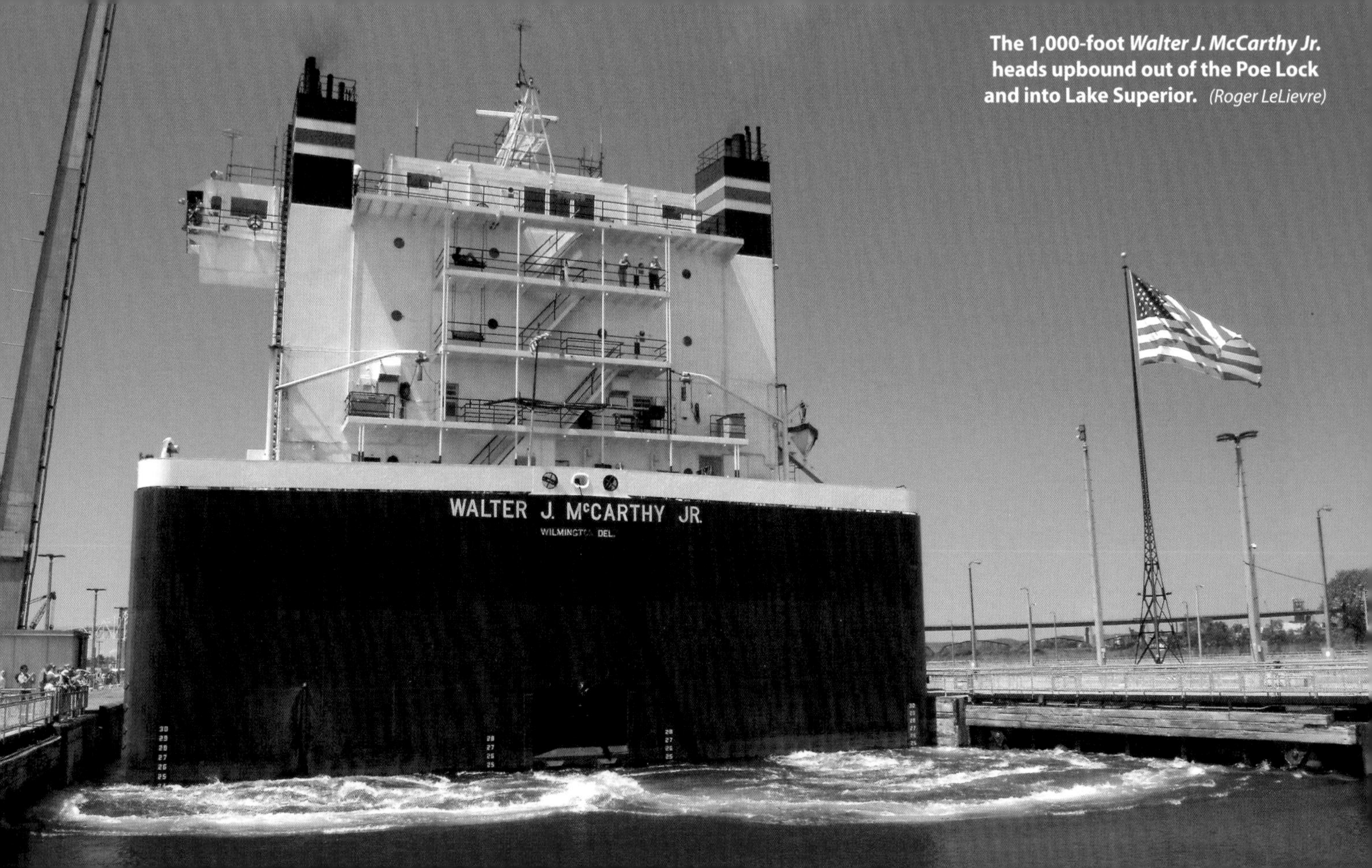

The 1,000-foot *Walter J. McCarthy Jr.* heads upbound out of the Poe Lock and into Lake Superior. *(Roger LeLievre)*

Canadian Soo Lock

The present Canadian Lock at Sault Ste. Marie, Ont., to the north of the much larger locks on the U.S. side, has its origins in a canal constructed during the years 1887-95 through the red sandstone rock of St. Marys Island on the north side of the St. Marys Rapids.

The most westerly canal on the Seaway route, the waterway measures 7,294 feet (2,223.4 meters), or about 1.4 miles (2.2 km) long from end to end of upper and lower piers. A 900-foot (274.3 meters) lock served vessels until the collapse of a lock wall in 1987 closed the waterway. In 1998, after $10.3 million in repairs, a much smaller lock opened, built inside the old lock chamber. Operated by Parks Canada, it is used mainly by pleasure craft, tugs and tour boats, which pass through toll-free.

There are several historic stuctures on the site – the administration building, superintendent's residence, the canalmen's shelter, powerhouse and the stores/ blacksmith shop, all built from red sandstone dug up during the canal's construction.

Soo Locks facts

The St. Marys River, running 80 miles (128.7 km) from remote Isle Parisienne at its north end to the restored DeTour Reef Light at its south end, connects Lake Superior with Lake Huron. It includes two engineering marvels: the Soo Locks at Sault Ste. Marie and the West Neebish Cut, a channel dynamited out of solid rock that allows traffic to pass to the west side of Neebish Island.

The Empire State Building is 1,250 feet tall. The largest vessel using the Soo Locks is 1,014 feet long. This vessel, the *Paul R. Tregurtha*, carried 3,219,646 net tons of cargo through the locks during the 1998 season.

There are about 150 major cargo carriers engaged almost exclusively in the Great Lakes and Seaway trade. That number is augmented by a variety of saltwater vessels, or "salties," that enter the system during the shipping season.

***Canadian Leader* heads into Lake Superior *(top)*. The steamer *Cumberland* at the Soo Locks around 100 years ago *(bottom)*.**

The Great Lakes shipping season runs from late March to late December. In the spring and fall, a small fleet of icebreakers operated by the U.S. and Canadian coast guards and commercial tugs help keep navigation channels open.

A vessel traveling from the Atlantic Ocean to Lake Superior through the St. Lawrence Seaway and the Soo Locks rises nearly 600 feet. The first lift, a total of 224 feet, is provided by the seven St. Lawrence Seaway locks that begin at Montreal. The Welland Canal, connecting Lake Erie and Lake Ontario and bypassing Niagara Falls, raises vessels an additional 326 feet. The Soo Locks complete the process with a 21-foot lift.

31,595,520 gallons of water are needed to fill the Poe Lock. To drink this much, one would have to drink 9,233 12-ounce glasses every day for 100 years. It takes about 12 minutes to fill the lock and 10 minutes to empty it.

One short blast of a vessel's whistle while in the lock means "cast off lines."

A red-and-white flag flying from a vessel's mast indicates a pilot is on board. Saltwater vessels pick up pilots at various points in their voyage.

During 1953, 128 million tons of freight were moved through the locks. This record still stands.

No tolls are charged at the Soo Locks (U.S. or Canadian locks).

In 2005, Soo Locks handled:

- Nearly 43 million net tons of iron ore
- More than 21 million net tons of coal
- More than 4 million net tons of stone
- Almost 4 million net tons of wheat
- 647,821 net tons of salt and 518,970 net tons of cement and concrete
- Other commodities locking through include petroleum, manufactured goods and industrial by-products.

FOLLOWING THE FLEET

These prerecorded messages help track vessel arrivals and departures.

Algoma Central Marine	**(905) 988-2665**	ACM vessel movements
Boatwatcher's Hotline	**(218) 722-6489**	Superior, Wis.; Duluth, Two Harbors, Taconite Harbor and Silver Bay, Minn.
CSX Coal Docks/Torco Dock	**(419) 697-2304**	Toledo, Ohio, vessel information
DMIR Ore Dock	Discontinued	Duluth vessel information
Eisenhower Lock	**(315) 769-2422**	Eisenhower Lock vessel traffic
Michigan Limestone docks	**(989) 734-2117**	Calcite, Mich., vessel information
Michigan Limestone docks	**(906) 484-2201**	Ext. 503 – Cedarville, Mich., passages
Presque Isle Corp.	**(989) 595-6611**	Stoneport, Mich., vessel information
Soo Traffic	**(906) 635-3224**	Previous day – St. Marys River
Superior Midwest Energy Terminal (SMET)	**(715) 395-3559**	Superior, Wis., vessel information
Thunder Bay Port Authority	**(807) 345-1256**	Thunder Bay, Ont., vessel info
Great Lakes Fleet	**(800) 328-3760**	Ext. 4389 – GLF vessel movements
Upper Lakes Group	**(905) 988-2665**	ULG vessel movements
Vantage Point, Boatnerd World HQ	**(810) 985-9057**	St. Clair River traffic
Welland Canal tape	**(905) 688-6462**	Welland Canal traffic

With an inxpensive VHF scanner, boat watchers can tune to ship-to-ship and ship-to-shore traffic using the following frequency guide.

Commercial vessels only	**Ch. 13 – 156.650 MHz**	Bridge-to-bridge communications
Calling/distress only	**Ch. 16 – 156.800 MHz**	Calling/distress only
Commercial vessels only	**Ch. 06 – 156.300 MHz**	Working channel
Commercial vessels only	**Ch. 08 – 156.400 MHz**	Working channel
Supply boat at Sault Ste. Marie, MI	**Ch. 08 – 156.400 MHz**	Supply boat *Ojibway*
DeTour Reef – Lake St. Clair Light	**Ch. 11 – 156.550 MHz**	Sarnia Traffic - Sect. 1
Long Point Light – Lake St. Clair Light	**Ch. 12 – 156.600 MHz**	Sarnia Traffic - Sect. 2
Montreal – mid-Lake St. Francis	**Ch. 14 – 156.700 MHz**	Seaway Beauharnois – Sect. 1
Mid-Lake St. Francis – Bradford Island	**Ch. 12 – 156.600 MHz**	Seaway Eisenhower – Sect. 2
Bradford Island – Crossover Island	**Ch. 11 – 156.550 MHz**	Seaway Iroquois – Sect.3
Crossover Island to Cape Vincent	**Ch. 13 – 156.650 MHz**	Seaway Clayton – Sect. 4 St. Lawrence River portion
Cape Vincent – mid-Lake Ontario	**Ch. 13 – 156.650 MHz**	Seaway Sodus – Sect. 4 Lake Ontario portion
Mid-Lake Ontario – Welland Canal	**Ch. 11 – 156.550 MHz**	Seaway Newcastle – Sect. 5
Welland Canal	**Ch. 14 – 156.700 MHz**	Seaway Welland – Sect. 6
Welland Canal to Long Point Light	**Ch. 11 – 156.550 MHz**	Seaway Long Point – Sect. 7
Montreal Traffic	**Ch. 10 – 156.500 MHz**	Vessel traffic
St. Marys River Traffic Service	**Ch. 12 – 156.600 MHz**	Soo Traffic, Sault Ste. Marie, MI
Lockmaster, Soo Locks	**Ch. 14 – 156.700 MHz**	Soo Lockmaster (call WUE-21)
Coast Guard traffic	**Ch. 21 – 157.050 MHz**	United States Coast Guard
Coast Guard traffic	**Ch. 22 – 157.100 MHz**	United States Coast Guard
U.S. mailboat, Detroit, MI	**Ch. 10 – 156.500 MHz**	Mailboat *J. W. Westcott II*

John G. Munson **unloads coal at Ontonagon, Mich.** *(Rod Burdick)*

The *Edward L. Ryerson* made three trips to Quebec City in 2007, her first-ever visits east of Lake Erie. Here she passes through the Welland Canal. *(Bill Bird)*

The Welland Canal

The 27-mile-long (43.7 km) Welland Canal, built to bypass Niagara Falls, overcomes a difference in water level of 326.5 feet (99.5 meters) between Lake Erie and Lake Ontario.

The first Welland Canal opened in 1829; the present (fourth) canal opened officially on Aug. 6, 1932. Each of the seven Welland Canal locks has an average lift of 46.5 feet (14.2 meters). All locks (except Lock 8) are 859 feet (261.8 meters) long, 80 feet (24.4 meters) wide and 30 feet (9.1 meters) deep. Lock 8 measures 1,380 feet (420. 6 m) in length.

The largest vessel that may transit the canal is 740 feet (225.5 meters) long, 78 feet (23.8 meters) wide and 26 feet, 6 inches (8.08 meters) in draft.

Locks 1, 2 and 3 are at St. Catharines, Ont., on the Lake Ontario end of the waterway. At Lock 3, the Welland Canal Viewing Center and Museum houses an information desk (which posts a list of vessels expected at the lock), a gift shop and restaurant. At Thorold, Locks 4, 5 and 6, twinned to help speed passage of vessels, are controlled with an elaborate interlocking system for safety. These locks (positioned end to end, they resemble a short flight of stairs) have an aggregate lift of 139.5 feet (42.5 meters). Just south of Locks 4, 5 and 6 is Lock 7. Lock 8, seven miles (11.2 km) upstream at Port Colborne, completes the process, making the final adjustment to Lake Erie's level.

In 1973, a new channel was constructed to replace the section of the canal that bisected the city of Welland. The Welland bypass eliminated long delays for navigation, road and rail traffic.

The average passage time for the canal is about 12 hours, with the majority of the time spent transiting Locks 4-7. Vessels passing through the Welland Canal and St. Lawrence Seaway must carry a qualified pilot.

There are also 11 railway and highway bridges crossing the Welland Canal. The most significant are the vertical-lift bridges that provide a clearance of 126 feet (36.6 meters) for vessels passing underneath. Tunnels at Thorold, Ont., and South Welland allow vehicle traffic to pass beneath the waterway. All vessel traffic though the Welland Canal is regulated by a control center. Upbound vessels must call Seaway Welland off Port Weller, Ont., on VHF Ch. 14 (156.700 MHz), while downbound vessels are required to make contact off Port Colborne. Cameras keep vessels under constant observation, and locks (and most bridges over the canal) are controlled from the center.

The Welland Canal

Lock up the perfect fun day out!

The **Welland Canals were built to circumvent the mighty Niagara Falls. Marvel as lake and ocean freighters are raised and lowered in the locks on their journey between Lake Erie and Lake Ontario.**

Welland Canals Centre at Lock 3
1932 Welland Canals Parkway,
St. Catharines, ON L2R 7K6
t **905-984-8880 ext. 226**
toll free **1-800-305-5134**
e **museuminfo@stcatharines.ca**
w **www.stcatharineslock3museum.ca**

THOROLD

Lock 7 Viewing Complex
50 Chapel Street South,
Thorold, ON L2V 2C6
t **905-680-9477**
toll free **1-888-680-9477**
e **thoroldtourism@bellnet.ca**
w **www.thoroldtourism.ca**

Call daily for ship schedules (April - December)

Motorcoach/Group Friendly!
Ship Viewing Platform - Always FREE!

The St. Lawrence Seaway

The St. Lawrence Seaway is a waterway extending some 2,038 miles (3,701.4 km) from the Atlantic Ocean to the head of the Great Lakes at Duluth, Minn., including Montreal harbor and the Welland Canal. More specifically, it is a system of locks and canals (U.S. and Canadian), built between 1954 and 1958 at a cost of $474 million and opened in 1959, that allow vessels to pass from Montreal to the Welland Canal at the western end of Lake Ontario. The vessel size limit within this system is 740 feet (225.6 meters) long, 78 feet (23.8 meters) wide and 26 feet, 6 inches (8.08 meters) draft.

Closest to the ocean is the St. Lambert Lock, which lifts ships some 15 feet (4.6 meters) from Montreal harbor to the level of the Laprairie Basin, through which the channel sweeps in a great arc 8.5 miles (13.7 km) long to the second lock. The Côte Ste. Catherine Lock, like the other six St. Lawrence Seaway locks, is built to the dimensions shown in the table below. The Côte Ste. Catherine lifts ships from the level of the Laprairie Basin 30 feet (9.1 meters) to the level of Lake Saint Louis, bypassing the Lachine Rapids. Beyond it, the channel runs 7.5 miles (12.1 km) before reaching Lake Saint Louis.

LOCK DIMENSIONS	
Length	766' (233.5 meters)
Width	80' (24 meters)
Depth	30' (9.1 meters)

The Lower Beauharnois Lock, bypassing the Beauharnois Power House, lifts ships 41 feet (12.5 meters) and sends them through a short canal to the Upper Beauharnois Lock, where they are lifted 41 feet (12.5 meters) to reach the Beauharnois Canal. After a 13-mile (20.9 km) trip in the canal and a 30-mile (48.3 km) passage through Lake Saint Francis, vessels reach the U.S. border and the Snell Lock, which has a lift of 45 feet (13.7 meters) and empties into the 10-mile (16.1 km) Wiley-Dondero Canal.

After passing through the Wiley-Dondero, ships are raised another 38 feet (11.6 meters) by the Dwight D. Eisenhower Lock, after which they enter Lake St. Lawrence, the pool upon which nearby power-generating stations draw for their turbines located a mile to the north.

At the western end of Lake St. Lawrence, the Iroquois Lock allows ships to bypass the Iroquois Control Dam. The lift here is only about one foot (0.3 meters). Once in the waters west of Iroquois, the channel meanders through the Thousand Islands to Lake Ontario and beyond.

Shell refueling tanker *Arca* alongside *Huntestern* in Montreal harbor. *(Eric Treece)*

MARINE MUSEUMS ASHORE

Information can change without notice. Call ahead to verify location and hours.

ANTIQUE BOAT MUSEUM, 750 MARY ST., CLAYTON, NY – (315) 686-4104: A large collection of freshwater boats and engines. Open May 11-October 18, 2007.

CANAL PARK MARINE MUSEUM, ALONGSIDE THE SHIP CANAL, DULUTH, MN – (218) 727-2497: Displays, artifacts and programs. Many excellent models and other artifacts are on display, plus the former Corps of Engineers' tug *Bayfield*. Open all year.

COLLINGWOOD MUSEUM, MEMORIAL PARK, 45 ST. PAUL ST., COLLINGWOOD, ON – (705) 445-4811: More than 100 years of shipbuilding, illustrated with models, photos and videos. Open all year.

DOOR COUNTY MARITIME MUSEUM & LIGHTHOUSE PRESERVATION SOCIETY INC., 120 N. MADISON AVE., STURGEON BAY, WI – (920) 743-5958: Many excellent models help portray the role shipbuilding has played in the Door Peninsula. Open all year.

DOSSIN GREAT LAKES MUSEUM, 100 THE STRAND, BELLE ISLE, DETROIT, MI – 313-833-7935: Models, interpretive displays, the smoking room from the 1912 passenger steamer *City of Detroit III*, an anchor from the *Edmund Fitzgerald* and the pilothouse from the steamer *William Clay Ford* are on display. Open Wednesday-Sunday.

ERIE MARITIME MUSEUM, 150 E. FRONT ST., ERIE, PA – (814) 452-2744. Displays depict the Battle of Lake Erie and more. Check ahead to see whether the U.S. brig *Niagara* is in port. Open all year.

FAIRPORT HARBOR MARINE MUSEUM AND LIGHTHOUSE, 129 SECOND ST., FAIRPORT, OH – (440) 354-4825: Located in the Fairport Lighthouse, displays include the pilothouse from the lake carrier *Frontenac* and the mainmast of the first *USS Michigan*. Open late May-early September.

GREAT LAKES HISTORICAL SOCIETY, 480 MAIN ST., VERMILION, OH – (800) 893-1485: Museum

(Continued on Page 138)

Ship Watcher's
Paradise
located in beautiful Duluth, Minnesota
VIKEN
1-800-430-7437
www.southpierinn.com
Named "Best Waterfront Hotel in Minnesota 2007" by the Official Best Of!
SOUTH PIER INN
on the canal

Steamship
William G.
Mather
Museum

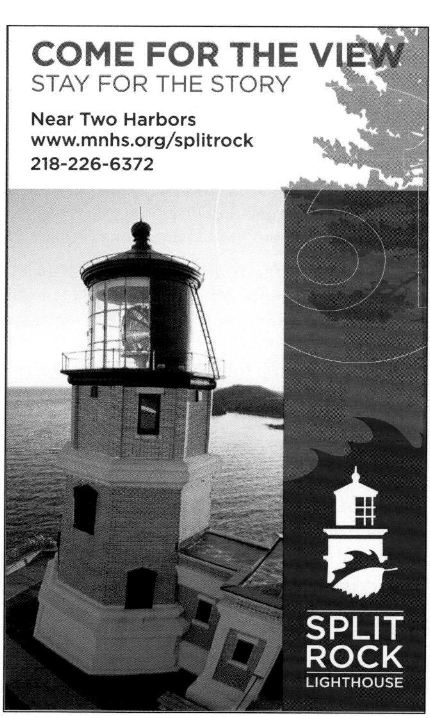
COME FOR THE VIEW
STAY FOR THE STORY
Near Two Harbors
www.mnhs.org/splitrock
218-226-6372
SPLIT
ROCK
LIGHTHOUSE

(Continued from Page 136)

tells the story of the Great Lakes through ship models, paintings, exhibits and artifacts, including engines and other machinery. Pilothouse of retired laker *Canopus* and a replica of the Vermilion lighthouse are on display. Museum open all year.

GREAT LAKES MARINE & U.S. COAST GUARD MEMORIAL MUSEUM, 1071 WALNUT BLVD., ASHTABULA, OH – (440) 964-6847: Housed in the 1898-built lighthouse keeper's residence, the museum includes models, paintings, artifacts, photos, a working scale model of a Hullett ore unloading machine and the pilothouse from the *Thomas Walters*. Open April-October.

GREAT LAKES SHIPWRECK MUSEUM, WHITEFISH POINT, MI – (888) 492-3747: Lighthouse and shipwreck artifacts, a shipwreck video theater, the restored lighthouse keeper's quarters and an *Edmund Fitzgerald* display that includes the ship's bell. Open May 1-October 31, 2007.

LE SAULT DE SAINTE MARIE HISTORIC SITES INC., 501 EAST WATER ST., SAULT STE. MARIE, MI – (888) 744-7867: The steamer *Valley Camp* is the centerpiece of this museum. The vessel's cargo holds house artifacts, models, aquariums, photos and other memorabilia, as well as the *Edmund Fitzgerald's* lifeboats. Tours available. Open May 15-October 15.

LOWER LAKES MARINE HISTORICAL MUSEUM, 66 ERIE ST., BUFFALO, NY – (716) 849-0914: Exhibits explore local maritime history. Open all year (Tuesday, Thursday and Saturday only).

MARINE MUSUEM OF THE GREAT LAKES, 55 ONTARIO ST., KINGSTON, ON – (613) 542-2261: The musuem's largest exhibit is the retired Canadian Coast Guard icebreaker *Alexander Henry*, which is open for tours and also as a bed and breakfast. Open February-November.

MARITIME MUSEUM OF SANDUSKY, 125 MEIGS ST., SANDUSKY, OHIO – (419) 624-0274: Exhibits explore local maritime history. Open all year.

MARQUETTE MARITIME MUSEUM, 300 LAKESHORE BLVD., MARQUETTE, MI – (906) 226-2006: Located in an 1890s waterworks building, the museum re-creates the offices of the first commercial fishing and passenger freight companies. Displays also include charts, photos, models and maritime artifacts. Open May 31-September 30.

MICHIGAN MARITIME MUSEUM, 260 DYCKMAN ROAD., SOUTH HAVEN, MI – (800) 747-3810: Exhibits dedicated to the U.S. Lifesaving Service and U.S. Coast Guard. Displays tell the story of various kinds of boats and their uses on the Great Lakes. Open all year.

OWEN SOUND MARINE & RAIL MUSEUM, 1155 FIRST AVE. WEST, OWEN SOUND, ON – (519) 371-3333: Museum depicts the history of each industry (but leans more toward the marine end) through displays, models and photos. Seasonal.

PORT COLBORNE HISTORICAL & MARINE MUSEUM, 280 KING ST., PORT COLBORNE, ON – (905) 834-7604: Wheelhouse from the steam tug *Yvonne Dupre Jr.* and a lifeboat from the steamer *Hochelaga* are among the museum's displays. Open May-December.

U.S. ARMY CORPS OF ENGINEERS MUSEUM, SOO LOCKS VISITOR CENTER, E. PORTAGE AVE., SAULT STE. MARIE, MI – (906) 632-3311: Exhibits include a working model of the Soo Locks, historic photos and a 25-minute film. Also, three observation decks adjacent to the MacArthur Lock provide an up-close view of ships locking through. No admission charge; open May-November. Check at the Visitor Center information desk for a list of vessels expected at the locks.

ST. CATHARINES MUSEUM, 1932 WELLAND CANALS PARKWAY ROAD – (905) 984-8880 or (800) 305-5134: Museum traces the development of the Welland Canal. Museum and adjacent gift shop open all year. Observation deck open during the navigation season. Check at the information desk for vessels expected at Lock 3. Gift shop has a wide selection of maritime books.

THUNDER BAY NATIONAL MARINE SANCTUARY, 500 W. FLETCHER ST., ALPENA, MI – (989) 356-8805: New research and musuem facility is the dry-land component of a collection of shipwrecks located off the northeast corner of Michigan's lower peninsula. Open all year; closed on Sundays.

WISCONSIN MARITIME MUSEUM, 75 MARITIME DRIVE, MANITOWOC, WI – (920) 684-0218 or (866) 724-2356: Displays explore the history of area shipbuilding and also honor submariners and submarines built in Manitowoc. The World War II submarine *Cobia* is adjacent to the museum and open for tours. Open all year.

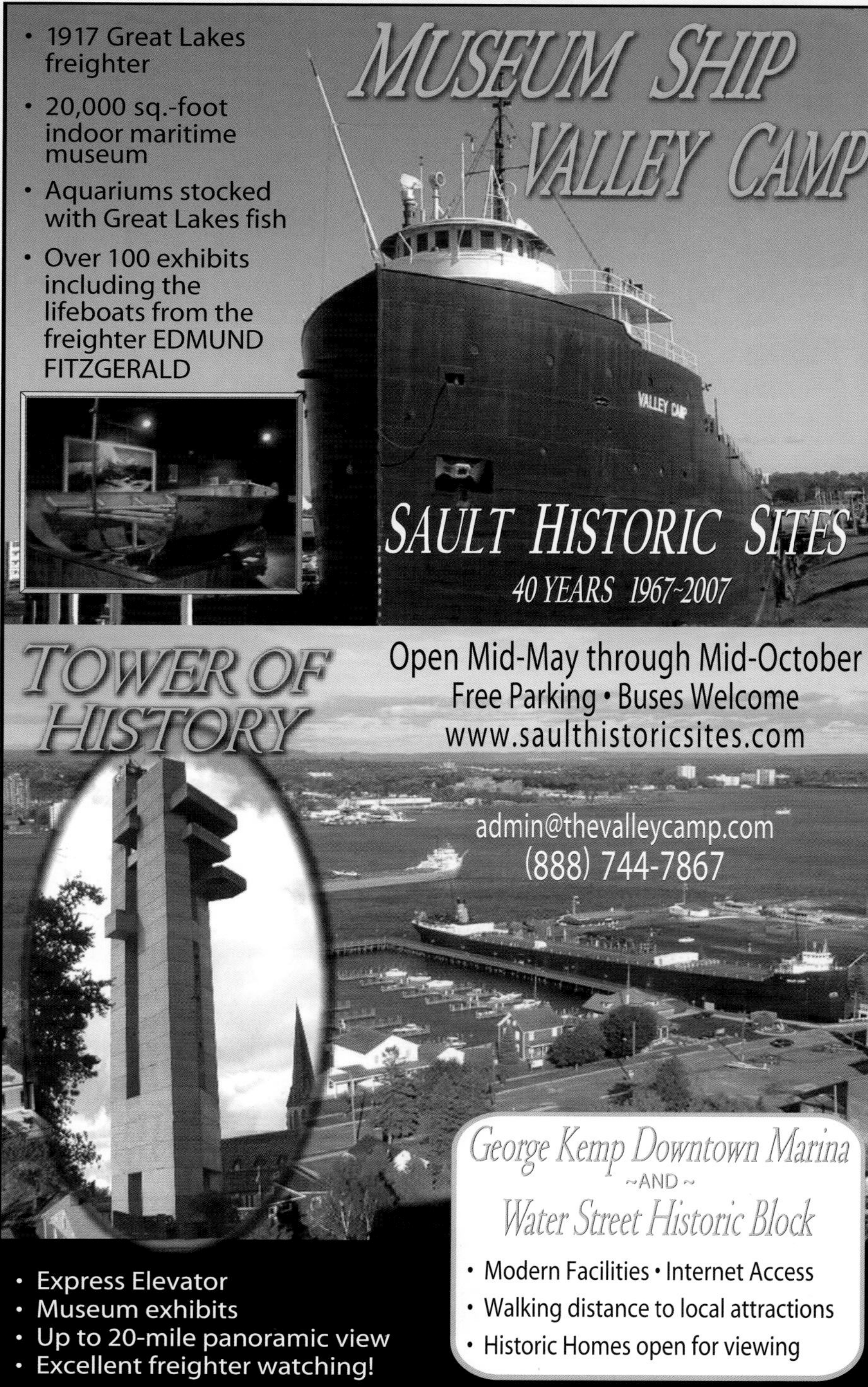

• 1917 Great Lakes freighter
• 20,000 sq.-foot indoor maritime museum
• Aquariums stocked with Great Lakes fish
• Over 100 exhibits including the lifeboats from the freighter EDMUND FITZGERALD
MUSEUM SHIP VALLEY CAMP
VALLEY CAMP
SAULT HISTORIC SITES
40 YEARS 1967~2007
TOWER OF HISTORY
Open Mid-May through Mid-October
Free Parking • Buses Welcome
www.saulthistoricsites.com
admin@thevalleycamp.com
(888) 744-7867
George Kemp Downtown Marina
~AND~
Water Street Historic Block
• Modern Facilities • Internet Access
• Walking distance to local attractions
• Historic Homes open for viewing
• Express Elevator
• Museum exhibits
• Up to 20-mile panoramic view
• Excellent freighter watching!

Colors of the Great Lakes and Seaway Smokestacks

A.B.M. Marine
Thunder Bay, ON

Algoma Central Corp.
St. Catharines, ON

Algoma Tankers Ltd.
Div. of Algoma Central Corp.
St. Catharines, ON

American Canadian Caribbean Line Inc.
Warren, RI

American Marine Constructors
Benton Harbor, MI

American Steamship Co.
Williamsville, NY

Andrie, Inc.
Muskegon, MI

Apostle Islands Cruise Service
Bayfield, WI

Arnold Transit Co.
Mackinac Island, MI

Basic Towing Inc.
Escanaba, MI

Bay City Boat Line
Bay City, MI

Bay Shipbuilding Co.
Sturgeon Bay, WI

Beaver Island Boat Co.
Charlevoix, MI

Billington Contracting Inc.
Duluth, MN

Blue Heron Co.
Tobermory, ON

Buffalo Public Works Dept.
Buffalo, NY

Busch Marine Inc.
Carrollton, MI

Calumet River Fleeting Inc.
Chicago, IL

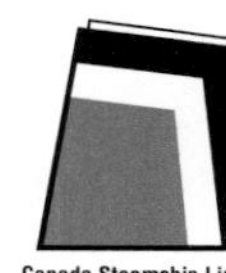

Canada Steamship Lines Inc.
Montreal, QC

Canadian Coast Guard
Ottawa, ON

Central Marine Logistics Inc.
Operator for ArcelorMittal
Griffith, IN

Chicago Fire Department
Chicago, IL

Cleveland Fire Department
Cleveland, OH

Club Canamac Cruises
Toronto, ON

Columbia Yacht Club
Chicago. IL

Croisières AML Inc.
Québec, QC

Dan Minor & Sons Inc.
Port Colborne, ON

Dean Construction Co.
Belle River, ON

Detroit City Fire Department
Detroit, MI

Diamond Jack's River Tours
Detroit, MI

Dragage Verreault Inc.
Les Méchins, QC

Duc D'Orleans Cruise Boat
Corunna, ON

Durocher Marine
Cheboygan, MI

Eastern Upper Peninsula Transit Authority
Sault Ste. Marie, MI

Edward E. Gillen Co.
Milwaukee, WI

Egan Marine Corp.
Lemont, IL

Equipments Verreault Inc.
Les Mechins, QC

Erie Sand & Gravel Co.
Erie, PA

Essroc Canada Inc.
Upper Lakes Group – Mgr.
North York, ON

Ferriss Marine Contracting Inc.
Detroit, MI

Fraser Shipyards Inc.
Superior, WI

Gaelic Tugboat Co.
Detroit, MI

Gallagher Marine Construction Inc.
Escanaba, MI

Gananoque Boat Line
Gananoque,ON

Gardiner Marine
Richard's Landing, ON

Geo. Gradel Co.
Toledo, OH

Goodtime Transit Boats Inc.
Cleveland, OH

Grand Portage / Isle Royale Transportation Line
Superior, WI

Gravel & Lake Services Ltd.
Thunder Bay, ON

Gravel & Lake Services Ltd.
Thunder Bay, ON

Great Lakes Dock & Materials
Muskegon, MI

Great Lakes Fleet Inc.
Key Lakes Inc. – Mgr.
Duluth, MI

Great Lakes International Towing & Salvage Ltd.
Burlington, ON

Great Lakes Maritime Academy
Northwestern Michigan College
Traverse City, MI

Great Lakes Towing Co.
Cleveland, OH

Groupe C.T.M.A.
Cap-Aux-Meules, QC

HMC Ship Managment
Div of Hannah Marine Corp
Lemont, IL

Hamilton Port Authority
Hamilton, ON

Hannah Marine Corp.
Lemont, IL

Hannah Marine Corp.
Lemont, IL

Heritage Cruise Lines
St. Catharines, ON

Holly Marine Towing
Chicago, IL

Hornbeck Offshore Services
Covington, LA

Horne Transportation Ltd.
Wolfe Island, ON

Illinois Marine Towing Inc.
Lemont, IL

Inland Lakes Management Inc.
Alpena, MI

The Interlake Steamship Co.
Lakes Shipping Co.
Richfield, OH

Keystone Great Lakes Inc.
Bala Cynwyd, PA

Kindra Lake Towing LP
Downers Grove, IL

King Co. Inc.
Holland, MI

Lafarge Canada Inc.
Montreal, QC

Lafarge North America Inc.
Southfield, MI

Lake Michigan Carferry Service Inc.
Ludington, MI

Laken Shipping Corp.
SMT (USA) Inc. – Mgr.
Cleveland, OH

Le Groupe Océan Inc.
Québec, QC

Le Groupe Océan Inc.
Quebec, QC

Lee Marine Ltd.
Sombra, ON

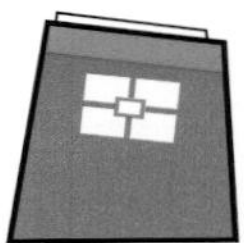

Lock Tours Canada
Sault Ste. Marie, ON

Lower Lakes Towing Ltd.
Port Dover, ON
Lower Lakes Transportation Co.
Cleveland, OH

Luedtke Engineering Co.
Frankfort, MI

M.C.M. Marine Inc.
Sault Ste Marie, MI

MacDonald Marine Ltd.
Goderich, ON

Madeline Island Ferry Line Inc.
LaPointe, WI

Maid of the Mist Steamboat Co. Ltd.
Niagara Falls, ON

Malcom Marine
St. Clair, MI

Manitou Island Transit
Leland, MI

Marine Tech Inc.
Duluth, MN

Mariposa Cruise Line
Toronto, ON

Maximus Corp.
Bloomfield Hills, MI

McAsphalt Marine Transportation
Scarborough, ON

McKeil Marine Ltd.
Hamilton, ON

McKeil Marine Ltd.
Hamilton, ON

McKeil Marine Ltd.
Hamilton, ON

McNally Construction Inc.
Hamilton, ON

Miller Boat Line
Put-In-Bay, OH

Museum Ship
CCGC Alexander Henry
Kingston, ON

Museum Tug Edna G
Two Harbors, MN

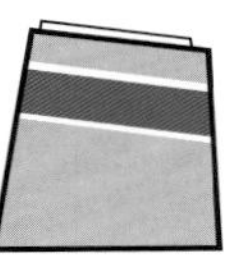

Museum Ship
HMCS Haida
Hamilton, ON

Museum Ship
Keewatin
Douglas, MI

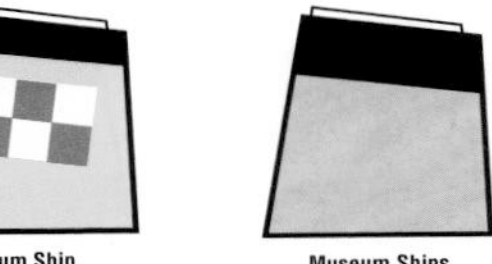

Museum Ships
USS Little Rock
USS The Sullivans
Buffalo, NY

Museum Ship
Meteor
Superior, WI

Museum Ship
City of Milwaukee
Manistee, MI

Museum Ship
Milwaukee Clipper
Muskegon, MI

Museum Ships
Norgoma (Sault Ste. Marie,ON)
Norisle (Manitowaning,ON)

Museum Ship
Valley Camp
Sault Ste. Marie, MI

Museum Ship
William A. Irvin
Duluth, MN

Museum Ships
Willis B. Boyer (Toledo,OH)
William G. Mather (Cleveland,OH)

Muskoka Steamship Historical Society
Gravenhurst, ON

Nadro Marine Services Ltd.
Port Dover, ON

Nautica Queen Cruise Dining
Cleveland, OH

Norlake Transportation Co.
Port Colborne, ON

Ontrario Ministry of Transportation
Downsview, ON

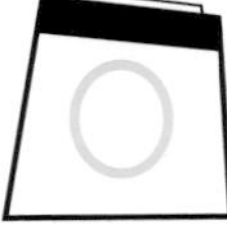

Osborne Companies Inc.
Grand River, OH

Owen Sound Transportation Co. Ltd.
Owen Sound, ON

Pere Marquette Shipping Co.
Tug Undaunted
Ludington, MI

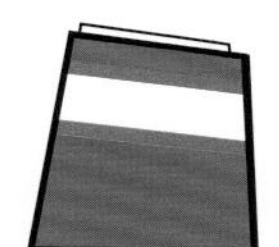

Provmar Fuels Inc.
Div. of Upper Lakes Group Inc.
Hamilton, ON

Purvis Marine Ltd.
Sault Ste. Marie, ON

Purvis Marine Ltd.
Sault Ste. Marie, ON

Rigel Shipping Canada Inc.
Shediac, NB

Roen Salvage Co.
Sturgeon Bay, WI

Ryba Marine Construction Co.
Cheboygan, MI

Selvick Marine Towing Corp.
Sturgeon Bay, WI

Shamrock Chartering Co.
Grosse Pointe, MI

Shoreline Sightseeing Co.
Chicago, IL

Société des Traversiers
Du Québec
Québec, QC

Société Québecoise
D' Exploration Minière
Algoma Central Corp. – Mgr.
Sainte-Foy, QC

Soo Locks Boat Tours
Sault Ste. Marie, MI

St. Lawrence
Cruise Lines Inc.
Kingston, ON

St. Lawrence Seaway
Development Corp.
Massena, NY

St. Lawrence Seaway
Management Corp.
Cornwall, ON

St. Marys Cement Inc.
Toronto, ON

TGL Marine Holdings ULC
Toronto, ON

Thousand Islands & Seaway
Cruises
Brockville, ON

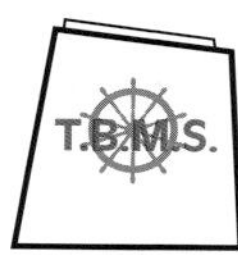

Thunder Bay Marine
Services Ltd.
Thunder Bay, On

Thunder Bay Tug
Services Ltd.
Thunder Bay, ON

Toronto Parks
& Recreation Department
Toronto, ON

Transport Desgagnés Inc.
Québec, QC

Transport Desgagnés Inc.
Québec, QC

Transport Igloolik Inc.
Montreal, QC

United States Army Corps of Engineers
Great Lakes and Ohio River Division
Cincinnati, OH

United States Coast Guard
9th Coast Guard District
Cleveland, OH

United States
Environmental Protection Agency
Duluth, MN / Chicago, IL

United States
National Park Service
Houghton, MI

Upper Lakes Group Inc.
Toronto, ON

Upper Lakes Towing Co.
Escanaba, MI

Vista Fleet
Duluth, MN

Voyageur Marine Transport Ltd.
Ridgeville, ON

Wendella Boat Tours
Chicago, IL

Zenith Tugboat Co.
Duluth, MN

On ships, as on buildings, stacks are used to vent exhaust smoke and provide an air draft for the boilers, if a vessel is so-equipped. Most modern vessels don't need a traditional smokestack, but most carry one for the sake of appearances.

Colors of Saltwater Fleets

Allrounder Maritime Co.
Manilia, Philippines

Amalthia Maritime Inc.
Athens, Greece

Anbros Maritime SA
Pireaus, Greece

Athena Marine Co. Ltd.
Limassol, Cyprus

Atlantska Plovidba
Dubrovnik, Croatia

B&N Moorman B.V.
Ridderkerk, Netherlands

Beluga Shipping GMBH
Bremen, Germany

Bernhard Schulte Group
Hamberg, Germany

Biglift Shipping BV
Roosendaal, Netherlands

Blystad Tankers Inc.
Oslo, Norway

Briese Schiffahrts GMBH & Co. KG
Leer, Germany

Canadian Forest Navigation Co. Ltd.
Montreal, QC

Carisbrooke Shipping PLC
Cowes, UK

Chartworld Shipping Corp.
Athens, Greece

China Ocean Shipping Group
Bejing, PRC

Clipper Wonsild Tankers AS
Clipper Elite Carriers
Copenhagen, Denmark

Coastal Shipping Ltd.
Goose Bay, ON

Commercial Fleet of Donbass
Donetsk, Ukraine

Commercial Trading & Discount Co. Ltd.
Athens, Greece

Common Progress Compania Naviera SA
Piraeus, Greece

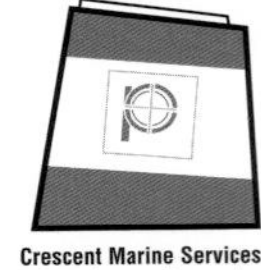

Crescent Marine Services
Copenhagen, Denmark

Crystal Pool Group
Helsinki, Finland

ER Denizcilik Sanayi Nakliyat ve Ticaret A.S.
Istanbul, Turkey

Eastwind Ship Management
Singapore, Singapore

Eitzen Chemical ASA
Oslo, Norway

Enzian Shipping AG
Berne, Switzerland

Euronav NV
Antwerp, Belgium

Far-Eastern Shipping Co.
Vladivostok, Russia

Fednav International Ltd.
Montreal, QC

Finbeta
Savona, Italy

Fisser & V. Doornum Kg GMBH
Hamburg, Germany

Flinter Groningen B.V.
Groningen, Netherlands

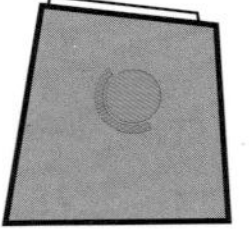

Fortum Oil & Gas
Fortum, Finland

Franco Compania Naviera SA
Athens, Greece

Hapag Lloyd
Hamburg, Germany

Harbor Shipping & Trading Co. S.A.
Chios, Greece

Intersee Schiffahrts-Gesellschaft MbH & Co.
Haren-Ems, Germany

Intership Navigation Co. Ltd.
Limassol, Cyprus

Isko Marine (Shipping) Co. SA
Piraeus, Greece

JSM Shipping
Jork, Germany

Jo Tankers, B.V.
Spijkenisse, Netherlands

Jumbo Shipping Co. S.A.
Rotterdam, Netherlands

Knutsen O.A.S. Shipping
Haugesund, Norway

Krey Schiffahrts GMBH & Co.
Simonswolde, Germany

Laurin Maritime Inc.
Houston, TX

Lietuvos Juro Laivininkyste (Lithuanian Shipping Co.)
Klaipeda, Lithuania

Lydia Mar Shipping Co. S.A.
Athens, Greece

Marbulk Shipping Inc. CSL International Inc. Mgr
Beverly, MS

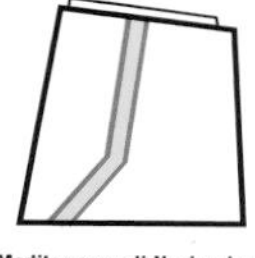
Mediterranea di Navigazione
Ravenna, Italy

Murmansk Shipping Co.
Murmansk, Russia

Murmansk Shipping Co.
Murmansk, Russia

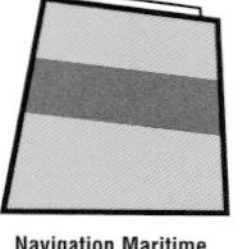
Navigation Maritime Bulgare Ltd.
Varna, Bulgaria

Novorossiysk Shipping (Novoship)
Novorossiysk, Russia

Oceanex Ltd.
Montreal, QC

Oldendorff Carriers GMBH & Co.
Luebeck, Germany

Olympic Shipping and Management S.A.
Athens, Greece

Onego Shipping & Chartering
Rhoon, Netherlands

Orion Schiffahrts
Hamburg, Germany

Polish Steamship Co.
Szczecin, Poland

Precious Shipping Public Co.
Bangkok, Thailand

Sea Observer Shipping Services
Piraeus, Greece

Seastar Navigation Co. Ltd.
Athens, Greece

Shih Wei Navigation Co.
Taipei, Taiwan

Shipping Corp. of India Ltd.
Mumbai, India

Siomar Enterprises Ltd.
Piraeus, Greece

Spar Shipping A.S.
Bergen, Norway

Stolt Parcel Tankers
Greenwich, CT

Teo Shipping Corp.
Piraeus, Greece

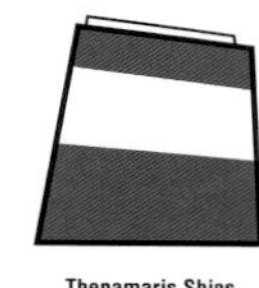
Thenamaris Ships Management Inc.
Athens, Greece

Torvald Klaveness Group
Oslo, Norway

Union Marine Enterprises S.A.
Piraeus, Greece

Viken Shipping AS
Bergen, Norway

W. Bockstiegel Reederei KG
Emden, Germany

Wagenborg Shipping B.V.
Delfzijl, Netherlands

Wagenborg Shipping B.V.
Delfzijl, Netherlands

House Flags of Great Lakes / Seaway Fleets

Acheson Ventures LLC
Port Huron, MI

Algoma Central Corp.
St. Catharines, ON

American Steamship Co.
Williamsville, NY

Canada Steamship Lines Inc.
Montreal, QC

Fednav Ltd.
Montreal, QC

Gaelic Tugboat Co.
Detroit, MI

Great Lakes Fleet Inc.
Key Lakes Inc. – Mgr.
Duluth, MN

Great Lakes Maritime Academy
Traverse City, MI

Great Lakes Shipwreck Historical Society
Sault Ste Marie, MI

Great Lakes Towing Co.
Cleveland, OH

Inland Lakes Management Inc.
Alpena, MI

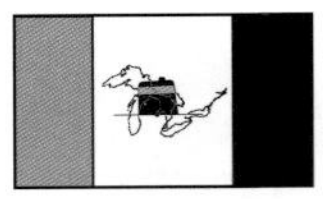

Interlake Steamship Co.
Lakes Shipping Co.
Richfield, OH

J.W. Westcott Co.
Detroit, MI

LaFarge Canada Inc
Montreal, QC

Lake Michigan Carferry Service Inc.
Ludington, MI

Lower Lakes Towing Ltd.
Lower Lakes Transportation Co.
Port Dover, ON / Williamsville, NY

McAsphalt Marine Transportation Ltd.
Scarborough, ON

McKeil Marine Ltd.
Hamilton, ON

McNally Construction Inc.
Hamilton, ON

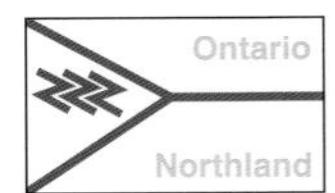

Owen Sound Transportation Co. Ltd.
Owen Sound, ON

Pere Marquette Shipping Co.
Ludington, MI

Purvis Marine Ltd.
Sault Ste. Marie, ON

Rigel Shipping Canada Inc.
Shediac, NB

Seaway Marine Transport
St. Catharines, ON

Transport Desgagnés, Inc.
Québec, QC

Upper Lakes Group Inc.
Toronto, ON

Voyageur Marine Transport Ltd.
Ridgeville, ON

Wagenborg Shipping B.V.
Delfzijl, Netherlands

Flags of Nations in the Marine Trade

Antigua & Barbuda

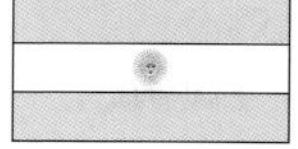
Argentina

Australia

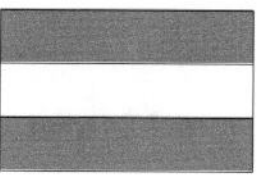
Austria

Azerbaijan

Bahamas

Bahrain

Barbados

Belgium

Bermuda

Bosnia & Herzegovinia

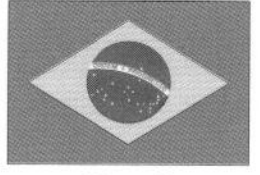
Brazil

Canada

Cayman Islands

Chile

China

Cote D'Ivoire

Croatia

Cyprus

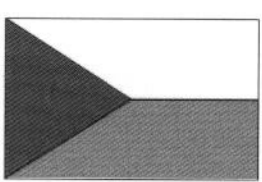
Czech Republic

Denmark

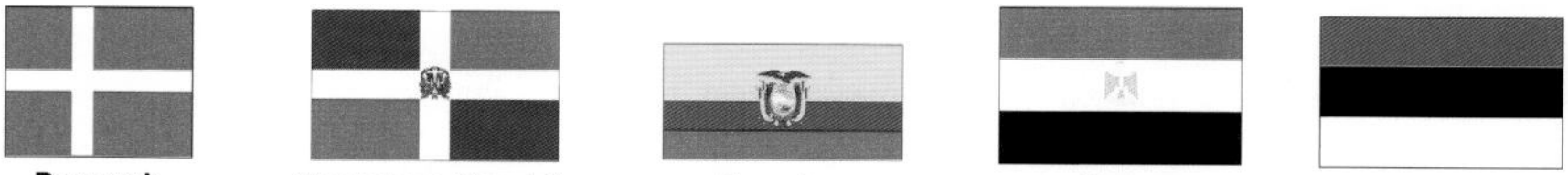

Dominican Republic

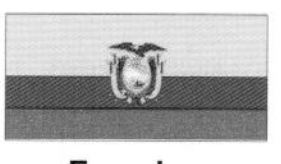
Ecuador

Egypt

Estonia

Fiji

Finland

France

Germany

Ghana

Greece

Guinea

Haiti

Honduras

Hong Kong

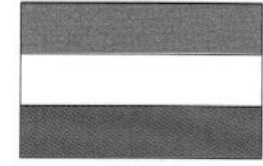
Hungary

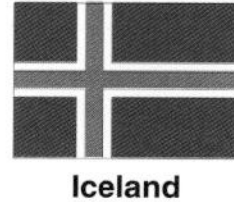
Iceland

India

Indonesia

Ireland

Isle of Man

Israel

Italy

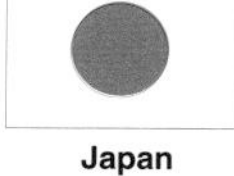
Japan

Korea-South

Latvia

Liberia

Lithuania

Luxembourg

Malaysia

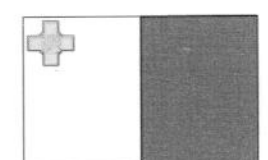
Malta

Marshall Islands

Mexico

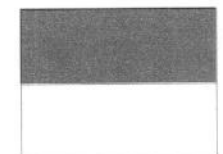
Monaco

Morocco

Myanmar

Netherlands

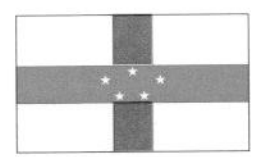
Netherlands Antilles

New Zealand

Nicaragua

N. Mariana Islands

Norway

Pakistan

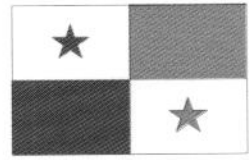
Panama

Peru

Philippines

Poland

Portugal

Republic of South Africa

Romania

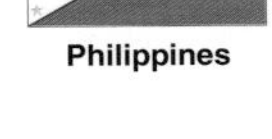
Russia

Singapore

Solomon Islands

Spain

St. Kitts Nevis

St. Vincent & The Grenadines

Sweden

Switzerland

Syria

Taiwan

Thailand

Trinidad & Tobago

Tunisia

Turkey

Ukraine

United Kingdom

United States

Vanuatu

Venezuela

Yugoslavia

Other Flags of Interest

International Shipmaster's Association – Member Pennant

Canadian Coast Guard Ensign

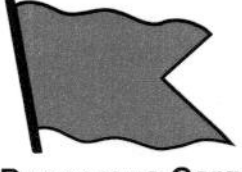
Dangerous Cargo On Board

Pilot On Board

U.S. Coast Guard Auxiliary Ensign

U.S. Coast Guard Ensign

U.S. Army Corps of Engineers

St. Lawrence Seaway Development Corp.

St. Lawrence Seaway Management Corp.

GREAT LAKES
MARITIME ACADEMY
Chart your course as a Merchant Marine Officer aboard the ships of the world. The Academy offers an exciting Bachelor's degree program which includes three semesters at sea and 100% job placement.
Lakes
Academy
1.800.748.0566 ext.1200 www.nmc.edu/maritime
Great Lakes Maritime Academy, Traverse City, Michigan

LAKE EXPRESS